Explaining Death to C...

SHELTON STATE COMMUNITY
COLLEGE
JUNIOR COLLEGE DIVISION
LIBRARY

DISCARDED

P9-CMP-931

DISCARDED

EXPLAINING DEATH TO CHILDREN

Edited by

EARL A. GROLLMAN

With an Introduction by
Louise Bates Ames

DISCARDED

BEACON PRESS   BOSTON

Copyright © 1967 by Earl A. Grollman

Library of Congress catalog card number: 67–24891

First published by Beacon Press in 1967

First published as a Beacon Paperback in 1969

Beacon Press books are published under the auspices of
the Unitarian Universalist Association

All rights reserved

Printed in the United States of America

International Standard Book Number: 0–8070–2385–X

9 8

Grateful acknowledgment is made to Little, Brown & Company and to
Gregory Rochlin, M.D., for permission to use as Chapter II a large portion of the chapter "Fears of Death" appearing in the book *Griefs and
Discontents,* published by Little, Brown & Company, Copyright © 1965,
by Gregory Rochlin.

Chapter V is based upon an article by Claiborne S. Jones which first
appeared in the December 1964 issue of *The Church Review,* published
by The Church Society for College Work.

To my children,
David, Sharon, and Jonathan,
who have helped me to understand more
fully the meaning of life. May I, through
this book, help them to accept more
maturely the meaning
of death.

CONTENTS

FOREWORD

SURELY, death is destined to remain among the certainties of life. The new hope for a better world in this time of war and racial strife is small comfort to a mortal in an uncertain world. To a child it is nothing.

Albert Camus said that "Men cannot live without meaning." We would say that of children, too. We go on to say that "meaning," the answer to "emptiness," is found beyond the fact of death. As we cannot protect ourselves from death so we cannot protect children. The traumatic experiences of life belong to both adulthood and childhood. Tragedy is the gift to all.

What is new in our day is the attention given to understanding the emotional needs of children. We are beginning to see children as human beings. Only an individual psychologically uninformed could say of a child who had encountered tragedy and who had become silent and passive, "He is taking it very well. He never cries."

There are occasions for tears, sometimes even in public—even if we are mature adults.

Mental health, the mental health of us all, child and adult, is not the denial of tragedy but the frank acknowledgment of it. Better to say to child or adult, "I could cry, too," rather than, "There, there, you mustn't cry."

Where can one turn in tragedy if no one understands or will admit that there is tragedy? But if tragedy can be admitted, we shall find our comfort in what we can mean to each other, and even in the kind of world that we can build, in the midst of tragedy. We reap from the depth of our own understanding and the genuineness of our own love. The child who is understood and loved can himself give understanding and love now and throughout life.

EARL A. GROLLMAN

INTRODUCTION

IF YOU KNOW EXACTLY what you'd say to a child of any age faced for the first time by the death of someone very close to him, and if you yourself have a clear and comfortable understanding of death and what it means, you don't need a book on the subject.

For the rest of us—professional people as well as parents —the present volume will prove to be of rather surprising help, interest, and pleasure. Death is a topic which fascinates and concerns us all. There are few who will not learn a great deal and who may not find their own thinking shaken up a bit by the wealth of advice and information and the highly varying points of view in these present chapters.

Your pleasure and satisfaction in reading this book can be great, but it will depend in part on the way you approach it. If you are looking for a single voice, a single style, a single philosophy, you may be disappointed. If, however, you can appreciate that here for perhaps the very first time under a single cover you are privileged to find in condensed and highly readable form thoughts on death of nearly a dozen different professional people most especially interested in the subject (rabbi, minister, priest, sociologist, anthropologist, research psychologist, school psychologist, psychiatrist, biologist, librarian), you will be richly rewarded.

Central to the presentation and most striking of all are the chapters by Rabbi Earl A. Grollman, Methodist minister Edgar Jackson, and Catholic Bishop Thomas J. Riley. Each comments on his own faith's attitude toward and beliefs about dying. What thoughtful discussions and what striking contrasts!

One of the most beautiful, warm, and positive discussions of death I have ever read is Rabbi Grollman's. It will not be news to Jewish readers, but it may be to many others, that Judaism has not wholly harmonized or integrated a concept of death and the hereafter even though there are certain central and unifying patterns. It does, however, emphasize the inevitability of death. It affirms life with such principles as "Better one day of happiness and good deeds in this world than in all the life in the world to come." In fact, major emphasis is given to the priority of life, even at the time of death. Death is considered as making life more precious.

The Reverend Edgar Jackson, with great frankness and flexibility, points out that many of the traditional teachings of the Protestant church with regard to death are too often not worthy of respect and not always rational. If we are to help children, we must tell them things which are both rational and helpful.

He suggests that even quite young children can be given pastoral counseling and that this counseling might best not be so much Bible oriented as people oriented.

Bishop Riley points out that "the problem of death is inseparably bound up with the problem of the nature and purpose of life" and emphasizes the traditional Catholic point of view which is that in the world to come the union of body and soul, interrupted by death, will definitely be reestablished.

The clear contrast here provided between the emphasis on death by these three qualified representatives of our three major faiths is one of the outstanding contributions of this book.

A significant and demanding theme which runs through the whole presentation is that if we as individuals and as a society could ourselves come to terms with death, we could do a better job in telling our children about it.

As the research psychologist, Robert Katzenbaum, comments, "How would the child develop his understanding of death if he grew up in a society that truly had solved its intellectual and emotional relationship to death?"

Nearly all of the authors touch on this theme, but the remarks of sociology professor Robert Fulton are perhaps the most challenging. He asks, bluntly, "Is Death dying in the United States?" He adds, "The collection of readings in this book is both an expression of and a reaction to a very significant change taking place in American society. Whereas death was once regarded as inevitable, it is coming to be viewed as the result of personal negligence or of an unforeseen accident. Death is now a temporal matter that man treats much as he would an avoidable illness or physical stigma."

Memorial services take the place of funerals. We speak of people "passing away," of flowers which "wither" or "fade." We seem to be trying to push death and the thought of death into the background if not denying it entirely. In fact, as the Reverend Jackson points out, a few generations ago parents could not talk about the beginnings of life but could confront honestly its end. Now parents openly talk with their children about sex and childbirth and the biological processes surrounding the beginning of life, but are strangely confounded when they try to speak of death and dying. They tend to hand on their own anxiety and negative attitudes.

And yet, as Claiborne Jones says so correctly from his biological point of view, no matter how you sidestep, you cannot do away with death. "The stubborn fact remains that the world of biology is the world of living *and* dying. . . . There can be no death without life and conversely there can be no life without death. At every biological level above the photosynthetic, every man's life depends upon the regular, orderly, uninterrupted occurrence of death after death after death."

All agree that only if the adult can come to terms with death himself, can he give a reasonable explanation to, and adequately deal with, the emotional reactions of his children. And that there is danger of increasing disruption of family life and other social relations by death in a society which increasingly is unable to accept or explain it.

Now for that important practical question—should children attend funerals? The answer from all authors is an unequivocal "yes," except perhaps for children under seven. As Jackson points out, children and ceremonials have a natural affinity, and actually children need more rituals not fewer. To deny children the chance to participate in important family events is to deny them important opportunities for therapeutic communication. It is through rites and rituals and ceremonies that people work through their feelings. While no child should be *forced* to participate, it would be wise to offer the opportunities that would be relevant to his needs. If participating in the funeral seems impractical, the child could visit the funeral home with a mature and competent adult who would answer his questions.

Rabbi Grollman concurs: "To shut a youngster out of the funeral experience might be quite costly and damaging to his future development. He is an integral part of the family unit and should participate with them on this sad but momentous occasion. However, if the child is unwilling, he should not be forced to go or made to feel guilty because 'he let the family down.' If he does not attend the funeral, it may be wise to provide an opportunity at some later time to visit the cemetery and see the grave."

And Fulton states specifically, "The wise management of grief in children as well as in adults revolves around two major factors: one, the encouragement and facilitation of the normal mourning process, and two, the prevention of delayed or distorted grief responses. In our society, the funeral possesses the potential to compel the individual to acknowledge his loss."

This is not only an extremely thought-provoking but an extremely practical book. Sensible advice abounds. Just a little of it here. The main suggestion, from the clergyman authors, seems to be not to try to reassure the child with falsehoods, not to teach him a lot of nonsense. Children need, at the time of death, not theology but an affirmation of the priority of life over death.

The child should not be subjected to theological assumptions having to do with revenge and punishment, Heaven or Hell. Rather, the experience should be explored in terms of its emotional meaning for the individual who encounters it. Then the emotional capital invested in a lost love object can be more readily withdrawn and reinvested where it can produce a healthful response in life. Most especially, says Rabbi Grollman, since no one knows God fully or understands the mystery of death, we should never impart a fanciful doctrine that the youngster will later need to unlearn. That is, parents should strive for the child's spiritual development rather than for positive acceptance of theological doctrine.

Children should not be entirely protected from participation in the grief of the adult. And above all, the value of taking part in the funeral service and ritual is stressed.

School psychologist Hella Moller further emphasizes that the child both at school and at home should be given the opportunity to talk about death and to air his own views and theories. Don't just talk *to* them. Get them to talk to you.

This collection of writings is further enriched with a chapter by Gregory Rochlin, a psychiatrist, as to his own experience with child patients and their notions about death. Anthropologists Diskin and Guggenheim broaden the presentation by describing the way children in different cultures respond to death. And Eulalie Steinmetz Ross, from the librarian's point of view, emphasizes the fact that books not only enhance life and death but that stories which discuss death provide a good way for the child to become acquainted with death in a relatively harmless way.

That all authors are qualified to speak on the subject is indicated not just by their professional and personal backgrounds but, more than that, by the authority with which they write on this subject.

Death is a universal and inevitable process and must be faced. This collection of readings should help any reader to face it more effectively.

LOUISE BATES AMES
Gesell Institute

Explaining Death to Children

PROLOGUE

Explaining Death to Children

"Before I can teach children about death, someone has to straighten me out!"

So said a sophisticated religious school teacher when asked how she explains death to her students. Her comment was understandable. Death touches the ebb and flow of the deepest feelings and relationships. Especially in Western culture, man has tended to seek refuge in euphemistic language. Movies and plays often treat death as a dramatic illusion. One of the reasons why many persons reject the aged is that they remind them of death. Discussion about death is relegated to a tabooed area formerly reserved for sex and dread diseases like cancer.

Fear of death is not only a cultural phenomenon but a part of being human. The knownness of life and the unknownness of death, the termination of the natural joys of living, the conclusion of the relatively controllable activity of life all create a pervasive dread of death touching every man.

Since no mortal has ever pierced the veil of mystery surrounding death, the teacher and particularly the parent are frightened at the thought of finality. Perhaps for this reason many adults try in every way to keep from children the idea of death. Parents wish to protect their offspring. Often because of their own anxieties, they rationalize by saying: "The youngsters are really too little to understand." Yet, the parents who try to hide their grief for the sake of their youngsters are rarely able to do so effectively. The gap between what the adults say and do and the underlying feeling that the children sense is likely to cause more confusion and distress than if the parents tell the child the truth.

There are no simple, foolproof answers to death, the most difficult of all questions. Not only children but adults differ more widely in their reactions to death than to any other human phenomenon. But in trying to help the children see death as an inevitable human experience and in sharing grief with them, the parents may be able to diminish in the process their own bewilderment and distress. Instead of feeling inadequate because they do not know what happens after death, adults should welcome their children's questions as occasions to explore the problem with them.

While insight is a gift, parents must first place themselves in a position to receive it. They must prepare themselves for it. They must be quiet and learn to listen to their children. They must sit down and watch the youngsters while they work and play. They must observe them in action and hear the tone and timbre of their voices. Let the youngsters tell the adults how they feel about death, what they think, what they know, where they want to go. Parents should respond by trying to let the youngsters know that they understand what the children are trying to say. Adults should try to answer the question in the spirit in which it is asked.

Children can understand the meaning of death.

Language has a different meaning for adults and children. Philosophical meanings are far too abstract for the very young. But this does not mean that they do not reach out for an understanding of death. The small child tries out the word "death" and rolls it around his tongue. He experiments with the appearance of death much as he experiments with his daddy's hat and briefcase to get the feel of "going to work." All children are concerned about death and frightened by it. Some have even said they do not wish to grow up, "because if you grow up, you get old and die."

Dr. Jerome Bruner, Director of the Harvard Center for Cognitive Studies, begins with the hypothesis that any subject can be explained effectively in an intellectually honest form to any child at any stage of development. Understandably, the knowledge may be imparted with symbolic imagery or intellectual reasoning.

It cannot be precisely determined what concepts of death

can be understood at a given age. Children differ in behavior and development. Some are responsible and stable; others are more immature and younger in relation to their years. Girls are generally more mature than boys. The ability to cope with the material will depend upon the maturity of the individual and his ability to cope with his problems.

In addition, environments vary greatly. The child's individual thinking is influenced not only by his biological equipment but by his adjustment to the world as understood through his family and social hierarchies. A young Jewish child in Nazi Germany would have a clearer insight into the reality of death than the small American lad whose parents believe that he should be shielded from any knowledge which might arouse painful emotions. The mourning task is initially dependent on this ability to have a concept of death and would differ from individual to individual as well as society to society. Age is but one of the factors affecting an understanding of death, to be contrasted to the unique religious, political, and social attitudes of the person and his group's dynamic cultural life.

"Some two-year-olds will have a concept of death, while five-year-olds will not," Dr. Robert A. Furman reports in a continuing study that is now in its twentieth year. "It is fundamental, however, to make a sharp distinction between a child's not mourning and his incapability of mourning." Dr. Furman dismisses the notion that a child may be incapable of grief. He also quotes a colleague who stresses that "mourning as a reaction to the real loss of a loved one must be carried through to completion."

In another recent study in Budapest, Dr. Maria Nagy studied 378 children between the ages of three and ten to determine their feelings concerning death. She learned that between these ages children tend to pass through three different phases. The youngster from three to five may deny death as a regular and final process. To him death is like sleep; you are dead, then you are alive again. Or like taking a journey; you are gone, then you come back again. This child may experience many times each day some real aspects of what he considers "death," such as when his father goes to work and his mother to the grocery. When the late President Kennedy's son John-John returned on a visit to the White House following the demise of his father and saw his father's secretary, he looked up at her and said: "When is my daddy coming back?"

Since the mother and father usually return from an absence, the child comes to believe that the people he loves will always come back again. Consequently, the youngster when told about the death of a member of the family may seem to be callous and possibly express an immediate sorrow and then seem to forget about it.

Between five and nine, children appear to be able to accept the idea that a person has died but may not accept it as something that must happen to everyone and particularly to themselves. Around the age of nine, the child recognizes death as an inevitable experience that will occur to him. Of course, these are all rough approximations with many variations, but they may prove to be of some value when children raise questions. Nagy's investigation also demonstrated three main questions in the child's mind: "What is death?" "What makes people die?" "What happens to people when they die, where do they go?"

What should parents say?

It is easier to suggest what *not* to say. Do not tell a child what he is incapable of understanding. Do not be evasive, but modify explanations according to the child's understanding. What is said is important, but *how* it is said has even greater bearing on whether the child will develop anxiety and fears or accept, within his capacity, the fact of death. The understanding of the very young child is, of course, limited. He doesn't ask for or need details. His questions should be answered in a matter-of-fact way, briefly, without too much emotion. Too complicated a reply often confuses the child.

Always remember to avoid philosophical interpretation.

Even adults find it difficult to comprehend abstruse concepts such as "ultimate reality" and "the absolute." Children, too, easily mistake the meaning of words and phrases, or take literally what is only an idiom. The result is that fantasies are inadvertently formed. One boy, hearing that God was high and bright, assumed that the weathercock on the barn must be God, for it was the highest and brightest object he knew. Difficult terms may slip by the child as he takes only the familiar words to weave them into a meaning of his own. Dr. Jean Piaget, the great developmental psychologist, points out that even when an adult supplies an answer, it is frequently only partially heard and inaccurately comprehended.

Even if the child does not fully understand the explanations given him, death will be less of a mystery and therefore less frightening to him. And he will, in time, ask further questions that permit further rational explanations. If his questions are answered frankly, he may even drop the whole matter for the time, satisfied that nothing is being hidden from him, relieving him of doubts and disturbing fantasies.

Often the children ask questions to test the parents. In answering, the parent needs to understand the train of thought leading to the question. Otherwise the reply he gives may be misleading. What is the child really asking? What does he mean when as asks: "What is going to happen to you, Mommy, when you die?" Is he in truth seeking a theological answer or is he searching for security in his anxiety? Perhaps he wants to know: "Who will take care of me?" Or, "Will Daddy die, too, and leave me all alone?" The best answer may be mostly nonverbal. The parent might hold the youngster close and say: "All of us hope to go on living together for ages and ages—for a longer time than you can even think of."

Parents who have their own religious convictions will naturally share them with the child. They may explain in an understandable way their belief in a life after death. Those adults who do not believe in a personal hereafter might say: "We really don't know. But this we do believe—the kind of

lives we lead will continue to be reflected in the lives of on-
coming generations. People the world over have different
approaches to this question which has no final answers. Each
one learns day by day that there is more to be discovered
about this important subject." This type of reply prompts
the child to go on thinking and probing. And even if there
are no definitive answers, he comes to understand that unanswered problems are also part of life.

In explaining death to children, the parent may proceed
from two areas of concern. There is the *interpretative* where
the religious concepts are explained. "There is a God; God is
a loving spirit; God's love transcends human experience;
God can be trusted." In addition, there is the *factual* area
where the adult draws upon scientific sources. In this sphere,
as far as the physical body is concerned, the parents should
make it clear that with death, life stops, the deceased cannot
return, and the body is buried. A less explicit explanation is
apt to result in more confusion and misinterpretation.

Should parents indicate their religious convictions, if any?

Of course, the approach will depend upon what the parents believe. Since religion deals with the meaning of life
and death, those with deep faith in God may find real comfort in their beliefs when one of their loved ones dies. Those
who believe in personal immortality often find the problem
of death less painful since there is a conviction that they
may one day rejoin their loved ones. Explanation of death
will vary according to whether it is seen as a beginning of a
new experience or an end to existence. Be honest and be
open. Children adjust most quickly when they are in on
things and have the help of those they love.

Essentially, the adult's aid to the youngsters will depend
very largely upon his own resources, his own attitude, and
the social culture and religious traditions affecting him. One
can answer the children's questions with sincerity and conviction only if one responds with feelings that are real.

How should the subject of death be introduced?

Since the subject matter is so sensitive, the first discussion should not concern the death of the child's mother or father. Nor should the explanation revolve around dogma, belief, or theology. Death and its meaning should be approached gently, indirectly, and unsentimentally. It might involve a discussion of flowers and how long they last. Or whether bees and wasps that sting humans should be destroyed. Or the springboard may be an immediate experience such as the death of a pet or a biblical story where death is mentioned. One should proceed slowly, step by step, according to the understanding of the child and the personal beliefs of the parents. Fear will be lessened when the discussion is focused not on the morbid details of death but on the beauty of life.

WHAT NOT TO SAY ABOUT DEATH

Would it not be wise to answer a child with stories and fairy tales about death?

Childish descriptions of death as eternal sleep are subject to much change and revision with advancing age. Adults must tailor fundamental knowledge and belief to the interests and capacities of the children. But the inability of the adult to tell the young the whole truth about death, even if it were available, does not give him the prerogative to tell a lie. The parents should never cover up with fiction that they will someday repudiate. To state "Now Grandmother is up in the sky with a beautiful pair of shining wings so that she can fly away" is not faith. It is imaginative fancy. And it is not helpful to the child. It simply gets in his way when he is having trouble enough distinguishing the real from the pretend.

Why do parents feel it necessary to give the child explanations of death that they themselves do not accept?

A parent may feel his own beliefs are too stark for a child.

He therefore attempts to affirm a conventional conviction about death which he does not hold. A mother, for instance, may comfort her young son on the loss of his father by saying he will live eternally, while she herself is mourning a husband irretrievably dead. Or a father may spin a tale of the heavenly happiness of the children's mother, while hopeless finality fills his own heart. In such cases the confused child, not able to bring awareness of the double-talk to the surface, develops a double dread of death. He panics not only at the loss but also at the agonized reaction of the bereaved parent.

Some pragmatic parents, while not exactly believing in the survival of personality, operate on the theory that they have nothing to lose and perhaps something to gain in answering, *as if* for example, life after death were a fact. Sometimes because the adults' own emotional reactions to death are so painful, they make statements to their children that are misconceptions of reality. They add to the child's own fantasies representing a realm halfway between the fully conscious and the unconscious thought of dreams.

What are some unhealthy explanations of death?

Mother has gone on a long journey. Again an untruth is stated that the child must later unlearn for himself. The parents are catering to misconception and fantasy. Freud remarked that, to the child, death means little more than departure or disappearance, and that it is represented in dreams by going on a journey.

To say, "Your mother has gone away for a very long journey for a very long time," is geared to provide some comfort for the child and to ease the strain of his mother's disappearance. But the child interprets this explanation to mean that his mother has abandoned and deserted him without telling him good-bye. Far from being comforted and holding the memory of the deceased dear, the child may react with anxiety and resentment. This is not surprising, for the adult's pattern of mourning is similar. How often has a widow castigated a deceased husband: "How could he do this to me? How could he leave me alone?" A euphemism of death is "when my husband *left* me."

The child may develop the delusion that someday the mother will return. Or unconsciously he may assume, "Mommy didn't really care enough about me so she stayed away." And if the mother only went away on a journey, why is everyone crying?

God took Daddy away because He wants and loves the good in heaven. The mother seeking to ease the burden for her child explained the death of the father: "We can't be selfish about it. If God wants Daddy because he is so good and so wonderful, we must be brave and strong and accept God's will and request." Despite the best of intentions to bring comfort, a questionable theology is introduced. Adults may understand that "the Lord giveth and the Lord taketh away" in the sense that many believe that the God who makes birth and life possible also makes death necessary. Despite hopes and fears, they cannot alter the unalterable: "Daddy is dead!" But to assert that God took the loved one because "he was good" is to question the posture of both religious and scientific reality. Why be good if God may reward us for our piety by death? If one lives to an older age, does this mean that he was not good? The righteous one may surely die young but may he not live to a ripe old age? To equate longevity of life with goodness is hardly a solution to a vexing problem. The child may develop fear, resentment, and hatred against a God who capriciously robbed him of his father because the man was loved by God. The youngster may become even more frightened when he thinks: "But God loves me too; maybe I'll be the next one He will take away!"

Daddy is now in heaven. "Mother, if Daddy is supposed to go to heaven, how is it that they buried him in the ground? He's heading in the wrong direction. How can God take Daddy to heaven if Daddy is in the ground?" And the child demanded in an active voice that the mother disinter the remains of the father. The parent in this case did not herself believe in heaven but took a deceptive and dishonest path. Many parents realize that the introduction of the traditional idea of heaven creates far more problems than it solves.

Grandma died because she was sick. The psychologist, Dr. Chloe, has asserted that small children equate death with illness and going to the hospital. People do become sick and die, but most everyone becomes ill many times and yet survives to live a long life. Will the child himself die if he has a cold, the mumps, the measles? How does the youngster make a distinction between a serious illness and one not quite so grave? The comparison of sickness to death only prolongs and intensifies the fear of death.

To die is to sleep. It is only natural to draw the parallel. Homer in the *Iliad* alludes to sleep (Hypnos) and death (Thanatos) as twin brothers, and many of our religious prayers entwine the ideas of sleep and death. Traditional Jews, for example, on arising from sleep in the morning thank God for having restored them to life again.

But one must be careful to explain the difference between *sleep* and *death;* otherwise, he runs the risk of causing a pathological dread of bedtime. There are children who toss about in fear of going to "eternal sleep," never to wake up again. Some youngsters actually struggle with all their might to remain awake, fearful that they might go off to the deceased grandfather's type of sleep.

Understandably, it is easier for the parent to respond with fictions and half-truths that also make him appear to know all the answers. But the secure adult has no need to profess infinite knowledge. It is far healthier for a child to share the joint quest for additional wisdom than for his immediate curiosity to be appeased by fantasy in the guise of fact. The child may be shocked to discover there is something his father or mother does not know, but he has to discover this as he grows. Deception is worse than the reality factor that the parents are not all-knowing. Why not admit the lack of understanding in this mysterious area of life?

How Does the Child Experience Grief?

Do children experience grief?

Of course, the child experiences a sense of loss and with it, sorrow. His grief is a complicated mechanism. He feels remorseful that a loved one is dead. On the other hand, he feels sorry for himself because he was picked out for personal pain. He is faced with many problems about which he is helplessly confused. He may believe that the departed has run out on him. His fears often give rise to anger with hostile feelings toward those who are closest to him. The knowledge that from now on there is nothing the child can do to "make up" to the deceased can be a very heavy burden. Yet, the parents who understand that a variety of reactions may possibly occur are well on their way to helping the child toward a more positive and more mature approach in dealing with the loss.

According to Dr. John Bowlby of Tavistock Clinic, London, each child experiences three phases in the natural grieving process. The first is protest when the child cannot quite believe the person is dead, and he attempts, sometimes angrily, to regain him. The next is pain, despair, and disorganization when the youngster begins to accept the fact that the loved one is really gone. Finally there is hope, when the youngster begins to organize his life without the lost person.

How does the child face the loss of a pet?

When a pet dies, the child is brought face to face with some of the implications of death—its complete finality and the grief and loss it inflicts. The youngster may experience some guilt because he feels he had not cared well enough for the pet and was in some way responsible for its fate. He may conduct in greatest secrecy an elaborate burial. To the adult, the ceremony may seem to be a thoughtless mockery of a very sacred religious ritual, but to children these burial rites are far from prank or ridicule. The youngsters engage in them with as much zest and enthusiasm as a mock wedding ceremony or secret initiation. This kind of "game" has profound meaning. Here is their real opportunity to work things out for themselves and play out their feelings and fears. Sometimes the "play" is accompanied by real sadness and tears which afford an opportunity to help them put the experience somewhat behind them. Parents may well suggest such a ceremony to a child whose pet has died.

There is the example of a small boy whose pet dog was killed by an automobile. His first reaction was one of shock and dismay. This mood was followed by outrage against his parents who he felt were guilty of the death because they did not take proper care of the pet. The boy behaved like the adult who rages against God for neglecting His charges. Yet, the anger against the parents was but a substitute for his own guilt, for the youngster had on occasion expressed the wish to be rid of "that awful pest." The child then insisted that as part of the burial service one of his favorite toys be buried with the dog. The toy served as a kind of peace offering to the offended pet. Now, the lad was freed of his own anxiety and could continue to function effectively in his everyday activities. Thus the ritual combined the dynamics of guilt, assuagement, and reparation which possess a similarity in the mourning behavior of adults.

Usually the child accepts the loss of a pet, constituting a step in acceptance of one of the many unpleasant realities of everyday living. More often than not, a new pet replaces the dead one, and life goes on much as it did before.

The child's loss of a brother or sister.

Although deprived of a sibling who had played an important role as caretaker or playmate, the child still has the security of the parents' presence. Yet it would be an error to assume that the death of a brother or sister is relatively unimportant, even though few conscious and readily discernible reactions may be detected. For the death of a child invariably affects the parents. Whether they turn more closely and protectively to the surviving child, or are so disturbed by their grief that they are unable to maintain a healthy parent relationship to him, the child will experience some modification of his life situation.

An older child's reaction to such a death may be the frightening realization that this could happen to him! Would it occur tomorrow, or next week, or next year? If the cause of death of an older sibling is not made clear, the younger child may take on babyish behavior to prevent himself from growing to that age when he, too, might die.

The youngster may try to replace the deceased person. He sees his parents grieving and he wants to make everything all right again. He may suddenly try to act like the lost brother in ways not suited to his own capacities and well-being. He may be burdened by the feeling that he must take the other child's place.

If he and his brother or sister were close, death may bring a long-lasting feeling of loss. His parents' grief, the many reminders around the house, and the abrupt cessation of a relationship that had been an important part of his life, all combine to make readjustment slow and painful. The situation may be further complicated by strong feelings of guilt because of past anger or jealousy toward the dead person, or because of failure to make the brother or sister happier while he or she was still alive.

What are some reactions to the death of a parent?

One of the greatest crises in the life of a child is the death of a parent. Never again will the world be as secure a place as it was before. The familiar design of family life is completely disrupted. The child suffers not only the loss of a parent, but is deprived of the attention he needs at a time when he craves that extra reassurance that he is loved and will be cared for. Here, too, the child's reactions are complicated by guilt feelings. Sometimes guilt evolves from earlier hostility toward the dead person, and from the feeling that the survivor bears some responsibility for his death.

Anna Freud points out that a child's first love for his mother becomes the pattern for all later loves. "The ability to love, like all other human faculties, has to be learned and practiced." If this relationship is interrupted, through death or absence, the child may do one of four things: remain attached to a fantasy of the dead person; invest his love in things (or work); be frightened to love anyone but himself; or, hopefully, accept his loss and find another real person to love.

If the boy loses a mother, he may regress to an earlier stage of development. His speech becomes more babyish. He begins to suck his thumb. He whines a great deal and demands the attention of adults. He says in effect: "Dear Mother, see, I am only a very little baby. Please love me and stay with me." Later on in life, because he was injured by his mother, the prototype of all women, he may believe that all women have a tendency to hurt men. To avoid being wounded by them, he loves them and leaves them before the girls can do what his mother did to him: hurt and abandon him. However, it cannot be overemphasized that these dynamics need *not* occur. For example, in a home where there is no mother, there are almost always mother substitutes—a housekeeper, an aunt, or an older sister. Even in time of death there can be an exposure to intimate relationship with some significant person.

The small boy whose father dies will feel the loss of a male person to imitate, a masculine foil with whom he can learn to temper his feelings of aggression and love. The mother, however, may contribute to the boy's difficulty. Deprived of a husband, she may try to make up for her own deprivation by trying to obtain gratification from her son. The boy feels he now possesses his mother and she will continue to gratify him completely. Therefore he need not look for pleasure elsewhere. From observations, one can cite many examples and consequences of doting mothers and spoiled sons. (The reverse may be observed in girls who lose their father or mother.)

In general, if a child allows himself to find someone else whom he can come to love and trust, it is a good indication that he has worked out his grief. If he has not, he may spend the rest of his years searching, consciously or unconsciously, for an exact replica of his childlike relationship with the lost person and be disappointed over and over again that someone else cannot fulfill his original needs. For example, we all know people who are very successful at their jobs but who are unable to maintain a devoted and continuous love relationship.

In times of death, should parents discourage the child from crying?

Children's capacity for grief is often not recognized. The thought of death does bring fear. Paul Tillich, the theologian, who has been a strong influence in American psychiatry, based his theory of anxiety on the belief that man is finite, subject to nonbeing.

Yet, is this the child's first experience with death? He has heard the word used before, and he may have been exposed to death. He has seen dead animals and dead insects. He knows flowers wilt and die. And he is afraid. Death strikes his own family or pet, and he cries as he expresses painful emotion. When the child gives vent to tears and sorrowful words, he feels somewhat relieved. By the display of emotions he makes the dead person or pet seem more worthy.

Too often, well-meaning people say: "Be brave! Don't cry! Don't take it so hard!" But why not? Tears are the first and most natural tribute that can be paid to the one who is gone. The child misses the deceased. He wishes the loved one were still with him.

The son and daughter whose father dies should express their grief. It is natural. They loved him. They miss him. To say, "Be brave!" and especially to the son, "Be a man!" sounds as if one were minimizing their loss and places an impossible burden upon the boy. Be realistic enough to say, "Yes, it's tough!" Make them feel free to express themselves.

Otherwise the adult deprives them of the natural emotion of grief.

Don't be afraid of causing tears. It is like a safety valve. So often parents and friends deliberately attempt to veer the conversation away from the deceased. They are apprehensive of the tears that might start to flow. They do not understand that expressing grief through tears is natural and normal.

Tears are the tender tribute of yearning affection for those who have died but can never be forgotten. The worst thing possible is for the child to repress them. The child who stoically keeps his grief bottled up inside may later find a release in a more serious explosion to his inner makeup.

Crying is the sound of anguish at losing a part of oneself in the death of one whom he loves. Everywhere and always, grief is the human expression of the need for love and the love of life.

Just as the parents should not deny the child the opportunity to cry, they should not urge him to display unfelt sorrow. He is likely to feel confused and hypocritical when told he ought to express a regret he does not honestly feel. There are many outlets for grief and the child must utilize those openings that most naturally meet his needs.

What are other possible reactions to death?

Death is an outstanding example of a traumatic event which threatens the safety of all the surviving members of the family. It could bring in its train these well-marked symptoms:

Denial: "I don't believe it. It didn't happen. It is just a dream. Daddy will come back. He will! He will!"

The child may frequently look as if he were unaffected because he is trying to defend himself against the terrible loss by pretending that it has not really happened. The adult may even feel that the youngster's apparent unconcern is heartless. Or the parent may be relieved and feel, "Isn't it lucky! I am sure he misses his father, but he does not seem to be really bothered by it." Usually, this signifies that the child has found the loss too great to accept, and goes on pretending secretly that the person is still alive. This is why it is so necessary to help the child accept reality by not conjuring up fairy tales and compounding the problem with: "He went away on a long journey."

Bodily Distress: "I have a tightness in my throat!" "I can't breathe." "I have no appetite at all." "I have no strength." "I am exhausted." "I can't do my homework." "I can't sleep." "I had a nightmare."

The anxiety has expressed itself in physical and emotional symptoms and is often brought on by visits from friends or the mention of the deceased loved one.

Hostile Reactions to the Deceased: "How could Daddy do this to me?" "Didn't he care enough for me to stay alive?" "Why did he leave me?"

The child feels deserted and abandoned. "Bad Mommy—she's gone away!" There may yet be another aspect. Think of a child's anger after he has been left by his mother for a day or two. Although he may not show much reaction just after her return, later he may turn on her angrily saying: "Where were you, Mommy? Where were you?" Similarly, the child uses this protest to recover the lost person and ensure that she never deserts him again. Although no amount of anger will make the loved one return, the youngster may still use it simply because the protest worked successfully in the past.

Guilt: "He got sick because I was naughty. I killed him!"

Guilt is often coupled with the expectations of punishment.

Hostile Reactions to Others: "It is the doctor's fault. He didn't treat him right." "Maybe he was murdered." "It is God's fault. How could He do this to me?" "The minister doesn't know anything—he keeps saying God is good."

The noisy anger is turned outward usually in the attempt to cope with guilt. The youngster may even be angry at sympathetic friends simply because they are not the deceased.

He doesn't want any substitutes—even as the very young child does not want anyone but his mommy.

Replacement: "Uncle Ben, do you love me, really love me?"

The child makes a fast play for the affection of others as a substitute for the parent who had died.

Assumption of Mannerisms of Deceased: "Do I look like Daddy?"

He attempts to take on the characteristic traits of the father by walking and talking like him. He tries to carry out the wishes of the deceased. Or the boy tries to become the father as the head of the family and the mate of the mother.

Idealization: "How dare you say anything against Daddy! He was perfect."

In the attempt to fight off his own unhappy thoughts, the child becomes obsessed with the father's good qualities. The falsification is out of keeping with the father's real life and character.

Anxiety: "I feel like Daddy when he died. I have a pain in my chest."

The child becomes preoccupied with the physical symptoms that terminated the life of the father. He transfers the symptoms to himself by a process of identification.

Panic: "Who will take care of me now?" "Suppose something happens to Mommy?" "Daddy used to bring home money for food and toys. Who will get these things for us?"

This state of confusion and shock needs the parent's supportive love: "My health is fine. I will take care of you. There is enough money for food and toys."

These are some of the reactions of children as well as adults. Some may never appear. Some come at the time of crises. Others may be delayed, since so often the child represses his emotions and attempts to appear calm in the face of tragedy. At one moment he may express his sense of helplessness by acting indifferent. A moment later the feeling of loss will take the form of boisterous play. The parents may detect what the child is thinking from some superficially unrelated questions that he may later ask: "Mommy and Daddy, where did the light go when I blew out the candles on my cake?"

What are some of the distorted mourning reactions?

The inability to mourn leads to personal disintegration, the upshot of which is mental illness. The line of demarcation between "normal psychological aspects of bereavement" and "distorted mourning reactions" is thin indeed, just as is the division between "normality" and "neurosis." The difference is not in symptom but in intensity. It is a *continued* denial of reality even many months after the funeral, or a *prolonged* bodily distress, or a *persistent* panic, or an *extended* guilt, or an *unceasing* idealization, or an *enduring* apathy and anxiety, or an *unceasing* hostile reaction to the deceased and to others. Each manifestation does not in itself determine a distorted grief reaction; it is only as it is viewed by the professional in the composition of the total formulation. The psychiatrist may detect its pathology in the hallucinations of his patients. He may observe its appearance in the obsessive-compulsive behavior where the bereaved attempts to relieve guilt in a variety of ways, such as extreme cleanliness. He may discover its overtones in psychosomatic diseases, such as the morbid anxiety as to one's own health, with conjuring up of imaginary ailments. In psychotic patients, there is seen the stupor of the catatonic, sometimes likened to the death state. Delusions of immortality are found in certain schizophrenics. If there are any doubts, the parent should seek special assistance for the child from the psychologist or child guidance clinic. Without such outside help, few parents, in the midst of their own grief, can give proper support for that child facing a severe mourning reaction.

Does a child really feel guilt?

There is a degree of guilt involved in every death. It is human to blame oneself for the person's death. Even if the adult knows he did everything in his power to prevent the death and to make the loved one happy, he is still apt to search his mind for ways that he could have done more. After the Cocoanut Grove fire in Boston, one woman could not stop blaming herself for having quarreled with her husband just before his death. Often, the recrimination is an attempt to turn the clock back, undo the quarrel, and magically prevent the loss.

Children more than adults are apt to feel guilty since, in their experience, bad things happen to them because they were naughty. The desertion of the parent must be a retribution for their wrongdoing. Therefore, they search their minds for the "bad deed" that caused it.

Often guilt is induced by the child's misconceptions of reality. One youngster was told that to live you must eat. Since she did not eat her cereal the morning her father died, she concluded that it was she who brought about his death.

Young children believe in magic. That is, if one wishes someone harm, the belief will bring results. When the little boy said in anger, "I hope you die, Mom," and the mother did die, the lad felt responsible and guilty.

Painful thoughts are recalled. "I was terrible to her." "I kicked her." "Why did I call her those awful names?" "What will happen to me?" "Will God punish me?" Any normal child has feelings of intense hostility toward another child or an adult. If this person dies, the youngster may feel that in some way his thoughts contributed to the person's death.

The living sometimes feel guilt simply because they are alive. They may feel they should be censured for wishing that the sick person hurry up and die. Or they feel they should be blamed because they secretly hope that their friends' mommies would die, so they won't be the only one without a mother.

The resultant behavior varies. There may be aggressiveness, with or without excessive excitability. There may be unsociability and obvious despondence. There may be a lack of interest and attention in class, or a degree of forgetfulness of ordinary concerns. It must be underscored that guilt is a normal reaction to the experience of death.

Helping the child to relieve the guilt.

From a commonsense point of view, the child's guilt is usually unreasonable. Therefore, it is important for the parents to help the child give vent to his anxieties. In his childish mind he may remember times when he may not have been so good to this person as he should have been. Let him know that all people try to be good and loving but do not always succeed. Nor does one have to. One does the best he can. Tell the child: "You did the best you could. You had nothing to do with his death. All people die." By all means possible, parents should avoid linking suffering and death with sin and punishment.

Explain to him that "wishing does *not* make it so." Try to recall those happy moments when the child did make the deceased very happy. For the youngster who is too young to give shape to his thoughts or to find the words which might relieve his guilt, the best therapy is through relationships with other people. Children learn self-acceptance by being accepted by others. They learn to trust through living with trustworthy parents and teachers. They learn to love by being loved.

THE FUNERAL

Should a child go to the funeral of a loved one?

Children cannot and should not be spared knowledge about death. When death occurs within or close to a family, no amount of caution and secrecy can hide from the child the feeling that something important and threatening has happened. He cannot avoid being affected by the overtones of grief and solemnity. All the emotional reactions a child is likely to have to death in the family—sorrow and loneliness, anger and rejection, guilt, anxiety about the future, and the conviction that nothing is certain or stable anymore—can be considerably lessened if the child feels that he knows what is going on and that adults are not trying to hide things from him.

Often a parent will ask: "Do you think the boys should attend the funeral service of their grandfather? They loved him very dearly. They were very close to him. I'm afraid that if they go they will become too highly disturbed. Don't you think it would be much better if they would stay in the home of some friend or some neighbor during the day of the funeral?"

The parent is usually expecting an affirmative reply to this last question. Parents intend it as a kindness when they shield the child from death, as they send him away to stay with a friend or relative and permit him to return only after the funeral. They are dismayed by the suggestion that the child share in the service honoring the life and memory of someone close to him. Yet recognized child authorities have come to the conclusion that not only is it correct to permit a child to attend a funeral but, from approximately the age of seven, a child should be encouraged to attend. A child is an integral part of the family unit and should participate with the family on every important occasion. The funeral is an important occasion in the life of the family. It may be sad—but it still is a crucial occasion in the life of every family. A youngster should have the same right as any other member of the family to attend the funeral and to offer his last respects and to express his own love and devotion. To shut a child out of this experience of sorrow might be quite costly and damaging to his personality. To deprive him of a sense of belonging at this very emotional moment is to shake his security.

If your child goes to the services at the chapel and cemetery, explain in advance the details of the funeral. Tell him people are buried in places called cemeteries with stones placed on each grave to tell the names of people who rest there, and the place is kept beautiful with flowers and trees for remembrance. Children are more relaxed and less disturbed if they observe the funeral than by the fantasies conjured up by fertile young minds.

If the child does not attend the interment service, he may come to the cemetery later with his family. This is advisable when the child cannot accept the reality of death. There is the case of a boy who was told his mother went on a journey. He became sullen and unmanageable. Whenever the mother's name was mentioned, the child would speak of her in the vilest language. Then finally one day the child was told the truth. He was then taken to the cemetery where he could visit the grave. The child was heartbroken for he now realized that she had really died. Yet he felt a lot better for the experience. At least now he knew what had happened. And most important he knew that his mother had not run out on him, had not abandoned him or deserted him.

It is difficult to determine whether an apprehensive youngster should be encouraged to attend the funeral. The parents' own judgment should be the best guide. Of course, the child is frightened and may need a little support. Yet, he should never be forced to go. If one can anticipate in advance that there will be hysterical outbursts, it might be wise to keep the sensitive child at home.

Some enlightened adults have helped a youngster feel that he still has an important role to play by asking him to stay home with someone he knows well to answer doorbells and telephones and run errands. After the funeral, he helps to receive friends. During the mourning period that follows, he should not be sent away. He should be given the chance to feel grief and mingle with the family.

The important fact to always remember is that just as children cannot be spared knowledge about death, they cannot and should not be excluded from the grief and mourning following death. With as much calmness and assurance as possible, the parent must give the child calm reassurance of love, not only by tone of voice but by warmth of arms. The parent must keep in mind that children will exhibit their grief differently from adults. A child who is deeply affected

by a sense of loss may try to find solace in active play or give
expression to his confused feelings by behaving in a noisy and
—by adult standards—"improper" manner. It's more important that the child be permitted to express his grief in
his own way at a time like this than that he be reprimanded
and his burden of guilt increased for the sake of convention
and propriety.

How Do We Help the Child Who Has Lost a Loved One?

The adult must understand the youngster's emotional
needs. This is accomplished not by cross-questioning but by
empathy, understanding, and love. Love contributes to the
child's security and gives him the feeling that he is valued. He
is then able to love in return.

A parent should encourage what Sigmund Freud calls
the "ties of dissolution." That is, reviewing with the youngster pleasant and unpleasant memories of the deceased. As
each event is reviewed, a pang of pain is felt at the thought
that the experience will never be repeated. As pain is experienced, the youngster is able to dissolve himself of his
emotional ties with the dead person. A gradual working over
of such old thoughts and feelings is a necessary part of the
mourning at any age, and a prelude to acceptance of the
death as a real fact.

Assist the child to unburden his feelings through cathar-
sis, confession, remembrance, and release. The child needs
to talk, not just to be talked to. He should be given every
opportunity to discuss the person who has died and be permitted to feel that, if he wishes to do so, he may even express antipathy as well as affection for the deceased.

Adults should encourage the child to accept the reality
of the death. The approach should include a sympathetic,
never-shaming attitude toward the youngster's age-appropri-
ate inability to sustain tearfulness and sorrow.

Aid the child to get out of himself. Perhaps, he might become more active in a youth group, a club, or a special
hobby, such as modeling clay and finger painting.

Respect the youngster's own personality. Avoid efforts to have him become an emotional replacement for the deceased. For example, increased physical intimacy such as sharing a bedroom should be tactfully avoided to prevent an exaggeration of the child's already present sense of guilt at having a dead parent's mate more to himself.

Demonstrate in word and touch how much he is truly loved. A stable and emotionally mature adult who accepts the fact of death with courage and wisdom will bring the truth to the youngster that the business of life is life. Emotional energy formerly directed toward the absent person must now be directed toward the living. This does not mean wiping out the memories of the deceased. Even in death, the absent member can and should remain a constructive force in family life and be remembered in love without constant bitterness or morbidity.

The necessity for carrying on day-to-day routines will aid the process of adjustment, and, in time, special interests and pleasures will again assume their normal place in the scheme of things—for both parent and child. The relationship between parent and child will be essentially the same as before death. When parents accept the reality of death and the need for life to go on, they and their children can maintain their own healthy relationships and find new ones to give meaning and purpose to life, permitting young personalities to develop and mature.

EARL A. GROLLMAN

Man defines the world in which he lives and patterns his behavior according to the definitions he has developed. Death is a biological change around which all sorts of social behavior have been centered. The sociological method is that scientific approach toward death that emerges from the interaction of the human being in the social group.

What are the shifts in contemporary life that shape attitudes toward death? How has the assassination of President Kennedy affected not only the parents but the children as well? For "death is a profound event not only for the individual but also for the society. The responses and reactions engendered by death have both a personal and a social immediacy."

At a time when theologians are discussing the "Death of God," the sociologist, Robert Fulton, is pondering "The Dying of Death." Dr. Fulton is a professor of sociology at the University of Minnesota, having previously taught at California State College (Los Angeles), University of Wisconsin, and Wayne State University. He is the editor of Death and Identity *(John Wiley and Sons). His new book,* Creative Education and Social Crisis, *was published earlier this year.*

CHAPTER I

On the Dying of Death

ROBERT FULTON

WHAT MUST FIRST BE SAID is that the collection of readings in this book is both an expression of, and a reaction to, a very significant change taking place in contemporary American society. This change, thus far, has been basically attitudinal in nature; whereas death was once regarded as inevitable, it is now coming to be viewed as avoidable if not, indeed, unnecessary. Death, as it has been traditionally defined, is dying. It will be the purpose of this chapter to describe the manner of this dying and to point out certain of its social consequences.

Death is the great rupturer. Since man first appeared on earth, death has been his constant companion and ultimate threat. The question "Why should man die?" has traditionally been answered in Western society within the framework of sacred doctrine. Man, according to this doctrine, was God's creature, and his death, no less than his life, was an act of Divine will. Death, for Western man, was a personal matter between God and himself. He believed moreover, that the very purposefulness of his death placed him at the center of existence and elevated him above all other creatures as the principal subject of creation. As part of a Divine plan, death was confronted openly, spoken of freely, and regarded as an inevitable event.[1] Shakespeare expressed this idea succinctly when, in *Henry V,* he said, "We owe God a death." For Western man, the recognition of death was a prime requisite for life as well as an integral dimension of his personal identity.

In contemporary American society, a profound shift can be observed in man's attitudes toward death. An increasing number of Americans no longer view death as the result of Divine displeasure or as the price of moral trespass; rather, in our modern, secular society death is coming to be seen as the result of personal negligence or of an unforeseen accident.

31

Death is now a temporal matter that man treats much as he would an avoidable illness or physical stigma. Like syphilis or some other infectious disease it is a personal embarrassment to be discussed only reluctantly with a physician. Death, like a noxious disease, has become a taboo subject in American society and as such it is the object of much avoidance, denial, and disguise.

The significance of the mass media for depicting our attitudes toward death as well as for molding them cannot be minimized. If we look for a moment at the way the films characteristically have dealt with death, and at the way films do so today, we can perhaps catch something of the change in attitude that we have attempted to describe.

Early film classics such as *Frankenstein* and *Dracula* clearly portrayed the traditional polarities within Christian theology, i.e., the polarity between spirit and flesh, good and evil, and life and death.[2] Within the dramatic structure of these films, death was understood as the justifiable punishment for those who trespassed against the moral order or as a ritual of purification for those who died championing it.

The struggle between these polarities could also be seen in our traditional western movie with great clarity. The hero, chaste, courageous, and God-fearing, was confronted with the appearance of evil in the form of cattle-stealing Indians, land-stealing foreigners, or gold-stealing bankers. Without compromise the hero righted wrong, as an instrument of justice he restored law and order, and as a servant of God, he reaffirmed the principle of faith.

The world in which good struggled against evil, and the spirit vied with the flesh, finds itself today forced to give way to a different definition of the order of things, and is compelled to retreat before the advances of what might be termed relativistic secularism.

In the new genre of film entertainment offered American society, epitomized by the James Bond thriller, the hierarchical world of Christian transtemporalism is no longer described; rather what is presented is an existential world in which good and evil reside in both friend and foe alike.

The image of modern, existential man portrayed on the screen today is that of a rational, intelligent, youthful man— a man who is functioning within an environment but who is not a part of it. His values are pragmatic and relativistic. His loyalties are to a group, movement, or state. Oftentimes he works in the employ of someone as little known to him and possibly as hostile toward him as his unknown adversary.[3] For a cause that transcends one's individual self our modern hero is expendable, as are those persons with whom he struggles. His claim to life—and it is a life abundant with power, wealth, and sexual pleasures—is made existentially dramatic by the fact that at any given moment he may have to give it up. Carelessness or expediency may cause him to receive a fatal thrust from his enemy or a deadly push from a "friend." Life for our contemporary hero in such a world is relative, immediate, sensual, and lonely, while his death is irrelevant. In contrast to traditional conceptions of social reality this emerging functional secularism offers us a new vision for man and the promise of a new social order.

When we turn our gaze away from the reflected image of the screen to the object of its illumination, contemporary America, it can be seen that sometimes entertainment as well as art mirrors life.

Historically it has been a basic proposition in American society that every man had the same claim to life. Equality of life has served as a fundamental underpinning to the structure of our society. The new ethic emerging in America, however, threatens to negate this proposition. The invention of the kidney machine in Seattle, Washington, several years ago for instance, raised the question of who should benefit from this machine.[4]

Initially, only one machine was available and its use, of necessity, was limited to a few patients. How were they to be chosen? Our religious and political philosophy would argue for a democratic selection; each man would have the same chance to life. However, the criteria[5] that were initially established contradicted this traditional philosophy and said in effect that some men have a greater claim to life than others. Of course, it has always been true that wealthy persons could afford better medical care than the poor, but it has never been an official medical proposition that a person of wealth had a greater claim to life than any other person. Now it has been established by an anonymous committee of seven, known portentously as the "Life and Death Committee," that one's right to a life-sustaining machine is a function of his potential or actual contribution to society. The young academic, the young doctor, the young lawyer, the executive on the way up, it is implied, have a greater claim to life than the unskilled, the unemployed, or the unwanted.[6]

Death in our society is no longer the wages of sin. Today it is seen as something that does not have to happen. Furthermore, the idea is being entertained that it is remotely conceivable that for a very significant minority, that death eventually won't need to happen at all. In this connection it should be noted that an attempt has already been made to freeze a man following his death in order that he may later benefit from future advances in medical technology and thereby be restored to life and good health.[7]

One strategy that has emerged in contemporary society to cope with the dying and death of our aging members in a more immediate way is the retirement city movement. This movement encourages the segregation and isolation of those most likely to die before they actually do so. Such a development in modern life allows us for the first time to avoid death almost entirely and to mute the grief and anguish of bereavement. Time and separation loosen family and friendship ties. Once an older person is emotionally separated from the members of his family or group his death will register but lightly upon them, if at all.

Another movement in American society that augurs for the privatization of death is the memorial society movement.

In a recent study this author surveyed members of eleven such memorial societies (or funeral reform societies, as they are called) across the United States.[8] Highly educated, and relatively low in traditional religious affiliation, and reporting an annual income twice that of the average American family, members of memorial societies could well represent the vanguard of future Americans. The study showed that this group desired to eliminate the body from the funeral, avoided funerals more often than the average American, and showed a greater reluctance than the average person to permit their children to attend a funeral ceremony. This last finding is of particular interest. Typically, families of the social, professional, and intellectual level of these respondents attempt to deal realistically with their children. They characteristically discourage such fantasies as ghosts, hobgoblins, Santa Claus, and the bogies of sex. Nevertheless, where death is concerned, they appear to behave contrary to form and seek to shield the ultimate truth from their children.

It would appear that temporal-mindedness and scientific skepticism are coterminous with death suppression. Complementing the memorial society members' expressed desire to shield their children from the dead is the practice of medical hospitals of shielding children from the dying. In two separate studies, Feifel[9] and this writer[10] have shown that the dying person often wishes to be surrounded by family and friends. Hospitals, nevertheless, typically prohibit children from visiting patients. When permitted to do so children are allowed only in specific areas and at designated times.[11]

Today in the United States more than 17,000,000 persons are now 65 years of age or older.[12] Never before in our history have we had such an aged population. Moreover, in ten years their numbers will total more than 25 million persons.[13] But what of this group and of those members who are, or presently will be, dying? And what of the dying person himself? How is he to view his death in the face of a society that increasingly seeks to deny the reality of his existence and at the same time attempts to avoid the reality of his death? How will American youth, brought up in a society that seeks to disguise death, greet the death of its elders?

These questions cannot be answered easily nor can the problems they present to us be solved readily. Medicare, increased Social Security, nursing programs, emerging terminal hospital facilities, modern medical technology, and new techniques for the utilization of body parts all suggest new attitudes toward dying and death as well as ways of coping with life different from what we have ever known before.

Franz Borkenau, a distinguished historian, has characterized our modern era as post-Christian.[14] With the disintegration of belief in immortality, Borkenau saw modern society prepared to embrace a nihilistic philosophy of despair and denial. He believed that modern secularism would ultimately deny the relevance of self so that death itself, finally, would be defeated. It was Borkenau's conviction that modern man yearned for some unity of identity beyond himself and that to avoid existential extinction he would abandon himself to some temporal absolute such as a racial, social, or national group.

Borkenau's thoughts have relevance and immediacy for our society. The specter of statism in Russia and China, of racism in the Union of South Africa and Rhodesia, in which the individual is subordinated to the needs and aspirations of the society, cannot readily be dismissed. Nor are we necessarily free from the urge toward a collective identity for self here in the United States. The ultimate significance of the late President Kennedy's statement, "Ask not what your country can do for you—ask what you can do for your country," can only be judged by history. It does not appear, however, to be in the general political tradition of the primacy of the individual upon which the political institutions of this society were founded. Nor does it follow a much older conception of man's relationship to the state which has also served as the cornerstone of American political and religious life, namely, the directive, "Render therefore to Caesar the things that are Caesar's; and to God the things that are

God's." It would seem that, politically, at least, the conception that a man is a unique entity, prior to the state, and having recourse ultimately to an authority beyond the state is in danger of being lost in America. The protest over Vietnam today in our schools and colleges and the part played by the "conscientious objector" may well reflect the belief of many that the self may still claim a primacy over the state. In this light then the so-called "Vietnik" rather than being a modern revolutionary is in fact a traditional conservative expressing the most fundamental principles of our society.

Perhaps in no other era have the gods played such cruel games with youth. While this present generation in America can be said to be the first "death-free" generation in the history of the world,[15] the prospect of sudden mass extermination by a nuclear attack hangs threateningly over their heads. Contempt for authority and impatience with the older generation reflect their hostile attitude toward this bittersweet inheritance. In such a world that has known two intercontinental wars within this century and presently contemplates a third, the question of a meaningless life is made more poignant for those who must at the same time contemplate what is for many of them a meaningless death.[16]

Thus we can see in contemporary society the emergence of different strategies and techniques designed ultimately to avoid a direct confrontation with death. Simultaneously we also can observe a nascent conception of the individual developing which would equate his worth as a man with his value to society. It is within this context that death must be viewed. Moreover, it is within this social environment that strives to achieve the death of death itself that its meaning in our lives must come to be understood. And finally, it is within such a context that we must articulate the modern meaning of life and death to our children.

Death, nevertheless, continues to evoke powerful emotions that need to be vented or calmed. That this is so was made evident with the assassination of President Kennedy. The country grieved at his death. The nation mourned openly not only as solitary citizens but also together as a society. As a society, it observed public as well as private expressions of grief; it participated in a funeral to which the whole world paid heed.

Public evidence for the private reactions to the death of the President is available. At least thirty-nine different surveys were conducted at varying intervals following the assassination.[17] While the studies were manifestly different in design and intent, certain common reactions are discernible. These reactions are best shown by the study of the National Opinion Research Center in Chicago which polled a representative national sample of 1,400 adults within a week of the assassination.[18]

The study showed the following results:

1. Preoccupation with the death was almost total.
2. Nine out of ten people reported experiencing one or more of such physical symptoms as headache, upset stomach, tiredness, dizziness, or loss of appetite.
3. Two-thirds of the respondents felt very nervous and tense during the four days.
4. A majority of the respondents confessed to feeling dazed and numb.
5. Most people—men and women—cried at some period during this time.
6. The event was compared most often to the death of a parent or close friend or relative.
7. There was a tendency to react to the assassination in terms of personal grief and loss rather than in terms of anxiety for the future or of political or ideological concern.

As the researchers themselves described it, the reactions of the American people during the four days following the death of President Kennedy appeared to have followed a well-defined pattern of grief familiar to medical practice. The funeral of the President channeled that grief and gave it poignant expression.

Grief is a response to loss. It is a definite reaction characterized by psychological and physiological symptoms. Erich

Lindemann, a psychiatrist formerly at Harvard Medical School and one of the first scholars to conduct research into the subject of grief, undertook a study in 1944 of 101 patients including the bereaved survivors of victims of the Cocoanut Grove fire in Boston.[19] He found that common to all patients interviewed was a remarkably uniform reaction including (1) sensations of somatic distress, such as tightness in the throat, choking, shortness of breath, etc.; (2) intense preoccupation with the image of the deceased; (3) strong feelings of guilt; (4) a loss of warmth toward others with a tendency to respond with irritability and anger; and finally (5) disoriented behavior patterns. These five characteristics of grief appear to Lindemann to be pathognomonic for grief. This syndrome need not appear immediately after a crisis, however, but may be delayed over a period of months or even years.

The duration of this grief reaction and the manner in which a person finally adjusts to his new social environment depends, Lindemann says, upon the success of what is called the "grief work," i.e., emancipation from the bondage to the deceased, readjustment to the environment in which the deceased is missing, and the formation of new relationships. Lindemann noted considerable resistance on the part of his patients to accept the discomfort and distress of bereavement. The patients chose instead, in many instances, to avoid the intense pain connected with the grief experience and to avoid also the expression of emotion necessary for it. Such a distortion of normal grief may well be the prelude to a morbid grief reaction which Lindemann and others have documented, and which may run the gamut of response from such psychosomatic conditions as asthma, ulcerative colitis, and rheumatoid arthritis, to antisocial behavior and possibly even psychosis.

That there is an intimate relationship between grief and psychosomatic responses is proposed by the psychiatrist Karl Stern and his collaborators.[20] They studied the grief reactions of twenty-five subjects attending an old-age counseling service. These investigators found that while there was a relative

paucity of overt grief and of conscious guilt feelings, the subjects did manifest a preponderance of somatic illnesses. Moreover, they reported there was a tendency on the part of the
subjects to self-isolation and to hostility against some living
person.

The relationship between grief and a person's subsequent
psychoneurosis is suggested by another research psychiatrist,
Herbert Barry, Jr.[21] His study of commitment to a mental
hospital causes him to conclude that maternal bereavement
before the age of eight can well be a sensitizing factor in the
development of a psychoneurotic illness.

Evidence supporting the relationship between antisocial
behavior and unresolved grief is provided in the study by
two other researchers, Mervyn Shoor and Mary Speed.[22] Their
report is based upon psychiatric consultations with fourteen
adolescents in the care of a juvenile probation department in
California. All fourteen came to the attention of the authorities because of their extreme delinquent behavior. In each
case, there had been a recent death of a close family member.
Prior to the time of the death none of the children had shown
such behavioral problems. Operating on the premise that
these fourteen boys and girls were acting out their grief
and were the unhappy victims of pathologic mourning, Shoor
and Speed were able to effect normal mourning processes
with some of their clients and to achieve a return to more
acceptable modes of behavior.

It is the conclusion of Geoffrey Gorer,[23] an English research anthropologist, that certain expressions of adolescent
vandalism may be a function of the refusal or the inability of
some youths to mourn. In a study of recently bereaved individuals he found that in contemporary Britain there was both
an individual repudiation and a social denial of grief and
mourning—a repudiation and denial which left the survivor
grievously alone and ill-equipped to cope with the myriad
of personal and social difficulties that are attendant upon a
death.

The personal consequence of this development, Gorer

found, was the appearance of a considerable amount of mal-adaptive response to death which he described as "the apathy of despair," "meaningless business," and "private rituals of mummification."

On the more public level Gorer hypothesizes a link be-tween the stigmatization of grief and public callousness. It is his contention that the present preoccupation with death and cruelty, coupled as it is with an excessive squeamishness concerning it, displays the modern irrational attitude toward this inevitable event. Such an attitude toward death makes of it, Gorer argues, something obscene or pornographic and ultimately invites the maladaptive and neurotic behavior observed.

These and other studies contribute not only to our under-standing of the dynamic nature of grief but also allow us to appreciate the importance of grief itself both for the indi-vidual and for society. The death of an important person is a crisis situation. The attitude we take toward it and the man-ner in which we treat it will be reflected in the mental and physical health of the survivors of the almost two million persons who die each year in the United States.[24]

Death is a profound event not only for the individual but also for the society. The responses and reactions engendered by death have both a personal and a social immediacy. The way in which each society copes with death, however, is deter-mined by its own set of ideas, beliefs, values, and practices. Some societies see death as an improvement in one's prospects and status. Others do not. Mourning or weeping over the loss of an individual is not everywhere considered appropriate behavior.

How an individual reacts to the death of another is de-pendent upon one's "status" and "role" in relation to the deceased. Edmund Volkart has pointed out that in American society the accepted definition of who is "bereaved" or who has suffered the main "loss" includes the parents and siblings of the deceased as well as his spouse and children.[25] In con-trast, among the Trobriand Islanders, according to Volkart, the emphasis is placed upon persons related to the deceased through his mother. His maternal kin share the status of "bereaved" and it is they who are seen as having suffered the major loss. They are considered to be "closest" to the deceased—more so even than the spouse. While he or she may "grieve" the death, this response is considered more obligatory and ceremonial than spontaneous in nature. In any case, the spouse is not considered to be bereaved in the same sense as the maternal relatives of the deceased.

Expression of grief can also be seen to be a function of the psychological value that one person may come to have for another within the family system itself. Since we as individuals mature and become distinct personalities primarily within the family structure, the number and kinds of identification, emotional or affective involvement, and the degree and strength of dependency on others will vary according to the range, frequency, intimacy, and quality of the interaction provided by the family.

Among the Ifaluk, it has been observed that the pain and distress of grief seem to disappear upon the conclusion of the funeral ceremony. Volkart suggests that this behavior can be explained in terms of the family system and the socialization practices that prevail among these people. Child-rearing among the Ifaluk is not the sole prerogative of parents and older siblings, but is shared by many members in the tribe who are as important to a child as are the members of his "own" family. The emotional relationships of the growing child and the mature adult therefore are diffused and dispersed among many persons rather than focused and centered on only a significant few. The death of a "family" member, therefore, does not have the same psychological impact it would have if those relationships were more exclusive. With one's emotional investment distributed more widely, the "other" person is not valued as a unique and irreplaceable personality within one's system of relationships. More important, rather, are the "roles" played by the interchangeable others and the functions these "roles" perform for the individual. The death of any one person in the community or family little disturbs the psychological self and grief is muted.

In contrast to the Ifaluk the range of interaction possible with our typically small family system is limited. Self-identification and personal dependency for a child in our society is channeled among the same few persons. These few persons become as a result unique and irreplaceable within the family structure.

The American family, however, is not only emerging as a limited, more emotionally intense social unit, but other changes are affecting it as well. Both within and without the family, shifts in values, beliefs, and practices promise not only to alter significantly our relations with, and evaluations of, others, but also promise to affect our social reactions and emotional responses to their deaths.

In our small, nuclear families the impact of death can be sharply different from the day of the extended, multigenerational family and the large rural homestead. Scientific and medical advances have greatly reduced infant mortality as well as extended the average life span of the individual. Moreover, the social and spatial mobility of contemporary Americans, their highly urbanized existence with its casual, impersonal contacts, means that the role of the bereaved person is in a continuing process of change. But bereavement is not only the experience of grief, it is also the acting out of that grief, as well as the public dramatization of the loss.

The funeral has traditionally been a part of that dramatization. While the funeral has served manifestly to dispose of the body and to publicly acknowledge and commemorate a death, it has also asserted the viability and continuity of the group.

In the course of a funeral reciprocal obligations of a family are remembered, reenacted, and reinforced; that is, the death is announced, the body is attended to, mourners are received, and a ceremony is provided. In this way, the role taken by a participant in the funeral not only reflects his position in society but also reaffirms the social order itself.

Further, the obligations placed upon all members of a deceased's family, such as style of dress, demeanor, preparation of food, and restricted social intercourse, both identify and demonstrate family cohesion. The extended kinship system beyond the family, moreover, is also acknowledged and affirmed at death. Members of the larger family console the survivors as well as participate in the funeral and possibly share in the expense of the ceremony.

Occupational affiliation and association in other social groups are acknowledged and represented in the funeral ceremony. Through the participation in the funeral of neighbors, friends, and colleagues an individual is presented with, and reminded of, the various parts and personnel of his social group. Participation in the dramaturgy, the visiting, the funeral service, the procession, the committal, the feasting, all add to the sense of being a part of a larger social whole, just as the strict order of precedence in the conduct of the ceremony reminds one that there is structure and order to the social system.

The funeral, finally, is a "rite of passage." As such it not only marks the completion of a life but also reaffirms the social character of human existence.

The definition of death, as it has been pointed out, is not a constant. The characterization of the funeral, given above, presumes that the equilibrium of the community's social life is disrupted by death. But as it has been argued, the definition of the individual in this society, and consequently the definition of his death, is changing.

This change in definition is abetted in part by the shift in the rate and pattern of mortality itself. Death in contemporary society is increasingly an experience of the aged.[26] Retired from their work, freed from their parental obligations, and often removed from the main current of social life, the death of the aged disturbs little the round of life today.

As we have seen, the death of a leader such as President Kennedy can seriously disrupt the functioning of our modern society. The vacuum he left in the political and social life of

America was sorely felt. For the common man, however, and for the average family, it is the death of someone in the middle productive years of life that will have a comparable effect upon his social and familial group. The death of the elderly, less relevant as they are to the functional ordering and working of contemporary secular society, does not compel such attention.

Coupled as this development is with the decline in belief in immortality, the funeral, as both a declaration of a person's status in society and as a religious rite of passage, becomes for many merely a means for disposing of the dead.

The social strain and the severe psychological tension that are reported today in connection with mourning and burial rites reflect the conflicts and structural dissolutions and attempted reintegrations that are so characteristic of our changing world.

The problems associated with death are beginning to polarize at two different points within the social structure. The first area of concern is the disengagement of the aged from a society that is becoming less interested in them as individuals or as functionaries within the social system. The second area of concern centers around children who in a nuclear family setting have the burden of coping with an irreplaceable loss through death—a loss made greater by the reduced number of significant persons in his immediate family. While these two issues are not unrelated, they do seem to constitute two foci around which the major problems of death, grief, and bereavement cluster.

Deritualization of mourning and the suppression of grief are growing apace in America. The death crisis that survivors must face, given the pattern of modern living, can be greater or more profoundly disruptive emotionally, if not socially, than ever before.

The recent reform movement in America that proposes we cope with death by immediate nonpublic disposal of the dead, and that we manage our grief by stoically denying it, is in sharp contrast with our social past as well as with our

present knowledge regarding the dynamics of personal, irrep-
arable loss. But, on the other hand, a ceremony that no
longer appropriately symbolizes the understood meaning of a
death, or fails correctly to dramatize the change that has over-
taken the living and the dead, can create only confusion, if
not anger and frustration, on the part of the bereaved. Some
young couples today, for example, see their life as a private
affair and choose a civil or nonpublic wedding as a result.
Reasons of practicality or economy can only partially explain
this choice. We must recognize that such a restricted ceremony serves to dramatize for them their place in the world
and their perception of that world. The same can be said in
the case of the funeral. A funeral that attempts to represent
relationships, ideas, or values which the individual no longer
believes in or holds true may serve to thwart and anger him
rather than achieve its intended end.

Though death may indeed be dying in the United States,
nevertheless we are still confronted with those who must die.
In a society which has a lessened evaluation of death there is
a strong tendency for many to respond to the death of another
by turning away. Like the divorced person of several decades
ago, ostracized and neglected, many bereaved individuals
today are to a large extent without traditional religious
resources or community support, and often lack the skills
necessary to deal adequately with their loss.

If we view the question of death from the standpoint of
personal loss, what we see is the imminent threat of increasing
disruption of family life and other social relations by death
in a society which increasingly is unable either to accept or
to explain it. The problem is further intensified moreover by
the fact that we have as yet no scientific way of demonstrating
whether the patterns of behavior we observe in attempting to
cope with the death crisis are functionally relevant. However,
in the light of research[27] the wise management of grief in
children as well as in adults revolves around two major factors: one, the encouragement and facilitation of the normal

mourning process, and two, the prevention of delayed and/or distorted grief responses.

In our society the funeral possesses the potential to compel the individual to acknowledge his loss. The ritual of the funeral when it is responsive to the social and psychological needs of the survivors, can facilitate what Lindemann has called normal grief work.

The presence of a child at a funeral permits the child to recognize that death has occurred. He sees that he is only one among several who is experiencing the loss. Further, depending upon his relationship to the deceased, he may receive comfort, support, and expressions of love and affection from relatives and friends who normally would not be so demonstrative toward him. Moreover, the law of Talion may also be operative.[28] The child may fear his own involvement in the death. The responses of the others can serve to assure him that he is not culpable. The child, by the nature of his inexperience with death, has a crisis to work through.

Children, the evidence would suggest, are little aided in this crisis by their well-intended parents or their friends who advise that they do not participate in the celebration of a death. To the contrary, such a decision may be interpreted by the child as an expression of wrongdoing on his part. When the funeral is over, the mourners return home sad and depressed. At this juncture the child is ignored. His tentative questions are brusquely answered or quickly silenced. Rather than being embraced and taken into the sorrowing group, he is sent away to ponder alone what has occurred.

There are those in America who would withhold from children, particularly, a knowledge of, or experience with, death.[29] It would appear to be in the best interest of children, however, that such ideas be resisted for it seems that the evidence compels us to recognize the fact that death is too personal an event to be left a private matter.

People often write about children's views. They make assumptions from articles and books they have read.

"How Younger Children View Death and Themselves" is not about youngsters. It records the children's own real feelings as told to the Director of Child Psychiatry Services at the Massachusetts Mental Health Center, and associate clinical professor of psychiatry at Harvard Medical School.

Dr. Gregory Rochlin has studied the reactions of children to death and has given us his personal observations as well as the results of his emphatic listening. He is the author of what may become a classic in this field, Griefs and Discontents *(Little, Brown and Company) from which this contribution is taken.*

CHAPTER II

How Younger Children View Death and Themselves

GREGORY ROCHLIN

IT IS THE CONVENTIONAL VIEW that the child does not know about death. This seems to be as true of culturally archaic peoples as of modern society. Death as a subject for discussion is commonly treated by adults as if it were a prohibited issue where children are concerned. Children may play death games endlessly (they often use the same theme, e.g., in Warsaw, Berlin, the Kalahari, the "wild" West) so long as no one takes that play seriously. When taken as a matter for sober consideration, evasiveness is clearly evident on the part both of the adult and of the child. Adults themselves are reluctant to acknowledge, as we have noted, the inevitable fate which waits us all, and hence are the least likely source of information. Moreover, there are often concerted efforts to deny the child an awareness of death. The inevitable discovery of death then becomes a private individual experience of great magnitude. What such a discovery means is not conveyed to young children either as a body of dogma or as a natural phenomenon, nor is what to do about it once the revelation occurs. The attempted solution to the problems the discovery raises is universal in the sense that children everywhere seem to find remarkably similar solutions.

The serious significance of death is no more wasted on the child than it is spared the adult. The child typically applies it not only to himself but also to others, and particularly to those upon whom he has learned to depend. Fears of the loss of an important person like a parent and the dread of abandonment arise demonstrably in young children, as I have shown elsewhere.[10,11]

A more trying burden is added to the child's existence when his fears and fantasies carry him on to the inevitable realization that the end of his existence as well as the existence of those who care for him may occur at some unpredictable

51

time or in some unforeseen way. These somber actualities weigh heavily enough to have a compelling emotional effect. When it is remembered that this process goes on in the early phases of development, its significance is all the more profound. As one would expect, far from adding to the stability of the child's world, this insight has quite the opposite effect.

Ordinarily very young children make discoveries about death. They have plentiful opportunities from which to draw such information. They stand often as a mute witness when the successful hunt calls its fruits to their attention. A trip to the market or the barnyard has a similar connotation. The more clearly the child comprehends that life is followed by death, the greater is the demonstration of the uncertainty of the future. As a result, through these everyday experiences in addition to the growing realization of his utter dependence upon others some kind of social harmony is made imperative. Thus a further repression of destructive and aggressive impulses becomes a safeguard or offers a refuge. And an adaptation to social conditions which promotes the child's development is thus augmented.

Conflicts and relations to unpleasant experiences, unwelcome ideas, or untoward thoughts are met too frequently to require proof. Long before the child has discovered death, he has acquired some experiences with frustration, the failure of fulfillment of many of his wants, and some practice at compromise with his demands. Confronted now with this fresh assault on his security, he refines a system of defenses which he has continued to perfect from those which were born of the loss complex and the dread of abandonment. This elaborate web of self-protective emotional devices is not only directed toward the grim realities, but also against the conflicts which they arouse within himself. In this way, I suggest, the need for self-preservation is converted further into a powerful social force which promotes and generates change and adaptation.

There seems little doubt that the young child learns rapidly that death means the absence of life, that life comes to an end. Despite this recognition of reality there is no pragmatic or philosophic acceptance. On the contrary, a rich variety of psychological defenses that the child has not only in readiness, but has to some degree perfected, is brought to bear on this problem. These include two rapidly developing orders of psychological processes: first, those which serve to modify or distort perception of an intolerable objective reality—in this case, the discovery of death; and second, those which will effect an alteration in subjective experience in order to overcome helplessness and a sense of loss through fantasies of omnipotence and invulnerability. Many of these defenses stem from a denial of the reality. Denial and negation are always to the fore of this problem, not only in the very young but throughout life—in the belief that death is not the end of life. The refusal to accept the finality that the dead are irretrievable bears out that the existing paradox of rejecting what is acknowledged is a manifestation of negation. Men are unwilling and hence unable to accept the fact that the dead are forever gone. The belief that the dead will return is born of the wish.

If we recognize that seeing is an especially important function to a particular child, being dead comes to mean not to see, yet the dead to such a child are conceived as seeing again. They can watch over and observe. Rather than having limits to their vision as they do during life, the dead acquire infinite powers of observation. For another child, being dead may be characterized as being motionless. Such a child believes the dead to be free, mobile—in fact whatever limitations in mobility the particular child may have experienced are believed not to affect the dead. The dead may move anywhere. The same reversal may apply to all or any functions. Being dead, instead of representing a giving up of functions and processes, comes to mean just the opposite. Powers previously limited are extended without boundaries.

In 1940, Sylvia Anthony's book *The Child's Discovery of Death*[1] appeared. Here is one of the rare studies of the subject. She found that school-age children thought readily of death. It appeared in their fantasies as well as in their play and it arose in response to suggestions of grief and fear, loss and separation. Death was commonly associated with ideas of retaliation and reparation. Paul Schilder and David Wechsler in 1934 had made a preliminary study, "The Attitude of Children Towards Death."[12] Their work was done through family questionnaires. They concluded that a thorough study done directly with children was necessary. Anthony's book confirmed their findings.

No further clinical study of children concerning their attitudes toward death was reported until 1948. In a classroom setting, Maria Nagy[9] put questions to a group of children aged approximately four to ten years, and encouraged them to make drawings and tell stories, to elicit their views on death. Although she provided little new information in her report, she succeeded in showing that the subject of death was a very important one even to the youngest child that she observed. Her conclusions were a reaffirmation of the work by Schilder and Wechsler and by Anthony.

During the next two decades, neither a critical review nor a deeper study of the subject was attempted. It is the purpose here to demonstrate not only that death is a matter of deep consideration to the very young child, as has been indicated by others, but also that his thoughts of dying are commonplace. They serve as important determinants in his emotional development. I shall show, moreover, that his behavior is influenced by such thoughts, which are decisive in respect to some of his lifelong beliefs.

The selection of children for my study was based on rather simple requirements: (1) that the children be at least three years old and less than five; (2) that they be capable of revealing in a play session some organized thinking which could be expressed both verbally and through their play; (3) that they come from protected environments in the sense that they would be urban (rural life is more directly exposed to birth, death, life), and have well-educated parents without any formal church affiliation.

The children were all of at least average intelligence.

They were free from any unusual circumstances such as serious separations, serious illnesses or mishaps, to themselves, siblings, or parents. They were not regularly indoctrinated in a set of religious beliefs. The children were carefully attended by their parents, and the home situations by reasonable standards would be considered stable. Except for the birth of a younger child, there had been no significant major events in relation to the principal people involved. All the children had a history of good physical health and no unusual or conspicuous emotional problems. They were observed during play in a series of appointments in a standardized child therapy room—equipped with a one-way mirror; conversation with the child was recorded through hidden microphones. The number of visits was determined by the accessibility of their fantasy play, which was to reveal unmistakably some of their central ideas about death, dying, or being dead. Three to five individual periods of play were required for each child.

Four examples follow which illustrate significant aspects of how young children cope with their knowledge of death. I had not previously seen the children. They were brought to me by a parent who was interested in the study. It was considered important to verify in advance that no more than cursory attention had been paid to the subject of death by the family, although this proved to be hardly necessary. The parents were sophisticated adults and had themselves had direct experience with the problem of a death, either professionally or personally. They were without exception reluctant to discuss the subject of death or dying with the child beyond offering him some reassurance on the infrequent occasion of a question from a child. Parents thought the children were too young to have much said to them of an expository nature. Even a precocious two-and-a-half-year-old was considered too immature to share in a discursive exercise, particularly on the subject of dying or death.

The aim was to provide a situation in which the child would play alone with the investigator. When the subject of death came up spontaneously, it would be explored as far as the child would permit, within a limited period of time and within the limits of anxiety that the investigator judged the child could comfortably tolerate. The aim was to demonstrate that the subject of death had been given considerable attention by the child and that it had produced an effect. For purposes of the study, it was important to show that the subject was readily accessible in any child and that ample thought had been given by the child to a subject on which he had not been indoctrinated. Extracts of transcripts of these play sessions are included in the appendixes at the end of this chapter.

Child A was a boy three and a half years old. In the past six to eight months he had asked his parents spontaneously when he would die or they would die. Following reassurance that this was some time distant, he was heard to mutter to himself that he wouldn't die. During this period, the maternal grandfather died. He was not well known to the child. The grandfather had lived in a distant city, and the child had seen him only on several occasions. In the two weeks that followed the grandfather's death there appeared to be no recognizable signs of a reaction, although the parents had expected that there might be one, since they themselves were disturbed by the event. Shortly thereafter, however, the child awoke over a series of nights with nightmares (meaning fears without any specific content). He would delay going to sleep each night. After some questioning it was evident that he had equated going to sleep with dying. (Could someone have said to him that grandfather had gone to sleep?) His questions were: "What clothes did grandfather wear when he went away?" Does it hurt to die?" He said that he himself was afraid to die. I shall not attempt to describe all that went on during the child's visits but will include all that was relevant to the problems we are concerned with.

The child picked up a small man doll and spontaneously put him under a truck. When I asked what was happening, the reply was, "The man will die." In response to the inquiry as to what then happens, he replied, "When people die they go under." This line of inquiry was short. The play shifted to killing the object the doll represented. "Then it will go away." Another variation occurred while he was playing in the sink with water and dolls—a member of the family goes down the drain and drowns. "When people are dead do they go down the sewer?" was his question. When death occurs to some object in an episode of play, that toy is actively used and is viable soon after in a later sequence of play. A series of illnesses occurs to the doll; infection and vomiting end in death. Deaths come from poisonous gas fumes. They also occur from being painfully killed after fighting against being hospitalized. These deaths occur regularly regardless of the individual's wishes or the will of the victim.

The association of being gone with death evokes anxiety expressed as fears of being left. The child immediately wanted to know his parents' whereabouts during this visit.

Injuries which may cause death, especially from a "hard fall," are dramatized by play with toys or the child actually taking the role of the victim. Each time, people return from the dead; I suggested that they may not, or then that they cannot, and the child insisted the opposite. To support his case he said that he saw a dead cat in a sewer and later it was not dead. Death in all instances is brought about by anything but natural events. Other causes of death are attacks by fierce animals, going out of the house without boots, being exposed to the elements, and swimming over one's head. If it is a child who dies, it continues to grow. The dead may get hungry and they must eat. Excremental functions continue after death. The child plays this out with toy bears he has shot, killed, and buried. They then continue their vital functions. They can also walk about. Some objects may remain motionless and not eat or speak but they are the ones whom the child wants to deprive of functions. Death is reversible. Life is a set of functions which one performs and which one may be deprived of. It is "death" to lose functions, but the functions are restored as before or even bigger than during life.

Child B was a girl four years and four months old. Within the year her paternal grandmother had died of chronic heart disease, a broken hip, and old age. The child needed repeated assurance after the grandmother's death that broken bones did not always mean death. When she was two she was first fearful about fish dying. When she saw them being caught by her father during the following summer, however, there were no further comments about the fish. She helped to catch a few fish, and by the time she was four was considered by the parents to be an accomplished fisherman.

References to being run over by a car or to broken bones, to fears of the dark, and death associated with sleep were characteristic expressions of anxiety in the year following the grandmother's death, although questions about death actually preceded the event.

The child's play was about children being lost, frightened, and even killed. All of this was going on in and about a doll's house. The subject of being dead and what happens to people who die focused on going to a graveyard in a box. After a while the dead come out of the box. The dead person does not remain there. While focused on killing animals, the play was restricted only to those to be eaten. Those that are not eaten may die and they come back to life. Animals may go to a hospital when ill and may die, but the expressed belief is that good animals or "nice ones" come back. Dead animals can take medicine and be restored. This was played out in considerable detail. The child played that she was good after pretending to be dead, which is a clear implication that she will return from the dead. Play that ended with breaking the doll's legs was concluded with no wish to talk of it further. Play about broken bones occurred occasionally, followed by shrieks asking for medicine to prevent death. The child admitted that this was frightening and wished not to continue with this fragment of play. The belief is clear in respect to the return to life; particularly if one is good, it is believed that dying may be warded off or the effects of dying may be reversed. The anxiety about dying is thus reduced or modified.

Child C was a boy three years and eight months old. While driving home with his parents one day, he witnessed a cat in its death struggles. The child's immediate fears were for his own cat. "What happens to cats and where do they go when they die?" were his repeated questions. A few weeks later there was talk in the house about Mozart. The child later asked who Mozart was. On learning that the composer was dead, the child provided a long list of people, asking whether they were dead or alive. He repeatedly asked, "Where do dead people go?" The grave as a hole in the ground held his interest. He did not express fears for himself, but he began to speak of his worry that his sister might die. He became a little anxious about her when she had a mild illness at the time. There is no doubt that there are many mixed motives in this concern, but regardless of what other conflicts there may be, the one about death is clear. There was frequent talk about dying during this time. When one is grown-up or when one is old, what happens if parents die—to the child, that it? There appears to be an invariably strong association between being dead and gone or going away, and being left.

This boy's play is particularly concerned with an animal that he shot, killed, and then took to a graveyard and buried. He did not know what happened after this until he thought of the animal being hungry. It could not come back, but it could eat earth. A variety of other creatures and objects were killed and buried, were hungry and ate. They could also talk although dead. The emphasis was placed on the sick and the old who die, people and animals alike. He himself would not want to die. If he had to die, he would "go," but only with his mother and father, but he had to be sure, however, to come back. He knows that if people die they stay away, but he himself will return.

Child D was a four-year-old boy whose grandfather had died during the previous year in a distant city. The death actually occurred on the child's third birthday. He was told that the grandfather had died of old age. The boy immediately wanted assurance that his mother and father were not very old. He told them that he himself did not want to be any older. For weeks afterward he repeatedly insisted that his grandfather was not dead. Then a contemporary of his father died of a heart attack. The boy insisted on knowing exactly where the heart was and the details of the attack. He was openly concerned with death and how often it comes unexpectedly. He repeated his assertion that when he died he did not want to be buried in the ground but wanted to be buried above ground. His play emphasized dolls who became ill and had nothing further happen to them. Planes would crash with no effect on the passengers. Operations on tonsils, being boiled in a tub or being burned, led to no harm. He did not want to talk about people being killed. It was, he admitted, too sad. Sometimes people are killed with a knife; however, if you take the knife out they live again. He once saw a dead bee, but he knew that it could come alive and that was why he did not bury it. "People get buried because they are no good." He will have to die and his father will die. He knows that this will happen. Sometimes, he hates his mother and he wants her to die.

Countless examples can be found readily if one listens carefully to children and collects their accounts. Thoughts which children express without any organized play session and which can be casually collected include the following: "Before you are born, you're dead, then you get born and you live again till you're very old, then you die and maybe you become just a little thing and then you start all over again"; or, "I'll live to be more than a hundred, because people I heard of live sometimes to be very old. I heard of a woman who lived to be a hundred and three. When I'm a hundred and three they'll find some way to make people live forever." These and similar reflections are readily available to whoever cares to explore them.

The young child's discovery of death is a great personal and private experience. The importance of a significant discovery often lies in what inventions it gives rise to. The conflicts which are aroused by the knowledge, the fears, and the recognition that life comes to an end bring out the child's entire store of psychological defenses. The old mental mechanisms which have developed from earlier conflicts over separation and the dread of abandonment receive an impetus to contend with newer problems.

The examples cited show that at a very early age well-developed mental faculties are functioning to defend oneself against the realization that life may end. An elaborate system of psychological defenses may be observed. At this period of life the logic used is implicit. A paradox such as "when the dead are hungry they eat," or "those who are killed return to life," needs no further explanation so far as the child is concerned. Wishes are not often distinguished from the facts; realities are altered to suit the wishes when questions about death arise. Magical thinking or homeopathic magic is an active process in young children and is seen when sleep and death appear to the child to be similar and then are accepted as the same. Magical ideas of contiguity are also common— for example, the fact that what is not wanted is disposed of through drains serves the child who is playing at the sink with the concept that unwanted and dead children and people may be discarded in sewers. Fears of death, like other concerns of the child, are in part mastered by repetitive play, as when planes are smashed and cars are wrecked over and over while harm to passengers is denied. The denial of the obvious may be so strong in a child that it leads at times to the complete negation that anything of consequence has taken place. It must be borne in mind that children, like prehistoric or contemporary or any people, who employ magical thinking neither subject it to analysis nor concern themselves with the abstract principles involved. Sir James George Frazer wrote in *The Golden Bough* (1947) about the magician, "he reasons just as he digests his food in complete ignorance of the intellectual and physiological processes which are essential to the one operation and the other."[2]

Dying is recognized by the child as an arrest of his vital functions. The child determines the living functions as those which he regards as essential to himself. The organs of locomotion and motor activity, or perception, of the alimentary, excretory, and respiratory functions, and the genital organs are vital to the child. When death is signified as a loss of any or all of these critical organs or processes, the child's reaction is to make use unwittingly of the many available psychological defenses. Death is reconstituted to become a liberation rather than its opposite. What limitations life may have imposed are transcended in death.

The child regards death as not due to natural causes but as a result of strife, defiance of authority and retaliation, hostility and the wish to satisfy aggressive, destructive, and sexual impulses. In sum, death is the outcome of certain relations between people. Morality is introduced very early by the child in the belief that the bad die before the good. The good are rewarded by a return from the dead. The bad remain dead. Wishes play an important role, as in the case of the boy who mutters to himself that he will not die but who becomes very solicitous about his sister when she has a trivial illness. His concern is that she may die.

The serious significance of death is not lost on the child. He knows that death is inevitable. The examples cited above reveal that elaborate defenses which have been aroused by the knowledge and fear of death are brought into effect. They represent an extension of earlier fears, the dread of abandonment or separation. These conflicts are not entirely allayed in childhood. They are only partially resolved, to a greater or lesser degree, because man is a social creature who exists only in the company of others, on some of whom he is intimately dependent, and who he knows will sooner or later leave him. He neither accepts final separation from those he loves nor his own inevitable end. His refusal to accept the human condition fires his conflicts and summons all his ingenuity to contend with those issues which begin very early in life. Taken in its totality, the reaction to the discovery of death, which defines fate as the uncertainty it is, leads both the child and the man into initiating an active civilizing process. He begins to propitiate and conciliate those who are superior, who are believed to direct and influence the course of events and his life. There is a powerful incentive to emulate these beings, to want the valued qualities which he has attributed to them. Thus defined, the child has fashioned a religion that he practices. The institutional aspects follow later in life.

Does the child's discovery of death lead him to recognize it as the extinction and finality of life? The foregoing data suggest that very young children seem to learn that life ends. They apply this information to themselves. To expect that the child would entertain adult conceptions of dying or death would not only be unreasonable but naïve. The facts of death like the facts of life, however, are to the child heavily embossed with every conscious and unconscious emotion at his disposal. These psychological vicissitudes do not serve the ends of reality, but rather quite opposite ends. The incentive to repress the real significance of dying may be judged from the powerful mental mechanisms which are brought into function in order to transcend death. What is remarkable is not that children arrive at adult views of the cessation of life, but rather how tenaciously throughout life adults hold to the child's beliefs and how readily they revert to them. The clinical facts show that the child's views of dying and death are inseparable from the psychological defenses against the reality of death. They form a hard matrix of beliefs which is shaped early and deep in emotional life. It appears not to alter throughout life. The concept of death fused with its amalgam of defenses is established as a core, around which a knowledge of the facts of life is wrapped. The knowledge will vary considerably in people and in different societies and cultures, but neither the core nor the defenses differ in any appreciable way. The core seems to be irreducible and unaltered. Although intellectual development modifies reliance on the more primordial defenses of childhood, it does not replace them. This is nowhere better illustrated than in times of crisis and especially in threats to life, when intellectual concepts

and thoroughly substantiated facts are often relinquished and
the elemental emotional mechanims of childhood are brought
into play.

Both child and man constantly and restlessly strive to overcome their limitations. If in so doing they destroy others, they
are only following the path of all living matter, whose goal is
to remain alive. There is no purposeless aim at destruction of
others or oneself; on the contrary, there are the most elaborate structures, both internal and social, against destroying
oneself and others. In his effort to solve the problems of life—
and among the principal ones is death—man has erected
elaborate institutions both within himself and with his fel-
lows. Societies come into conflict with each other and man is
inevitably drawn into their defense. Some of his institutions
become dangerous to other people. The solution to the problem which this poses is not to get rid of man, as many imply,
but to eliminate those of his works which are menacing. It is
misleading to think that if you scratch a man you will find
an ape. You find a man who will defend himself and his faith,
which is but the affirmation of what he believes.

I have attempted here to present some aspects of an immediate and universal life problem. It may be studied simply,
under clearly defined conditions which may be reproduced
easily anywhere.

The thought of dying is an unforgettable experience. It
occurs much earlier in life than is generally believed. It
reveals itself to be among the powerful engines of change in
man's development, gives rise to his religious beliefs, and
advances his civilizing process.

The engine of change works in large measure in relation
to the limitations that life imposes. The limitations, as I
have shown, whether in the young child or in the adult, are
perceived as anathema. What we learn is how early in life the
conflict has its onset. The task, therefore, is to transcend one's
bounds. What is to be observed is that the instincts of self-
preservation manifest themselves psychologically earlier than
has been supposed. It is my belief that the condition of ig-

nominy is of necessity converted into a belief in distinction or being chosen, and that the threat of loss is made over into restitution. The realization of death produces a parallel effect. A transformation begins to take place which persists throughout life. Its ends are to defy an intolerable reality.

It has been correctly assumed that instincts of self-preservation must be present in early life. This remained to be demonstrated. Freud, as might have been expected, anticipated this in his 1914 paper "On Narcissism."[7] He wrote that his concept of narcissism received reinforcement "from the observations we make of primitive peoples and children. In the former we find characteristics . . . [of] an overestimation of the power of wishes and mental processes, the 'omnipotence of thoughts,' a belief in the magical virtue of words, and a method of dealing with the outer world—the art of magic. . . . In the child of our own day, whose development is much more obscure to us, we expect a perfectly analogous attitude towards the external world." At that time, he had little direct data either on primitives or on little children. His remarks, although more anticipatory than based on fact, are no less correct. He speculated that what threatens the self would be countered by the narcissism of the individual, and thereby a balance would be struck, an equilibrium established (homeostasis). He knew that difficulties hampered a direct study of narcissism, and felt that the principal means of access to an understanding of this central process would probably remain in the analysis of paraphrenics [schizophrenia], which would give us insight into the psychology of the ego. At that time, nearly fifty years ago, the intensive research into young children was not anticipated.

Some of the young child's cardinal characteristics—his belief in the omnipotence of wishes and the power of magic; his imperishable egocentricity; his sense of helplessness coupled with a dependence upon others in authority whose favor he must solicit in coping with the loss complex and the dread of abandonment—play a critical part in the development and exercise of highly complex and essential mental mechanisms of defense. The child has a deep and pervasive concern with causality, in which the factors of change, of accident, and of caprice are suspended in favor of a closed determinism. The emergent momentous discovery of death strengthens and profoundly and permanently influences and governs the child's conduct. The chief ingredient of the child's cardinal characteristics, his belief in magic, are compounded into a religiosity. While the variations in religious expression are dictated in large measure by time, geography, local physical conditions, particular cultural levels, and social circumstances, the principles show no alteration. From this view, the socialized, institutional, and formed aspects of religion of later life appear to be an evolved system of governing beliefs which rests upon a deeply rooted foundation that is fashioned in the early years. Actually, religious beliefs develop not so much by way of indoctrination as by the inevitable, specific, emotional conflicts of early childhood. Indeed, it is difficult to imagine how even a child subject to the most irreligious indoctrination would escape them. Religiosity thus plays a fundamental role in human experience. The significant, essential, and primary basis of religious belief is thus established far in advance of the final edifice, which, without it, would never have either its remarkable durability or its universality.

I have tried to show that the painful facts that people die, that limitations of one's powers exist, that life itself has limits and is uncertain in its duration, are all evident to the very young child. It appears that these threats to life and this recognition of reality are joined by the development of narcissism. The more closely death is encountered or limits to one's powers confronted, either early in life or as its end approaches, the more narcissism is relied upon. Narcissism is in fact an engine to recover, restore, and even to extend one's powers; to make restitution for loss; to transcend life by immortality. May narcissism then not be a principle of development—a *narcissine* principle—that has its origins in the psychology of childhood? Draconian in its persistence, it is this aspect of our own childhood psychology which constantly, although not exclusively, governs our contention with our awareness of our own inevitable but unpredictable end.

The two conditions of life a young child learns are that he has limitations and that he will die. These discoveries that each child makes for himself are abhorrent to him. In recent decades, since the child has been the object of direct psychological study, it has been found that at a very early age he knows his own fate and understands it to be true for others as well, but also he has erected emotional defenses against what he has learned.

These great discoveries, which have a lifelong effect, are at the root of melancholic discontent. It is these discoveries, moreover, that give rise to specific fears of being abandoned and isolated. The child's knowledge of what he has learned remains a permanent source of disquiet about reality; nothing is durable, and what is highly prized may be no exception to the rule. Hence, the disturbing import of possessing limitations, and of the certainty of dying at some unpredictable time, compels the development of elaborate defenses against a fate that cannot be escaped. The child does not rely solely upon himself, however. He turns to those upon whom he depends and who care for him. But the mere fact that he is in their charge is not enough to make him feel secure. Their fate, identical with his, must be altered. Therefore, he invests them with all the magical powers and privileges that he has taken upon himself. When he solicits their favor, they may be powerful enough to sway fate in his behalf. He expects little from a fate that is not cajoled into being kind. Self-inspired, unconsciously the child fashions a set of beliefs that counter all the disquieting details that he has acquired about living and dying.

The reactions which develop to mitigate fate are not confined to childhood. Only an uninformed view of psychological development would consider that the child's greatest discoveries, having had their impact in infancy and childhood,

remain principally as recollections of events; that once having
had an enormous influence, they are then carried into adult
life only as memories. Since no period in life is free from
losing what is valued, the past is thus constantly being re-
newed and linked to the present. The anticipation of what
losses may come ties the past and the present to the future.
In later development, the more intellectual and derived
values, that is, those of high purpose and principle, the altru-
istic and philosophical ones and the cardinal virtues, are *par-
venus,* elevated late to a high station but precariously placed.
In a crisis, they are quickly deposed to give way to the older,
more firmly established values of childhood. Thus in each
encounter with a limitation, with every curtailment of a
function, a failure or a loss, it is the inability rather than
the unwillingness to accept them that is plain. When there
is uncertainty of fulfillment, or a discrepancy between desire
and desert, and when life itself is endangered, intellectual and
logical reasoning are not left to hold the field alone. (This is
not to say that reality is excluded, but that the use of fantasy
is coupled with it rather than relinquished in the face of
reality.) High-wrought emotional processes aim at undoing
all dangerous and repugnant losses and limitations. Operating toward these ends as an engine of change is restitution.

Each phase of life has its characteristic means of finding
or fashioning restitution for the limitations and losses that
are encountered during it. Even so, the earlier methods of
young childhood are not discarded for newly acquired methods of later periods. It is as though they were an old pharma-
copoeia at hand in which the recipes never suffered deletions.
However much the new remedies improved over the old, both
are retained and used.

Efforts at restitution take place at all times. There are
conditions throughout life that challenge the self-preserving
instincts and the self-serving aims. Both the instincts and the
aims may be satisfied only by favoring oneself. Between the
demands of narcissism and the dictates of reality, conflicts

arise. It is the human condition to rediscover this paradox throughout life. In the conflict between narcissism and reality, necessity requires that narcissism be put first.

"Actually we can never give up anything; we only exchange one thing for another, what appears to be a renunciation is really the formation of a substitute or surrogate."[3] These remarks by Freud first appeared in 1908, in a short paper, after he had included them in a lecture the year before. They may be found, slightly modified, in several of his later writings and also in some of his personal correspondence. They were not elaborated upon. The context in which these comments were written is the attachment to what is pleasurable and thus valued, fears of loss, and transience as an experience leading to sorrow. Freud did not incorporate his observations into his conceptual structure or explanation of narcissim. But it is narcissism which his observations concern.

The most skeptical observer would agree with the neglected fact that narcissism is a stable lifesaving process which holds the seeds of discontent as well as those of restitution. The idea that discontent in the mental life of children is no more than the frustration of their simple wishes neglects the fact that it is their utter dependence upon those who care for them, their lack of skill and mastery, their feeble influence upon the environment, the experience that their wishes are not always fulfilled and that they can lose what they value, that leave them fully aware of their plight. The child must confront these facts of life and find reality-eroding narcissism. Reality compels discontent. A solution is found to the conflict.

However, the discontent which reality compels is mitigated through the use of negation, an important mechanism. Negation allows intellectual acknowledgment of a hostile reality, which it dismisses at the same time as emotionally unacceptable.[4] The fact that this mechanism is present in the three-year-old child has been overlooked. Negation is found to intervene on behalf of narcissism in order to spare the child the oppressiveness of a too burdensome reality. Negation, which is part of the process of repression, is a defense used to resist the sense and the fact of limitations on the self that reality imposes. The child is no more willing than the adult to accept his limitations or to accept his end. When reality confronts narcissism, adult defenses are not to be distinguished from those of the child. Freud reported them fifty years ago in his treatment of the concept of narcissism. He did not, however, indicate the tenacity or the durability of these defenses, or that they served a basic need in the elaborate process of restitution for the limitations and losses experienced and anticipated in life. It is still customary to relegate these mechanisms to children, so-called primitive peoples, and to those adults who are childlike or "primitive." Freud wrote: "In the latter [referring to children and primitives] we find characteristics which if they occurred singly, might be put down to megalomania: an overestimation of the power of their wishes and mental acts, the 'omnipotence of thought,' a belief in the thaumaturgic force of words, and a technique for dealing with the external world—'magic'—which appears to be a logical application of these grandiose premises. In the children of today, whose development is much more obscure to us, we expect to find an exactly analogous attitude towards the external world."[5]

The psychological development of children is not now as obscure as it was half a century ago. As Freud surmised it would be, the child's world of magic has been fully acknowledged. It is known to persist in the child for an indefinite period and it is also, in some uncertain measure, present in the adult. The general assumption, in the past and also currently, has been that magical thinking rests upon the use of fallacious premises. In addition, it has been assumed that enlightened intelligence replaces the world of magic. The latter assumption is founded upon the premise that reason is more appealing than unreason and that, true to the beliefs of John Locke, where reason is offered, the irrational yields. Common experience shows that reason does appeal within limits as a means of adapting to reality. However, when reality contains danger or uncertainty that reason cannot penetrate, another system of thinking is manifested. It is the oldest one, magic.

When narcissism is menaced, reason seems to have little effect; it is the world of magic that is relied upon. There is no time in life when the archaic system of magical thinking may not be invoked. Striving to extend one's limits, to fulfill ideals, to recoup losses of self-esteem, of functions, and of valued objects, to reduce anxiety about an uncertain future and even to evade one's death,[13] will not be satisfied by appeals to reason. The rational system of thinking will inevitably reach its bounds in failing to provide gratification that is sought for wishes that narcissism requires. The result is that the archaic system is never altogether relinquished, regardless of one's level of intelligence and reason, because the demands of the wishes are far beyond what may be rationally satisfied by reason or rationally justified.

Freud's monumental work, "The Psychopathology of Everyday Life,"[8] reveals that it should be possible, at least theoretically, to demonstrate the processes of the mind in its smallest details. The work is so thorough that little has been added to it by other authors since its first appearance in 1901. It was not within the scope of Freud's work to include the psychopathology of everyday magic, that is, the expression of the archaic system of thinking in daily existence. He made many references to it throughout his voluminous work, but he did not place everyday magic with everyday psychopathology.

It may be argued that the two are not often distinguishable. This, while correct, is the best reason to attempt defining the distinction. So little study has been done on this aspect of everyday life that there is no significant psychoanalytic literature to cite. For reasons that seem indeterminate, the daily use of magical thinking in support of narcissism throughout life has not been studied much by psychoanalysts. It is paradoxical that a science attentive to unconscious moti-

vation and to the irrational in man should have neglected
definitive studies of the archaic system of thinking in everyday life. Studies of this subject have been carried out principally in relation to the most serious emotional disorders, the
psychoses, and to a far lesser degree in relation to the thinking of young children. Perhaps the explanation for this lack
may be in the restricted view of narcissism that has prevailed.

Narcissism, to judge from the extensive writings upon the
subject, is regarded primarily as a condition of childhood
that needs to be converted from one of egoism and egocentricity, characterizing early development, to one of object
relations, in which narcissism is relinquished for the love or
for the sake of another and valued person. Or it is considered
in its disorders, as displayed in the psychoses and neuroses.
Freud explained that "certain special difficulties seem to me
to lie in the way of a direct study of narcissism. Our chief
means of access to it will probably remain the analysis of the
paraphrenias [psychoses, especially the schizophrenias]." In
the same paper he states that hypochondria and the "behavior
of human beings in love, with its manifold differentiation in
man and woman," offer ways of studying narcissism.[6] Freud
had not anticipated that the direct study of children would
provide one of the most profitable sources for the study of
narcissism. But the question that Freud poses, What brings
narcissism into being?, goes begging.[14]

Freud takes off from the point that narcissism exists and
he goes on to considerations of its vicissitudes. But the way
in which the feeling of self-regard, that is, narcissism, evolves
is not extensively discussed except as "a measure of the ego,"
to use his phrase. ". . . what various components go to make
up that measure is irrelevant," he adds; "everything we possess or achieve, every remnant of the primitive feeling of
omnipotence that experience has corroborated helps to exalt
self-regard." He admits the importance of the subject and
the difficulty of surveying it. He attributes the development
of the ego to a departure from primary narcissism which
leads to a vigorous attempt to recover it. For ego develop-

ment to take place, some of the instinctual aims are deflected and recovery of what has been sacrificed by the way of instinctual satisfaction is attempted. "This departure is brought about by means of displacement of libido to an ego-ideal imposed from without, while gratification is derived from the attainment of this ideal," [6] he wrote. "Self-regard is in part primary—the residue of childish narcissism [primary narcissism]; another part arises out of such omnipotence as experience corroborates (the fulfillment of the ego-ideal) whilst a third part proceeds from the gratification of object libido." [6]

The achievement of object relations is a process of departure from concern solely with primary needs, in which they are given up and invested in the need for another person. The human condition is that instinctual needs (as they are expressed in primary narcissism) are not self-sustaining. Contrary to Freud, human survival does not rest solely upon the primordial instincts; it rests also upon another person (or persons) upon whom one has come to depend. Ego development is thus defined; survival is thus insured. Therefore, survival depends upon departure from the primary state.

It was Freud's observation that "normal adults show that their former megalomania has been subdued and that their mental characteristics from which we inferred their narcissism have vanished," [6] that is, undergo repression. These characteristics that Freud refers to return readily and with viability in the course of everyday psychopathology. Magical thinking does not seem to be remote when, in the dream, all the characteristics of our former megalomania are often present. Our movement from the world of reality to the one of magic is commonplace. We are never entirely in the one or the other at any given time. Rather, we are chiefly in the one while not having given up the other. The extent to which we live in a world of magic can, as yet, only be surmised.

Appendix

Case A:

A boy, 3 years 6 months old. The action takes place in a doll house which is furnished with the usual household goods. A family of dolls (mother, father, brother, sister, and baby). First the dolls are being knocked from the chairs.

A: They fall down and get hurt.
Dr.: How?
A: From falling down.
Dr.: What now?
A: To the hospital.
Dr.: Then what?
A: Get shot with a needle.
Dr.: But he doesn't want it.
A: That's what he's going to get.

An interval now. The play continues with shifting the dolls to a sink, with running water. The child indicates that the dolls are frightened.

Dr.: They are scared?
A: Put him in there and he'll die.
Dr.: Will he?
A: Yup.
Dr.: Then what?
A: No more. He'll be all gone. He died. He goes down the pipe.
Dr.: Not really.
A: Yup. Down the sewer. He gets died. The pipe and the sewer is where he goes down. *(He eats candy and then says)* They have to have some food.
Dr.: But they're dead.
A: They have to eat.
Dr.: Food for the dead ones?
A: Yes, they're hungry. *(He puts another doll down the drain.)* They're all dead. They come back.
Dr.: If you're dead, don't you stay dead?
A: No, you grow again. You don't stay dead.
A: I shoot that *(rubber toy bear)* dead. The bear went down the sink. He's gone.

Dr.: When it's dead it's gone?

A: I shoot him again.

Dr.: But he's dead.

A: Yes, I'm going to eat him for supper. Then he'll be gone. *(Runs water over the toy bear.)*

Dr.: What are you doing now?

A: He's drinking it *(the bear)*.

Dr.: I thought he was dead.

A: He can drink now.

Dr.: Can dead bears drink?

A: Yes.

Dr.: They can? *(The bear is filled with water again.)*

A: I'll drink out of the bear.

Dr.: Then what?

A: I'll grow to be a bear.

Dr.: You'll do what?

A: I'll grow to be a bear.

Dr.: Is that what happens?

A: Yes.

Dr.: Suppose you eat a chicken?

A: Yup. *(Drinks from the bear again.)* He's walking in a pond *(refers to the bear on the edge of the sink)*.

Dr.: You said he was dead.

A: He can still walk.

Dr.: Really? Can dead people walk?

A: Yup.

Dr.: Oh! I thought dead bears couldn't walk.

A: Yes they can. They can eat.

Dr.: They can walk and eat? Anything else?

A: No.

Dr.: Can they talk?

A: I'm going to turn the water off.

On another occasion the action takes place between a group of toy soldiers and a plane.

A: The soldiers get hit with a plane. He's dead.

Dr.: You killed him?

A: Yes.

Dr.: What happens?

A: He goes bye-bye.

Dr.: Now you are hitting that man.

A: I'll get him down here *(the drain)*.

Dr.: Down there?

A: Yes, down in the sewer.

Dr.: Is that where dead people go?

A: Dead things get in sewers.

Dr.: They don't want to go there.

A: Yes, they do. They're already in.

Dr.: Well—

A: He comes to get him out. *(Ambulance comes to the sink.)*

Dr.: To take him out?

A: No, we'll take him to the hospital.

Dr.: Isn't he dead?

A: He's still dead in the sewer. Now he's going to throw up in the sewer.

Dr.: Maybe he doesn't want to be in the sewer.

A: He's going to scream.

Dr.: He's dead.

A: He doesn't have to go to the hospital. He's going to have to get shot with a needle.

Dr.: He doesn't want that.

A: But he is. Two men are going to take him. He's going to get gasoline in his mouth.

Dr.: He doesn't want it.

A: He'll get it.

Dr.: What happens if you put gasoline in his mouth?

A: What?

Dr.: What happens?

A: He dies.

Dr.: If he dies?

A: They're all gone.

Dr.: Will he stay gone?

A: Yes. If he's gone he can't come home. *(He puts doll once more in drain.)*

Dr.: You're putting them all in the sewer. Are they dead or alive now?

A: Alive.

Dr.: Alive?

A: They are all in the sewer again.

Dr.: But then they're dead.

A: They can be alive again.

Dr.: Dead people can be alive again?
A: They're wet. I put gasoline on them.
Dr.: That's enough, isn't it?
A: No. I want more. He's left behind *(designating a doll).*
Dr.: Why is he left behind?
A: He did something.
Dr.: What?
A: Nothing!
Dr.: He did do something?

The play with dolls goes back to the sink again.

A: He went over his head. Too deep. He has to be over his head.
Dr.: You're going to put him in over his head?
A: Yes.
Dr.: Why?
A: Well, I like to be mean to him.
Dr.: He says, "Don't be mean to me."
A: I'm going to be.
Dr.: He says, "Don't."
A: I'm going to be.
Dr.: You're going to be mean anyway?
A: Yes.
Dr.: Really?
A: He's going to be killed.
Dr.: He says, "Don't kill me."
A: He is.
Dr.: He says, "Please don't."
A: Going to put water on him. Going to put gasoline on him.
Dr.: Then what?
A: Nothing.
Dr.: Nothing?
A: He's down the pipe. He's killed and gone.
Dr.: You brought him out.
A: He's back.
Dr.: He was dead.
A: Yup, but he's back.

Another interval. He picks up a dog.

A: The dog is going to have a shot.
Dr.: What's wrong?

A: He has a temperature. See, the man is in the sewer and I'm taking him out.

Dr.: Wasn't he dead?

A: Not now. He's looking in the pipe.

Dr.: What for?

A: To see if dogs and cats are in the sewer.

Dr.: How do they get there?

A: People put them in the sewer.

Case B:
A girl, 4 years 4 months old. On this occasion the action takes place around the doll's house. There is a mother, a father, a little girl, and a baby boy.

B: The lights are out. It's dark.

Dr.: If the lights are out?

B: The kids get scared.

Dr.: What is there to be scared about?

B: They would get lost.

Dr.: Anything else?

B: They could get killed.

Dr.: In the dark?

B: They might have an accident. They couldn't see where to go. Not know where they're walking.

Dr.: They might get killed if they couldn't see where they're going?

B: Well. They might walk into the woods by mistake. I'm pretending they're in the woods.

Dr.: And if they get killed?

B: They die.

Dr.: Then?

B: They go in the graveyard.

Dr.: Have you seen a graveyard?

B: I once saw someone get buried.

Dr.: Did you really see it?

B: Well— No.

Dr.: What happens when people are buried?

B: I don't know. I saw my great-grandma killed.

Dr.: You saw your great-grandma killed?

B: She got too big and too old.

Dr.: When they get too old they die?

B: Yes. My mother told me people die. They get buried. Before they get buried they just get in a box and they put them in a truck.

Dr.: Then?

B: *(Silence)* I wish you would say the words. What I was trying to think of.

Dr.: What words?

B: They have all kinds of boxes.

Dr.: For different people?

B: Big sizes.

Dr.: Then after the people are in the boxes and buried?

B: They come one. Somebody digs the dirt off them.

Dr.: They can't do it themselves?

B: No. They take the box out. I'm thinking where they go.

Dr.: Where dead people go?

B: In the woods.

Dr.: They go in the woods? Do they do anything?

B: How can they do anything when they're dead? In the box.

On another occasion in the playroom she picked up a rifle saying, "I'm going to play with a gun and shoot."

Dr.: What?

B: I'm going to shoot animals. I'll keep them and save them and eat them. *(Shoots animals.)*

Dr.: Which animals will you shoot?

B: Just the ones to eat. I don't shoot the elephant *(a rubber toy).* I wouldn't kill him. We'd save him for a pet.

Dr.: What happens to animals that die?

B: They don't get buried.

Dr.: What else?

B: They go to animal doctors and get fixed.

Dr.: After they die?

B: Yes.

Dr.: They don't stay dead?

B: No.

Dr.: Maybe you are mistaken.

B: Only if they get dead. They go to the animal hospital and they get fixed.

Dr.: Does it happen to people too?

B: No.

Dr.: People stay dead but animals don't?

B: Because animals are more nice.

Dr.: And animals only stay dead if you eat them?

B: I'm going to shoot myself.

Dr.: Kill yourself? Don't do that.

B: Yes. I'm dead.

Dr.: Now what will happen?

B: I'm going to get buried.

Dr.: Can't we take you to a hospital?

B: Yes. O.K. Now you fix me.

The play shifts to dolls. One is dead, taken to a doctor, and given medicine.

Dr.: Can dead people eat medicine?

B: Yeah. They swallow it.

Dr.: I thought they couldn't eat when they're dead.

B: They can. Give her more medicine. (*The doll is given medicine.*)

B: She isn't dead any more.

Dr.: Is she alive?

B: Yes.

Dr.: Just as she was before?

B: Yes.

On another occasion the child began with the following statement:

B: Remember the day I shooted myself? Let's do it again.

Dr.: You're going to shoot yourself? What will happen?

B: Nothing. I get shot in the arm. I don't fall dead. Only if I get shot in the eye.

Dr.: Then you're not dead because of the arm shot.

B: You fall dead if you get shot here.

Dr.: Where?

B: Because that's the heart. Right here.

Dr.: If you get shot in the heart, do you get killed?

B: Yes, if you get shot in the head you could get dead.

Dr.: But I could take pills so I won't get dead.

The play then shifts to puppets.

B: Get the right medicine. I believe I have a broken bone.

Dr.: How did you get it?

B: Because I fell out of a plane.

Case C:

A boy, 3 years 3 months old. The setting is a tabletop with a small family of dolls (mother, father, boy, girl, and baby), rubber elephant, bear, and tiger.

C: Let's run a truck over him *(the bear)*. O.K. Let's put him in a graveyard.

Dr.: He doesn't want to have it happen.

C: I'm going to put him in the graveyard.

Dr.: Maybe—

C: I'm going to put him there. He can talk and eat dirt sometimes.

Dr.: What else?

C: Let's shoot him again.

Dr.: I thought he was dead.

C: I just wanted to wound him, so he's going to be more killed.

Dr.: But he is dead?

C: I'm going to kill him once more.

Dr.: What happens?

C: He will have to lie down in the graveyard. He's dead. When they get very old they die.

Cats die when they get too old.

The play shifts now to a toy rubber tiger.

C: He is going to growl and bite.

Dr.: Who?

C: It bites different kinds of animals.

Dr.: You don't want to get bitten?

C: Sometimes my sister does.

Dr.: She bites you?

C: She tries. But I kick my foot. I want to shoot another animal. *(He takes a gun and fires away and then says)* Smoke came out of the gun.

Dr.: What happened?

C: I burned him. I'm going to shoot his head.

Dr.: I'll watch you do it.

C: I'm going to make a bigger hole. Maybe I can smoke him up. Now he's just got dead. They have to go to the graveyard.

DR.: I wouldn't want to stay.

C: I'd be sorry not to see my house. My mother and daddy would come with me to the graveyard.

DR.: What if they did not?

C: Then I wouldn't go. When grown-ups die, they die. People who die have to stay there.

DR.: Well, what happens?

C: They can eat inch worms. Can I make a big lobster? *(He begins to work with clay, and I help him to fashion a lobster. After we have completed this he says)* He's going to bite.

DR.: What will he do?

C: Let's take his mouth off.

DR.: What for?

C: So he won't bite.
   (He then picks up a rifle and shoots the house.) Should I kill the house?
   (The lobster bites the boy and then the boy turns and says) I'm going to make him flat as a pancake. *(With that he detroys the lobster.)*

Case D:
A 4-year-old boy. The action takes place in the kitchen of the doll house. D says that the mother is washing the dishes.

DR.: Why is she washing them?

D: To get the germs off.

DR.: What are germs?

D: They make people sick.

DR.: Did you ever hear of anyone being sick?

D: No. They take medicine and it makes them better.

Action shifts to an airplane that he flies to Chicago. He puts the family of dolls in the plane. All fly off. Suddenly the plane crashes.

DR.: What happens?

D: It ran out of gas.

DR.: And the people inside?

D: They have to go to the doctor.

The plane flies once more, crashes again, and burns.

D: He's going to check the gas.

DR.: What about the people?
D: They have to run. Nobody gets hurt.

*Action returns to the doll house kitchen now. The mother is
cooking dinner.*

D: Baby is sick and he needs medicine. *(While he is saying this, D
    eats candy and drops one on the floor. He says)* Are there
    germs on the floor?
DR.: Some.
D: I hate them. (But he eats the candy he dropped.)

The action shifts to shooting rifles at the dolls.

DR.: What happened?
D: The baby gets killed. He won't live forever.
DR.: Why not?
D: You're just not alive any more.

*The action goes back to the doll house. He fills a tub with water
for the baby to bathe.*

D: I'm going to fill it with hot water.
DR.: Hot?
D: It's going to be very hot. Roasting hot. He's going to get a
    roasting bath. The baby has to get it. He's burned. Now I'm
    going to shoot the baby.
DR.: What will happen?
D: *(Will not answer.)*
DR.: You don't want to say.
D: I don't like to talk about it. It's too sad. *(Suddenly)* Oh,
    they're still alive.
DR.: What's going on?
D: If you killed them with a knife and you take the knife out
    then they're still alive.

*The action changes to filling a plane with passengers. The plane
crashes. Before it falls to the ground the doors open and all the
people fall out.*

DR.: You know that if people fell out they could get hurt.
D: No. I don't know that.
DR.: What do you think happens?
D: You bury them.

*He plays again with a plane roaring about the room, crashes it.
The pilot is not hurt at all. He then goes to the blackboard and
draws a "wrecked-up house."*

D: It has ghosts.

DR.: What are they?

D: They scare people. But there is no such thing my father says.
    (He draws a small figure who he says has run away scared.)

*The play shifts to a rifle. He shoots animals—elephant, bear,
tiger—and kills them.*

D: They get buried.
    Last night I found a dead bee.

DR.: Did it look dead?

D: He got killed. Someone stepped on him and it got dead.

DR.: Dead like people are dead?

D: They're dead but they're not like dead people. Nothing
    like dead people.

DR.: Is there a difference?

D: People are dead and bees are dead. But they're put in the
    ground and they're no good. People.

DR.: Are no good?

D: After a long time he'll get alive *(the bee)*. But not a person.
    I don't want to talk about it.

DR.: Why?

D: Because I have two grandfathers alive.

DR.: Two?

D: One.

DR.: What happened to one?

D: He died a long time ago. A hundred years ago.

DR.: Will you live long too?

D: A hundred years.

DR.: Then what?

D: I'll die perhaps.

DR.: All people die.

D: Yes, I will have to.

DR.: That is sad.

D: I have to anyway.

DR.: You have to?

D: Sure. My father is going to die. That is sad.

DR.: Why is he?

D: Never mind.

DR.: You don't want to talk about it.

D: I want to see my mother now.

DR.: I'll take you to her.

D: I know where dead people are. In cemeteries. My old grandfather is dead. He can't get out.

DR.: You mean where he is buried.

D: He can't get out. Never.

Since children present such a wide range of behavior and development, generalizations about them are usually worthless.

Before one can teach concepts about death, he must first understand the age and the ability of the child to comprehend these thoughts. Is the youngster able to distinguish animate from inanimate objects? Does he have a concept of the living as opposed to nonliving? How does he understand time in terms of the past, present, and future? Does he have sufficient secondary-process thinking to comprehend that since something is dead, it can no longer do certain things? How is the structure of the subject of death represented in terms of the youngster's way of viewing things?

Robert Kastenbaum, Ph.D., has outlined developmental approaches of different ages in their understanding of death with tangible guidelines and suggestions.

Dr. Kastenbaum is the Director of Psychological Research, Cushing Hospital, Framingham, Massachusetts, and is co-editor of Omega, *a quarterly newsletter concerned with death and bereavement. A new book* Psychology of Death, *is now in press.*

CHAPTER III

The Child's Understanding of Death: How Does It Develop?

ROBERT KASTENBAUM

THE TAPE MEASURE and the scale faithfully report upon the physical growth of our children. How tall will David become? What will be his physical characteristics as an adult? Usually we can estimate the future growth with a fair degree of accuracy. We guess that David will attain a height of 5′ 10″, but would not be taken aback if the figure proved to be 5′ 8″ or 6′. Astonishment would reign, however, if David's growth should cease at 3′ 6″, or soar to 8′ 10″. We would be even more startled if, having attained a certain height, weight, and maturity of body, David should then begin to dwindle and return to a more infantile physical structure.

Guidelines for mental, emotional, and social growth have been offered by many developmental psychologists and their colleagues in related fields. Although these guidelines frequently are quite useful and are based upon substantial observation and research, we have come to recognize that the child's psychological development is a more "iffy" proposition than his physical growth. We do not mean to introduce a sharp distinction between psychological and physical growth. That would be an unfortunate return to a naïve form of doublethink. And we do not mean to imply that physical development is a simple, guaranteed process that we can take for granted; patterns of nutrition, sleep, exercise, and so on make their influence felt.

What we do mean to suggest is this:

(1) Whether we consider psychological development as a whole or in any of its parts, most generally we will (a) observe a greater range of variability than is the case with physical development and (b) experience greater difficulty in determining precisely which factors exerted precisely how much influence in leading to the observed behavior.

89

And this:

(2) In certain areas of psychological development we will encounter even greater difficulties because we lack a truly convincing
idea of the "goal" or "maturational outcome," what the
process of growth is moving *toward*. Such is the case with the
concept of death.

Mulling over the first point for a moment, we note that
a normal child may revert to more infantile forms of thought
and behavior on occasion, although reversion to a more infantile state of physical development is extraordinary. Furthermore, many of us have observed that a given child may
evidence a form of behavior, insight, or talent that far ex-
ceeds that shown by a given adult who is in full possession of
his matured physical and, presumably, psychological structure. Psychologically, then, a child may be "ahead" or "behind" his physical growth and his chronological age, and for
a variety of possible reasons. We appreciate the relationship
between psychological and physical aspects of growth but do
not equate them, nor do we expect to find the relationship
identical from child to child or in the same child from age
to age.

These background considerations, familiar as they may
be, are worth keeping in mind as we explore the child's
understanding of death. Here we encounter all the logical
and methodological problems that confront us in the general
study of child development, but with two further complications. The first complication has already been mentioned,
but requires a bit of elaboration. How far has a child at a
certain age advanced toward a mature concept of death? How
far must he still travel? What are the critical points and the
strongest factors at work in his development of this concept?
How can we help the child to develop a mature concept of
death, and how can we determine when he needs our help?
Questions such as these imply that we all know very well what
constitutes a mature concept of death. Most investigators and

advice-givers seem to make this assumption. But are we justified in doing so?

Man's social and intellectual history strongly suggests that the concept of death has undergone a number of fundamental changes through the centuries.[3] We certainly did not begin with a clear, universally held "mature" conception of death. Ah, but surely *we* have "the" mature conception of death *now!* One can slip into this follow-up assumption as naturally as one eases his feet into a comfortable old pair of slippers. To accept this belief, however, seems to require the additional conviction that the history of ideas has reached both its climax and its final resting place in our very own generation. Ideas of death may have been transformed over and again in past epochs, but now our notions are here to stay. No doubt some people are willing to overlook the multitude of new developments in fields ranging from biological research to theology, developments that bear directly upon our conceptions of death. But at least on these pages it will be doubted that we have attained even a close approximation to a perfected conception of death.

What attitude, then, might we take toward the child's conception of death? Of course, we can continue to compare and contrast the child's views with views that are held by adults. (Both plurals are intentional: adults as well as children show a variety of outlooks toward death.) But we might also observe the child's changing orientation toward death as a phenomenon deserving study and respect in its own right, not merely as a stepping-stone toward some ideal concept.

This point leads us to the second major complication in attempting to fathom the child's understanding of death—this "complication" is ourselves, the parental generation and adults in general. Many observers have claimed that the typical adult in the United States prefers *not* to view death, defending himself against a straightforward appreciation of death with a variety of escapist, diversionary, sugar-coating,

and covering-up behaviors.[5, 17] The psychiatric experiences of
Albert Solnit and Morris Green [26] suggest that adults' own
problems in coming to terms with death can have particularly unfortunate effects upon the thought and behavior of
their children, especially when the children themselves happen to be seriously ill. Is it more "mature" to avoid the
thought of death at all costs than it is to have a matter-of-fact
curiosity about the subject? As we will see below, many young
children enter a phase during which they speak of death in
an open, factual manner without a heavy overlay of sadness
or anxiety. Yet some years later these children may become
adults who are tongue-tied on the subject of death, offering
to their own children cliché and evasion rather than candor
and depth. We do not mean that the five-year-old necessarily
has a more mature concept of death than do his parents—but
we do mean to suggest that uncertainties, anxieties, per-
plexities in the adult world may complicate rather than
facilitate the child's quest for understanding.

How would the child develop his understanding of death
if he grew up in a society that truly had solved its intellectual
and emotional relationship to death? The answer to this
question we do not know and, so, we do not know the outer
limits or full potentialities of development during the childhood years. But we do know something about the development of death ideas within our own society. Having now
some appreciation of the problems involved in attempting
to *interpret* children's concepts of death, we can proceed to
consider *observations* and *descriptions*. At the conclusion
of this rather brief survey, we will return to the problem
of interpretation or meaning.

DEVELOPMENT OF THE BASIC CONCEPT OF DEATH

*The Idea of Death as Part of General
Intellectual Development*

There is a close relationship between development of ideas
about death and intellectual development in general. It is

necessary to appreciate how strongly the child's concept of death is dependent upon the total pattern of mental processes and resources available to him at a particular stage in his development. Consider, for example, the statement: "I will die." This recognition of personal mortality is not as simple as it might appear. It involves a complex integration of concepts, some of which are quite abstract, and all of which require a process of emotional growth. The three words, "I will die," are easy enough to say—a young child might learn to utter the sounds. However, the concepts implied by this statement are not within the reach of the young child's mind.

Let us examine this statement in some detail—not exhaustively, because a thorough analysis of this "simple" proposition would probably demand its own book. The person who states, "I will die," and knows what he is talking about has developed many concepts, a few of which will be illustrated here:

(1) *I* am an individual with a life of my own, a personal existence.

(2) I belong to a *class* of beings one of whose attributes is mortality.

(3) Using the intellectual *process of logical deduction,* I must arrive at the conclusion that my personal death is a certainty.

(4) There are *many possible causes* of my death, and these causes might operate in many different combinations; although I might evade or escape one particular cause, I cannot evade all causes.

(5) My death will occur in the *future.* By future, I mean a time-to-live that has not yet elapsed.

(6) But I do not know *when* in the future my death will occur. The event is certain; the timing is uncertain.

(7) Death is a *final* event. My life ceases. This means that I will never again experience, think, or act, at least as a human being on this earth.

(8) Accordingly, death is the *ultimate* separation of myself from the world.

Even this incomplete analysis indicates that "I will die" requires self-awareness, logical thought operations, conceptions of probability, necessity, and causation, of personal and physical time, of finality and separation. The available evidence strongly suggests that the young child lacks almost all the mental operations required to form the separate concepts which are integrated into the recognition of personal mortality.[1] The one possible exception is *separation,* as will be discussed below. It should already be clear that one cannot attain a well-developed concept of death without also possessing the intellectual tools for comprehending all the fundamental conditions of life.

From Infancy Through Toddlerhood

Much intellectual development takes place during the first months after birth. The toddler "knows his way around" and seems definitely to have "a mind of his own." However, this mind does not yet range into the realm of conceptual thought. Fully occupied in acquainting himself with his immediate world, the very young child does not deal in remote abstractions such as futurity and death. Arnold Gesell and Frances Ilg [7] and Anthony Sylvia[2] probably speak for most developmentalists when they declare that during the first two years or so there is no understanding of death.

Granting that the infant and toddler seem to lack *conceptions* of death, we might nevertheless explore the possibility that certain *experiences* and *behaviors* of the very young child imply a relationship to the state of nonbeing. This approach is difficult to evaluate because there is no direct access to the mind of the child who has yet to develop language skills. Here we are limited to observing behavior and guessing about its possible relevance to death. Adah Maurer is perhaps the most articulate advocate of the view that even the infant is already experimenting with, let us say, the "pre-idea" of death.[16] She recalls to us that one of Millicent Shinn's classic observations in *Biography of a Baby* [25] concerns the infant's alternations between sleeping and wake-fulness. These alternations may endow the infant with a basic appreciation of the difference between being and nonbeing. Elsewhere we have taken this same observation as the starting point for a theoretical interpretation of the development of psychological time concepts throughout the lifespan.[11] Maurer emphasizes the implications of the baby's rhythmical alternation of mental states for the maturation of death concepts.

She suggests that "By the time he is three months old, the healthy baby is secure enough in his self feelings to be ready to experiment with these contrasting states. In the game of peek-a-boo, he replays in safe circumstances the alternate terror and delight, confirming his sense of self by risking and regaining complete consciousness. A light cloth spread over his face and body will elicit an immediate and forceful reaction. Short, sharp intakes of breath, vigorous thrashing of arms and legs removes the erstwhile shroud to reveal widely staring eyes that scan the scene with frantic alert-ness until they lock glances with the smiling mother, where-upon he will wriggle and laugh with joy. . . . To the empa-thetic observer, it is obvious that he enjoyed the temporary dimming of the light, the blotting out of the reassuring face and the suggestion of a lack of air which his own efforts enabled him to restore, his aliveness additionally confirmed by the glad greeting implicit in the eye-to-eye oneness with another human."[16] Adding that the term, peek-a-boo, stems from Old English words meaning "Alive or dead?", Maurer points out that "the simple nursery games, usually brushed off as unimportant if not downright silly, may prove to be a key factor in the establishment of an autonomous individ-ual."

Maurer also interprets the very young child's interest in games of disappearance-and-return as little experiments with nonbeing or death. "During the high-chair age, babies per-sist in tossing away a toy and fretting for someone to return it. If one has patience to replace the toy on the tray a dozen or twenty times, the reward is a child in ecstasy." The child is doting on the joy of reappearance. Gradually he comes to suspect that some things do not return; they may, instead, be "all-gone!" And "all-gone!" is frequently one of the child's first and most popular phrases. After he begins to appreciate all-goneness, the toddler continues his experiments with being and nonbeing in many ways. Maurer cites three examples: "Offer a two-year-old a lighted match and watch his face light up with demoniac glee as he blows it out. Notice the willingness with which he helps his mother if the errand is to step on the pedal and bury his banana peel in the covered garbage can. The toilet makes a still better sarcophagus until he must watch in awed dismay while the plumber fishes out the tinker toy from the overflowing bowl."

We have seen an 18-month-old boy experiment with the possibility of placing a dead bird on a tree, trying to explain to his father that the bird would then fly again. A week later, he insisted that autumn leaves be replaced on the tree. Both experiments failed in their direct objectives (as, indeed, many of his father's experiments have failed), but there was the definite impression that David had taken a small step or two toward conceptions of separation, finality, and death.

It is rather clear, especially from psychoanalytic contributions, that separation can arouse the most profound anxieties in children as well as adults. How the young child experiences and attempts to come to terms with separation situations might well influence his subsequent ideas of death, the ultimate separation—but also contribute to the shaping of his basic character structure.

Perhaps the toddler is experimenting with *experiences* of separation, loss, and nonbeing more than we realize. Perhaps these experiences provide the foundations for his later *conceptions*. Perhaps as Maurer and some others have suggested, these very early flirtations with death play an important role in the child's general mental, emotional, and social development.

The Childhood Years

By the time of his third birthday the child often has a rather impressive command of language. He is able to participate in prolonged conversations, listen to long stories, and concoct his own monologues. It is obvious that words are important to him. In fact, much of his energy seems to be devoted to transforming what he hears from adults and what he himself experiences into his own words. You tell him a story or a bit of news, and he excitedly retells it to you. He is on the look-out for new words, especially "big" or "important" words that he can incorporate into his own repertoire. This development of language skills alerts us to the fact that the child's mind is now acquiring some freedom, range, and versatility. Although Jean Piaget[21] and others report that genuine *conceptual* operations are not available to the child until he is close to puberty, it is evident that even the three-year-old has begun to enjoy the "world of ideas" on at least an entrance level. We would then expect the child both to think more about death and related topics, and to share his views with adults. No longer are we limited chiefly to inferences from his nonverbal behavior.

Several investigators have attempted to specify the precise chronological age at which particular ideas of death first show themselves. However, for the purposes of this rather brief sketch, which does not permit side trips to methodological details, we will be on safer ground if we attend chiefly to the general sequence of development and not take the specific age references too seriously. We will offer some age references, but only as a rough guide.

Curiosity is one of the young child's strongest traits. We are all acquainted with the popular stereotype of a confrontation in which the embarrassed parent hems and haws about "the facts of life" while the child's mood slumps from eagerness to dismay. Although the adult in our society is likely to equate "facts of life" with the processes of conception, reproduction, and birth, the child usually is searching for a broader view. It is important to him that he gain some understanding of his origins *and* destination, birth *and* death. Where was he before he was? Is it possible that he might go back there again? If he is growing up, does this mean Daddy and Mommy are growing down? Questions such as these begin to occupy the child. (The philosophic implications of these questions have occupied some of the best minds of every generation—yet the parent may casually dismiss these inquiries as inconsequential or amusing.)

Generally, the child's first answer to his birth-and-death questions is based upon assumptions of *continuity* and *periodicity*. The preschooler believes that identity, who-he-is, has no limit in time. Indeed, he does not yet grasp the concept of final limits or of linear, nonrepetitive time. Periodically, one's condition changes. Somewhat in the same way as you sleep and wake, sleep and wake, so you "are made dead" and return to ordinary life. Even while dead, you still "live," although perhaps in a more restricted style, as while asleep.

Maria Nagy,[19] for example, found that children between the ages of three and five denied death *as a final event.* The state of being dead is temporary. The child *knows* that grandfather is "dead"—yet he will suddenly ask, "When is Grandpa coming for supper? Tonight?" The deceased could be more-or-less dead. One child may argue that the dead can hear but not talk, while another child argues that some dead people are hungry, and some are not. Although Nagy's investigation involved Hungarian children, it would appear that her conclusions have application across national boundaries. A rather neglected earlier study by Colin Scott[24] tends to be consistent with Nagy's work, although he studied adult Americans by the method of retrospective questionnaire. Many adults recalled having ascribed various degrees of life to the dead. Among the more frequent childhood ideas were that the dead felt smothered, were asleep, breathing gently, or that they felt cold.

The young child's tendency to regard death as temporary and life-death as alternating states usually meets with a mixed reaction. Adults and older children are likely to inform him that death is a one-way street. This proposition is difficult for the young child to comprehend, so he probably continues to think in terms of temporary death although perhaps no longer speaking of it as such. The same people who break the news that death is permanent may also tell ghost stories to the young child, or regale him with visions of the afterlife that seem to involve a return to life. Furthermore, an almost constant parade of life-unto-death-unto-life dynamics moves in front of his eyes as he watches his favorite animated cartoons on the tube or the screen. Notice how many temporary deaths are encountered by the characters of a typical animated cartoon within even a single episode. The "death" itself can be quite convincing—hero or villain is drowned, crushed, dismembered, etc. But an instant later—without explanation and often without loss of a single whisker—the character returns for his next escapade. So it is that the child occasionally finds his view of death flatly contradicted by "those in authority," but also receives strong reinforcement for some of his modes and themes of thought through both personal contact and mass media. We do not yet know what kind of effect the treatment of death on television and other mass media has upon the shaping of the child's thoughts and feelings, nor how this effect compares with the influence of direct personal contacts.

During this early phase in the development of thought, the child seems to regard death chiefly as a separation, a departure. It is clear enough that the dead person or animal is not here with us—and that is probably the most important "fact of death" for the young child. Any separation or prospect of separation, especially from a parent, is likely to arouse thoughts of death. Sensitive parents appreciate that their child may not always differentiate between a short (to us) absence and a long or permanent separation. Accordingly, they will make it clear that Daddy will be back "soon," or "for supper tomorrow night." The child recalls that Grandpa went away, and people said he went to the cemetery. He has not come back . . . yet. Daddy is not making *that* kind of trip. If the child has been given a runaround on the topic of death, then he finds it particularly difficult to know when death is *not* involved. As Earl Grollman [9] has observed, "Evasive answers like 'she went to sleep' or 'she went on a long journey' only compound the tension by blurring the difference between fact and fancy."

Even the young child seems to recognize that death is something "special" although he is not able to comprehend precisely what it is that makes death so special. An interesting experiment by Alexander and Adlerstein [1] demonstrated that children as young as five years old showed more emotional reaction to "death words" than to other types of words. The emotional reactions were measured by galvanic skin responses (GSR) and by the length of the delay between hearing a word and offering a response to it (latency measure on a word association task). While the five-year-old might not be able to formulate what would usually be considered as an accurate definition or concept of death, he nevertheless responded to death stimuli in a "special" way. This study also serves to remind us that our *relationship* to death—at any age—is more complex than what we *say* about death.

Other characteristics of the young child's view of death have been reported by a number of observers.[2,7,19,23] There is general agreement that the child begins with a matter-of-fact orientation. His "cool" or "detached" inquiry into death is accompanied by two important assumptions. The young child seems to believe that death is accidental rather than inevitable. "If you get runned over, then you be dead!", or "He is so old. That is why he be dead." That is, one dies under certain conditions. These conditions may or may not occur. If one does not get "runned over," very sick, or old, then one does not die—and one does not *necessarily* encounter a death-dealing situation sooner or later. The equally significant corollary assumption is that the child himself will not die. He is not very sick, he is not old, and he does not intend to become very sick or very old. Therefore, if he is a good boy and takes care when he crosses the street, then he will not be made "all dead."

It is roughly in the age range from four to six that the child often is prone to misinterpret superficial or even irrelevant signals as being intrinsically involved in death. Becoming increasingly aware that death is something that is both important and disruptive, he seeks to isolate those phenomena which "mean" or "cause" death. Did somebody die in a hospital? Then one must stay away from hospitals, because being-in-a-hospital equals death. A school counselor has told us of a terrified child who has been informed that his baby sister's death was caused by a white rabbit that happened to be in the house at the time. Naturally enough, the boy feared that he might inadvertently encounter a white rabbit some place and, consequently, die. As there is no telling when or where a white rabbit might cross one's path, there is also no way of containing death in a safe, isolated compartment. Sadly enough, in this case it was a parent who gave the child the anxiety-arousing misinformation. Often the parent can recognize that the child is forming an unrealistic association between death and a particular object, place, person, or condition. This insight can be followed by reassurance and explanation.

With the first apprehension that death is something formidable, the child attempts to gain control through what for him is a rational analysis of the situation. So it is that one of the first testing grounds of the child's reasoning abilities is the problem of death, which perhaps is also the ultimate challenge to man's powers of comprehension.

From approximately age five onward, the child seems gradually to be accommodating himself to the proposition that death is final, inevitable, universal, and personal. Many six- and seven-year-olds seem to suspect that their parents will die some day, and that the same fate might be in store for them. However, they now may speak less about death and seem to hold this topic in less regard. It seems rather typical for the full recognition of death to be delayed several years beyond the first premonitions. Perhaps the child is still too vulnerable emotionally to accept the implications of his own new thoughts about death. Perhaps it is necessary that his thoughts be attuned more completely to mastering the realities of daily life. In any event, there is the impression that in mid-childhood the youth can neither "deny" nor "accept" death as an authentic aspect of his own life. Some kind of compromise seems necessary.

The somewhat limited information available suggests that the compromise involves an acknowledgment that death is "real," but "real" in an external and distant sense. Nagy[19] has observed that between the ages of five and nine, there is a strong tendency to interpret death in anthropomorphic terms: death is a person. "Death exists but the children still try to keep it distant from themselves. Only those die whom the death-man carries off. Death is an eventuality. . . . Death is still outside us and is also not general." The death-person may be imagined as a separate person or as himself being dead. Among her illustrations, Maria Nagy reports the following conversation with a child aged 6 years, 1 month:

CHILD: Puts on a white coat, and a death face.
INTERVIEWER: Who?
C: Death. Frightens the children.
I: Has he frightened you already?
C: I'm not afraid. I know it's just a man who has put on a death face. He was in the circus once.
I: Now don't tell me about that man but about real death. What is death, really?
C: Real death? I don't know. It has big eyes and white clothes. It has long legs, long arms.
I: But that's not really death. That is an "uncle" dressed up like death.
C: No. I went to church. I saw the real death. He went toward the park.
I: But that was a man dressed up like death.
C: But death has eyes as big as the squares on this table. Death is also only a man, only it has bigger eyes.

The death-man usually is regarded as a creature of the night, whether he is based upon the image of a person the child has actually seen (as in the circus man in the illustration above), or the image of death as the dead. A girl 7 years, 11 months of age defines death as "A dead person who hasn't any flesh any more, only bones." Her twin brother gives a very similar definition: "Death is a skeleton."

The protective nature of death personifications is emphasized by Nagy: "Only those die whom the death-man catches and carries off. Whoever can get away does not die."

Most ten-year-olds seem to have made the transition in both mental development and emotional security: they now express an understanding of death as a final and inevitable outcome of life. No longer is it a question of hiding under the bed covers to escape the death-man. From children ten years and a little younger, Nagy heard definitions such as the following: "Death is like the withering of flowers." ". . . the termination of life. . . . We finish our earthly life. Death is the end of life on earth." "Death is something that no one can escape." "Everyone has to die once, but the soul lives on."

Around this time, children have also improved their ability to recognize the difference between animate and inanimate objects. The general concept of death is difficult to develop until the child has had enough experience with the world to learn what is *alive*. The young child tends to attribute life to the clouds that move about his head and to the automobile that seems to contain its own principles of activation and motion. Investigators disagree somewhat concerning the processes by which children learn to distinguish the living from the not-living, and the exact ages at which the distinctions generally occur. But the evidence suggests that most children have made a close approximation to the adult's view of the living and not-living by age ten if not before.[10, 14, 22, 27] The work of Piaget,[20] Anthony[2] and others further suggests that as the child approaches adolescence he is equipped with most of the intellectual tools necessary to understand both life and death in a logical manner. He now has completed his basic development of concepts of time, space, quantity, and causality. This gives him a framework within which the idea of death can be placed: death is one general principle or process among many other general principles or processes. The world is a more comprehensible and predictable place. Death can be understood *in relation* to "natural law" in general; it is no longer a phantom or will o' the wisp.

Adolescence

The child has come a long way from "peek-a-boo!" to his appreciation of death as the inevitable termination of life. But in adolescence he encounters new problems and opportunities; the child's understanding is no longer sufficient. Rapid transformations are being experienced in every sphere —physical, social, emotional, cognitive. He now is approaching adult stature and appearance—but can he behave as an adult, and does he want to? The advent of sexual maturity offers dazzling possibilities for gratification and growth— but how is one to cope with the new risks and responsibilities involved? Socially, he is becoming more of a participant in the "big world" outside his family circle—can he "make it"? What self should he put forth? Emotionally, he is much more self-conscious than the child, becoming acutely aware of himself as an individual person, and of a whole new set of yearnings and fears. Intellectually, his mind now has the power not merely to view life, but to review and preview. With an increased ability to think symbolically, to "think about thought," the adolescent can philosophize, daydream, plan, criticize, imagine. Possibility is as important to him as reality. He begins to explore the alternatives, the options that lie before him.

Sooner or later the adolescent is likely to turn his new intellectual resources to the subject of death. Previously he had been led to believe certain propositions about "life after

death"—now he may be inclined to examine these propositions critically. Furthermore, it is not enough to acknowledge
the bare reality of death. Somehow, this reality must become
integrated into his total view of life. As the adolescent begins
to form his own purposes and make his own decisions he
becomes aware that all his hopes, expectations, ambitions,
require *time* for their actualization. The adolescent stands
here, at a certain point in time. Off in the distance, on the
other side of time, stands death. This new self that he is developing and these new purposes that are emerging confront
a natural enemy in death. To grow up and lead one's own life
in one's own way—this is certainly a tremendous prospect.
But one grows up . . . to die. What sense does that make?

Some adolescents—in general, the brighter ones—devote
a good deal of direct thought to the subject of death. Many
others shy away from a direct exploration of death, yet show
great concern on a less direct, less conscious basis. At earlier
age-levels we could indicate the most typical solutions to
the problem of death. These solutions were closely related to
the child's current level of mental development. However, in
adolescence the outcome, the solution, is not so easily predicted. The youth endowed with normal intelligence has
enough "mental freedom" to arrive at many different solutions; he is not restricted by absence of symbolic reasoning
powers as was the child. The adolescent's understanding of
death will be shaped by his own life experiences. "Attitude"
or "viewpoint" is just as significant as basic mental ability.
Although some limited information is available regarding
adolescent attitudes toward death,[12,15,18] there are not many
generalizations that would be useful to our purposes.

We are accustomed to think of adolescence as a time of
emotional fireworks—upheavals, explosions, smolderings,
and, through it all somehow, growth. Perhaps, however, more
recognition should be given to the exciting and formidable
intellectual task that faces the adolescent. At the very time
that everything is changing inside and around him, he must
begin to develop a comprehensive and stable conception of

the adult-world-with-him-in-it. He must explore and create while at the same time reevaluating and doubting. So far as "pure intellect" is concerned, the adolescent can hold his own with the adult. Obviously, he lacks the adult's experience of the world—the latter being a mixed bag of anecdotes and strategies, satisfactions and frustrations, insights and blind spots. Perhaps the adult can offer to the adolescent his own most constructive encounters with death and receive, in turn, the advantages of the youth's fresh quest for understanding.

A FEW IMPLICATIONS

Any attempt to describe the child's exploration of death runs the risk of artificiality. Our emphasis upon a single aspect of development might all too easily convey the erroneous impression that ideas of death enjoy a completely separate career. Actually, thoughts about death are intertwined with the total pattern of personality development right from the beginning, influencing and being influenced by all the child's experiences. Furthermore, it is artificial to close the book with adolescence. The person who stays alive psychologically continues to modify his orientation toward death throughout his entire adult life. As a young person starting his own family, as a middle-aged citizen with many deep commitments and obligations, and as an elderly individual moving toward exitus, yesterday's child encounters qualitatively different life situations. The meaning of death shifts as the quality of life shifts. Certain basic concepts tend to remain firm (e.g., death as inevitable and final), but the full range of implications demands reexamination. The adolescent and his grandfather cannot simply exchange orientations toward death. It is appropriate that each of them develop a distinctive orientation. This does not mean that one of these orientations necessarily is more "true" or "mature" than the other.

We are suggesting that it might be more useful to think of a continuous process of *maturing* rather than a short-term process that terminates in a fixed *maturation*. It is true that in the earlier stages—infancy and childhood—the developmental process can be witnessed in its most obvious and flamboyant forms. Later developments are likely to be more subtle, having to do with new perspectives and arrangements rather than radically different ideas.

Although the individual reorganizes his understanding of death many times, he does not completely discard his earlier forms of understanding. As adults, we still are able to view death through the eyes of the child and the adolescent—for example, most of us are able to personify death and, in fact, do so more often than we might realize. The earlier ideas generally remain suppressed, being dominated by the adult's own forms of understanding. Nevertheless, the child within us has not completely lost his voice. And it is a voice to which we might listen and learn, at least on occasion.

In *The Psychology of Death,* my co-author and I have offered a more detailed and systematic account of the individual's relationship to death.[13] Several topics pertaining to childhood (e.g., the child's immediate and long-range reactions to bereavement, his intellectual and emotional response should he himself be stricken by a fatal illness) have been omitted from the present discussion because justice could not be done to them with just a few words. Other topics that are applicable to a broader range than childhood (e.g., "psychological death," social "death systems") are also important in developing a full perspective on the child's situation. The reader is invited to explore these and related topics in the books listed in the bibliography.

Here it remains to be said that we, as parents, have a superb opportunity to foster our children's development throughout their entire life-span—not simply for the next few years—by respecting their efforts to puzzle out the meaning of death. The more our children feel that they can approach us with their ideas on *any* subject and receive an interested, dependable hearing, then the more likely they are to share their meditations on death. A certain inner freedom and intellectual honesty is required on our own parts, is it not?

Somehow we must keep developing and reevaluating our own orientations toward death if we are to be open and useful to our children in this area.

We do not mean to leave the implication that parents should attempt to hurry their children through relatively early phases in the understanding of death. This advice has sometimes been given or implied by others. But we do not see any particular advantage in pressuring a youngster into being anything other than a natural person at his own age-level. If the subject of death does not embarrass or dismay us, if we can appreciate and respect the child's view of reality without losing our own, then we are in a position to foster his development through life with the beginnings of an enlightened orientation toward death.

Social scientists frequently use a technical term, Ethnocentrism. *It describes the commonplace custom of viewing life through one's own eyes in terms of one's own small social, cultural, and national milieu.*

Anthropologists have attempted to fill this "creditability gap" by bringing to light the many different approaches by different peoples throughout the world.

Dr. Martin Diskin of the Anthropology Department of the Massachusetts Institute of Technology and Dr. Hans Guggenheim of Educational Development Corporation and the Massachusetts Institute of Technology, have presented an analysis of the ways in which various children of diverse ethnic groups have met the challenge of death. What are these traditions that are common to all of us? The chapter contains an important discussion of the child and death in cross-cultural perspective.

CHAPTER IV

The Child and Death as Seen in Different Cultures

MARTIN DISKIN AND HANS GUGGENHEIM

IN MANY CREATION MYTHS, the end of Man's innocence and childhood and the creation and sudden awareness of Death fall together. It is the knowledge of death that constitutes a powerful symbol between what might be called a prolonged, innocent childhood and adult maturity. Although man shares with animals the inevitability of biological death, man alone, among all living species, is unique in having a symbolic system powerful enough to recognize the transitory nature of Life. The symbolic system that enables him to do this is Language. It is partly through language, myth, and ritual that man has attempted to explain and cope with the potential threat of death to the existence not only of the individual but of society.

Anthropology is the study of man, and is concerned with universal aspects of human experience. The essence of this perspective is to study the individual as a member of a group with shared customs, values, and beliefs that are part of culture. Such individual cultures vary widely in particulars, but can be seen to fall into patterns. If this were not the case, a science of man would, of course, be impossible.

In various cultures it is possible to observe regularities and patterns in the relationships between the modes of subsistence, e.g., hunting and gathering or agriculturists, forms of social organization such as the band or the tribe, the mythologies of peoples that serve to explain the universe wherein they live and their place within this universe, and rituals that serve to help maintain this universe in order. Although we often suspect and observe such cultural regularities, it is by no means clear whether a belief causes people to behave in a certain way, or whether, because they like to behave in certain ways, they believe what they do.

111

In what follows, we will attempt to show how the patterns of behavior of children at funeral rituals of one society correspond to the beliefs that the society holds about death (a part of mythology), the relationship of parents to their children (a part of social organization), and the distribution of land and valuables at the death of a parent (an aspect of ecological adaptation). We will pick a culture representative of a large group of societies, one in which people practice ancestor worship. We can expect individual attitudes toward death to be related to the belief in the existence or nonexistence of ancestors, and to the role that these ancestors are thought to play. Explanations for such attitudes can be found either in the belief systems themselves, in the social organization, or in the subsistence base of society. The approach presented in this chapter will not take psychological motivation into account. The child's attitudes, finally, must be understood in terms of the process of socialization of the society and the way in which the development of sentiments toward parents and kin and corporate groups serves society to perpetuate itself.

Anthropologists are aware of the striking variation in definitions of death that exist in different cultures. We are accustomed to think of death as that state that occurs after normal body functions cease. As we use the term, the transition from life to death occurs in an instant. However, we may observe that some practices that surround death in the United States seem aimed at giving the idea of death sufficient time to become real. In other words, for the living, death is not instantaneous but rather requires some time to take place and become accepted. The practice of unveiling is, for some Jews, an occasion for the survivors to prove to themselves that the deceased is indeed gone and that the necessary adjustments have been made in the intervening year. The finality of the death is symbolized by the headstone which is normally erected at this time.

Among the Kota of southern India two funeral ceremonies are conducted for every death: the first, called the

Green Funeral, shortly after death, and the second, the Dry Funeral, approximately one or two years after death.

> According to Kota belief, the dead have not left the world of the living until the Dry Funeral has been conducted. A widow continues to be her deceased husband's wife until this second ceremony, and if she becomes pregnant in the interval between funerals, the child is his and shares in his property. The stated purpose of the Dry Funeral is to dispatch to the other world the spirit of the deceased which, if left to linger in this world, is a source of harmful pollution to the living. This objective is always assumed to have been successfully accomplished once the ritual has been performed.[6]

Among the Kota, then, death is seen as a process which can take as long as two years. For other people, such as the Hopi Indians, the same process may take three days.

Accepted causes of death are conditioned by general understandings concerning the world. We know, for example, that among the Azande of the Sudan-Congo every death is attributed to the result of malevolence of a sorcerer. The Azande understand that a man dies because a granary has fallen on him, but they ask, "Why did the posts supporting the granary rot and fall at the precise instant that the man was sitting in its shade?" The question and its answer for the Azande are understandable in light of the general view the Azande have of the world.[2]

The Jivaro of Ecuador believe that there are various kinds of souls, each one possessing different characteristics that can harm or help the owner. The most important kind of soul to possess, *arutam,* guarantees its owner that he cannot be killed by any form of violence, poison, or sorcery. Here, if such a person dies, everyone knows that his death is natural, i.e., through disease. Or if such a person is killed, then it is said that he did not possess the soul to begin with. The acquisition of such a soul is part of the process of leaving childhood. Without it, a boy cannot become a man. While boys begin at about the age of six in their quest for an *arutam* soul, it is said that if they do not find one by the time of puberty, they will die. For males then in this society, death is a test for the possession of an *arutam* soul. Childhood for males, in like fashion, means the time before an *arutam* soul is obtained.[5]

In American society, the causes of death are a function of belief systems that have their roots in experimental science and careful observation of biological phenomena, such as the germ theory of disease. However, in reporting causes of death, it has been observed that conventional "explanations," such as heart failure, often mask other conditions that are not socially acceptable, such as syphilis or suicide. The wide variation in defining death reflects the variety of ways of looking at the universe. Death is only one of many phenomena that must be explained for man to make sense out of his environment.

It is at the time of death that the important groups that constitute a society are seen most clearly. It might even be said that a funeral is one of the best occasions for viewing a society in its fullest extension and in the most formal sense. This fact has impressed so many anthropologists that it is commonplace to view funerary ceremonies as "a reaffirmation of the solidarity and a restoration of the structure of social groups that has suffered loss."[3]

Social structure is the way of organizing social groups into the totality we call society. Most societies have various ways of organizing themselves. For the anthropologist, simpler societies are useful to study because we may often see important organizational principles in somewhat clearer form.

We see, for example, that an individual's place in society affects the impact his death has on society. The place an individual occupies is determined by a number of attributes. Among them are his position in the life cycle (age), his general rank in an economic or religious sense (caste or class), his degree of influence or authority (political), as well as the relation of the individual to his group of kin (kinship).

Among the Aymara of Bolivia the form of burial is closely related to the age of the deceased. For example, stillborn infants, or miscarriages, are simply disposed of. Small children are buried somewhat like adults but with much less ceremony and without the usual sadness that accompanies funerals there. At children's funerals no animals are sacrificed nor are the special mourning clothes worn. For the death of an adult special behaviors are considered necessary in order to help him in his journey to the afterworld. The immediate survivors often wear special garments (sometimes everyday garments turned inside out) ; they sometimes cut their hair and usually have to obey a series of restrictions on their behavior such as not eating certain foods or being prohibited from remarriage (in the case of the surviving spouse) for periods of a year or more.[7]

Social ranking has great importance for death practices. Where the social world is divided into fixed groups that have religious definitions such as castes in traditional Indian society, the burial practices for Brahmins differ from that of low caste individuals such as sweepers or barbers. In class structured societies such as many European societies, the United States, etc., the nature of mortuary practice reflects the deceased's position as seen in the public display of symbolic paraphernalia such as the number of people who attend, the quantity and quality of flowers, and vehicles.

Where the deceased has occupied an important political position, those obligations that were owed him in life are often complied with after his death as well, such as the offering of animal sacrifices and food offerings. Not uncommonly, important political figures must have their funerary arrangements reflect their power and generosity, and their families are obliged to feast the mourners in a style that relates to their importance.

However, the most widespread social arrangement that affects the nature and shape of funeral ceremonies and the behavior of the participants is the way in which the group of survivors is related to each other and, therefore, to the deceased. In order to understand this, we must examine some of the ideas that are included under the heading of kinship studies. All people recognize kinsmen in a systematic fashion that includes a special terminology and provides guidelines for behavior. Such a kinship system often regulates marriage and inheritance, exacts vengeance for offenses against its members, jointly stages certain ceremonies, often recognizes deceased members of the group and does them homage, and owns property.

Everyone is born into a kinship system, and, in many societies, the order of birth specifies a person's status both within his kin group and in society at large. For example, the first son in a Chinese family is held to be more important than the other children. As the family, or kinship group, grows and changes with time, the status of each member correspondingly changes. It is customary for anthropologists to note the ritual observances that accompany these changes in many societies. Baptisms, bar mitzvahs, and marriage ceremonies are such observances (*rites de passage*) that mark the entrance of individuals into new statuses within a kinship social system, while mortuary rites are those that mark his exit, or more properly speaking, his assumption of a new status, that of a dead kinsman.

The vacating of a given status position changes the relationships of those that were left behind, just as the entrance of a new individual changes them. The birth of a son radically alters the status of a wife in the Hindu family from that of a practical servant to her mother-in-law to one of importance as mother of an heir with new rights and privileges. Among the Netsilik Eskimos the death of a father changes the relationship between two brothers who had once been equally subservient to their father, the experienced hunter. The elder brother takes on some of the father's authority. Rituals at the time of death of a parent are therefore concerned with the adjustment of roles of those who were left behind rather than with the sentiments of the individuals left behind. Authority, wealth, and obligations have to be redistributed.

This can be seen in the case of the attitudes toward death

among the Edo, studied by an English anthropologist, R. E. Bradbury.[1] The Edo of the Kingdom of Benin in Nigeria number about 200,000, most of whom live in compact village settlements spread over some 4,000 square miles. The Edo are a patrilineal society, that is to say a society that traces its descent through the father's line, and they are ancestor worshipers, as are many of the peoples of Africa and Asia. Attitudes toward death among the Edo are conditioned by the deceased's social status and the extent to which he has achieved, as Bradbury puts it, "his social destiny." The death of a man who dies at a high age with many descendants is a time for rejoicing, while he who dies without a son believes that he cannot enter the society of his dead kin and associates, since his survival as a social being depends on the mortuary rituals conducted by his children. At these rituals, the chants that are heard repeat the central theme of Edo existence: "that is what we bear children for." In this way the funerary ritual becomes the symbolic fulfillment of the ideal child-parent relationship among the Edo.

The relationship between the father and the eldest son is a particularly close one among the Edo. It is the eldest son who inherits the father's house, his wives, the bulk of his father's movable property, and authority over his siblings. Such a system is called primogeniture and is characteristic of many societies, among them those of feudal Europe. In such systems, relationships between fathers and sons were usually strained, since one knew that he was to replace the other. However, among the Edo there exists an unusually close identification and relationship between the father and his eldest son, who is identified as the "son of the corpse." This close relationship leads to particular tension and strains as both men grow older and is recognized in the ritual.

The Edo divide the universe into two spheres of existence: that of the living, and that of the dead in which a supreme God, deities, and supernatural powers reside. The society that inhabits the world of the dead is almost as complex and stratified as that of the living, and it is the duty of the eldest son to perform a ritual that will separate out the various qualities of his father to various configurations of spirits, who have different meanings for the various social groups to which he belonged. At the same time, he is to "plant" his father as an ancestor and to dedicate a shrine to him at which he can serve him. If the eldest son is too young to appreciate the significance of the rituals or to understand the meanings surrounding these observances, he is instructed by elders. This coaching may serve to help him move into adult status. While the father is thus transformed into an ancestor, who will watch over his descendants, he is also implored to return in a new reincarnation. Bradbury points out that the paradox that seems to appear in this action has a deep meaning: the ancestor is seen as the perpetual guardian of good and evil and judge of kin morality, and at the same time as a reservoir from which the group draws strength and renewal. Thus Edo ritual and symbolism are based on the recognition that the continuity of the descent group involves the redistribution and redefinition of statuses and the orderly transmission of jural authority through the generations.

We will give here only a very brief outline of the complex and impressive rituals that take place at an Edo funeral, concentrating on the activities of the children, and in particular on those of the senior son. Following the death of the father, the senior son is asked to bring a new white cloth, a mat, a sponge (a bundle of fibers), soap, and a small earthenware bowl, together with his other siblings present, to sprinkle the body of his father. After this washing, the father is laid out in the white cloth. A goat is killed to honor the dead as a begetter of progeny:

> My father, behold the goat I come to kill for your *ekun,*
> the *ekun* you used to beget us all. Protect me, protect
> all my relatives, protect my children, so that we may be
> able to "bury" you, so that we may meet no hindrance
> while we are doing it.

Following this prayer, the female relatives of the deceased make a soup out of the intestines of the goat for an offering to the dead man. This is done in an attempt to placate him, since it is feared that in his loneliness he might attempt to draw his wife and children after him. The fear of danger emanating from the recent dead is quite common.

Among the LoDagaba of West Africa ashes are smeared on the children's faces in order to disguise them from the deceased, to make him think that they are grandchildren. Transvestism is also employed to disguise the children, who, regardless of sex, are made to wear the dresses of adult women, because the LoDagaba believe that the dead are actively endeavoring to maintain the network of social relationships that had surrounded them in life, possibly by abducting the souls of those closest to them.

After the Edo sacrifice, friends present cloth to the children symbolizing the end of past conflicts, and reasserting the ideal father-child relationship. This is to mark the transition from one status to another, the dressing being the responsibility of the "parent." As Bradbury sees it, to give cloth in the dead man's honor symbolizes the changing status of the father from a living man to an ancestor, as well as the changing status of the child, who has to serve the father in his old age and after death in a new intensified spirit of obedience and respect.

The interment now begins, with the dead being placed in the grave, his feet pointing toward the west, where Ughoton, the old port of Benin, is located, from where the dead are believed to embark in canoes on their voyage to the spirit world across the sea and the dome of the sky. While prayers are being said for the survival of the father as an ancestor and for his reincarnation as a great and happy man, children, led by the senior son, throw chalk and cowries on the grave. Suddenly their mood changes, and the children and grandchildren burst out into spontaneous and uncontrollable grief. The children and the older sons may be deeply moved, but the oldest son may show no sorrow at all, to no one's surprise or shock. He will walk around and boast in an arrogant attitude: "Look, look, what I am doing for my father. May my children do the same for me." Observers will explain this: "He is proud that he is burying his father. He is glad that he has survived to inherit his father's property and wives. . . . The child who eats the inheritance does not weep for the dead." The older son now admonishes his younger siblings: "You should weep no longer, the weeping is to fulfill our custom. You should be happy now, because our father died of old age, and none of us went before him."

But for him and his siblings, the death of the father means different things. The eldest son has now inherited the property and authority of the father, an authority enhanced by the funeral ceremonies. His own social status and social role can be fulfilled now that his father is out of the way. The conflict and ambivalences between his deep affection for the father and his desire for such fulfillment are now being resolved in the ritual obligations that he will be able to perform for the deceased. For the younger brothers the story is different. They exchange the authority of a perhaps indulgent father for that of a brother who may be less well disposed toward them. Bradbury adds that the senior son's grief may be very sincere indeed, and that, in contemporary Edo society, where senior sons may have reached a higher status than their fathers' during their lifetime, there is no need and no evidence for ambivalent attitudes.

The funeral rituals last for six days. On the evening of the sixth day, a child may be chosen to represent the dead man himself. Attired in their finest robes, the other children and grandchildren come and kneel before him, offering a few pennies, and receiving in turn a few pieces of coconut, or kola nut, and, since the "father" is not permitted to talk, some pieces of advice through an "interpreter." Bradbury tells how such exhortations include explanations that the father will not cease to look after them, nor to stop punishing them if they do wrong. Then, the "father" goes outside to dance with his children for the last time. They sing:

> *My father, you will come back soon*
> *you will go and you will come back*

and then:

> *This is what I wanted*
> *when I wandered about looking for a child*

With these songs, final leave taking of the father is accomplished, and at the same time, the reception of the father into the company of his kin. Now the planting has to take place, which means that an altar for the father will be prepared by the senior son. He prays:

> My father, Idehen, who has slept, I have buried you. Behold the goat, the palm wine, behold the four kola nuts that I have brought to introduce you into the house. This is the place where you will come and eat now. Let me not die. Let my children not die before me.

SUMMARY

The Edo material points out several interesting things. First, the meaning of death is seen in the Edo conception of the next world where the ancestors dwell and supervise the activities of the living. Without being connected to an ancestor, an Edo is not a full citizen or adult. Therefore the mortuary rituals serve as a transition from the status of child (for the eldest son) to that of adult.

Death alters the place of individuals in a social structure and the enactment of rituals often reestablishes relationships among the survivors. Here we have seen how the children who survive an Edo man fit into a new kind of family group depending on whether they are senior or junior sons. The public ritual also provides for the orderly transfer of property to the correct heirs.

The sentiments and attitudes held by the participants in this ritual are structured by the cultural and social circumstances and are demonstrated publicly.

Conclusions

It is not uncommon for adults to decide that children are not able to undergo funerary rituals or are too immature to appreciate their significance. In a myth from New Guinea, it is told how a very young girl became betrothed to a warrior. (The girl says, "This is a grown man you've married me to: I'm only small.") The husband who went to battle was killed. Her relatives do not tell her of the death of her husband ("She's not a grown woman, that she should weep for him"), and the funeral is conducted without her knowledge.[4]

Discretion and caution must be observed in our society as well, in regard to the readiness of children to participate in death rituals. Premature exposure to sometimes frightening aspects of ceremonies may be harmful to children. In American society, where there is not one culture but many subcultures and a great deal of racial, ethnic, and religious differentiation, it is hard to predict when children are ready to participate in funerary rituals. For example, a young boy had the meaning of death so strongly impressed upon him by having to see his dead and beloved grandfather at the funeral parlor that afterward, seeing a turkey in his mother's kitchen made him associate the death of the turkey with the death of his grandfather, and caused him to refuse to eat meat.

The above suggests that when children are participants in death rituals, they require continued care and attention to insure that the experience is properly assimilated and not a source of later difficulty.

The nonanthropologist will be interested in alleviating the immediacy of suffering, disruption, and emotional disturbance caused by death to children, rather than in the complexities of scientific research and the behavior of strange and distant peoples. For him there is perhaps a lesson in what we have tried to say in an Indian story about Buddha: Once, the Buddha was stopped by a young woman who had long been childless, and who, after many years, had given birth to a son. The child, playing among the bushes, was bitten by a poisonous snake and died. Pleading with the Buddha to restore her son to life, she received the answer: "Go, and bring me some mustard seeds from the home of people who are not mourning a death." The mother began to wander about, in search of such a house, but, after many years, returned empty handed. Seeing her return, the Buddha said: "When you departed, you thought that you and you alone were the only one who had ever suffered a loss through death. Now that you have returned, you know differently. Now you know that the law of death governs us all."

Any comprehensive discussion of death should include its biological aspects. "The world of biology is the world of the living and of the dying, of the dead and yet unborn."

Admittedly, the understanding of this discipline might occasion the greatest difficulty. The nomenclatures of the biologist are different than that of our common everyday vocabulary or even the psychological words that are now so familiar to the lay reader.

Yet, it is necessary to present not only a clinical analysis of the physiology of death but a discussion of the entire field of the biological phenomenon of death. The approach is academic but the result is infinitely rewarding.

Claiborne Stribling Jones is the Assistant to the Chancellor and professor of zoology at the University of North Carolina at Chapel Hill. Dr. Jones has been the recipient of the Fleming Research Prize at the University of Virginia and is listed in American Men of Science *and* Who's Who.

CHAPTER V

"... In the Midst of Life ..."
(Reflections on Some Biological Aspects of Death)

CLAIBORNE S. JONES

DEATH IS OF COURSE an archaic word in contemporary American life—people pass away, pets are put to sleep, flowers wither or fade, and the euphemistically valiant never taste of death. Yet the stubborn fact of it remains, as much a biological problem as the continuing problem of life, for the world of biology is the world of the living and of the dying, of the dead and of the yet unborn. It is a truism that an adequate biological definition of death requires and presupposes an adequate definition of life; and since the latter is by no means as yet a matter of general agreement, we are forced into the uncomfortable ambiguity of acknowledging the occurrence of death while being able to characterize it only in such relatively meaningless terms as "the irreversible cessation of those processes which distinguish the living from the nonliving and which permit (compel?) expression by the individual of its distinctive qualities as an organism."

Perhaps our cultural conspiracy to dispose of death by sweeping it under the rug may, regardless of its indefensibility, be to some extent attributable to the absence of any adequate definition of death as a biological phenomenon. However that may be, it will be the intent of this chapter not to engage in the presently fruitless attempt to arrive at any such definition, but instead to illustrate some aspects of the problem of definition, in the hope that this may provide a useful background for a consideration of death from standpoints other than the physicochemical or merely biological.

It is difficult to exaggerate the dimensions of this problem of definition, as may be apparent in what follows later, but in the very beginning we should take into account for later reference that

(a) except when it results from misadventure, death can hardly be considered as other than the culmination of the aging process, and this at once introduces not only the problem of time, but also the problem of "times"—e.g., solar, sidereal, biological (including thermal, photoperiodic, developmental, radiation exposure, experiential, etc.);

(b) "instantaneous" death by misadventure provides no escape from the time problem, for except in the almost unimaginable event of total atomization, death does not occur simultaneously in all tissues of the body, and the bull's "moment of death" may easily be as elusive as the matador's "moment of truth";

(c) since death is a function of time, it is more than a merely semantic question whether an organism, at any given moment in time while admittedly "alive," is more accurately adjudged to be "living" or "dying"—or both, in varying degrees at different times (Euripides put it better: ". . . for who knows if this thing that we call death is life, and our life dying . . .");

(d) no matter how we understand its meaning, in terms of our current concern death clearly comprises a unique event in the life of an individual organism, yet in at least some cases the individual itself is no more susceptible of completely satisfactory definition than are other taxonomic categories such as the species.

Consider first, for example, the problems of definition posed by an "organism" such as plasmodium, the protozoan parasite which causes mammalian and avian malaria. (It is fairly representative of a number of forms, some plant, some animal, many unicellular, some metazoan, exhibiting a regular and required life-cycle.) In the life-cycle of plasmodium, the needle-shaped *sporozoite,* introduced with the mosquito's saliva into the vertebrate blood stream, penetrates a red blood cell of the vertebrate host where it becomes an amoeba-like *trophozoite* which, as a *schizont,* undergoes fission to produce a cluster of daughter *merozoites.* These escape from the red cell as its membrane ruptures, and each may infect another red cell to repeat this part of the cycle, which operates on an incredibly precise time schedule. Some of the merozoites, however, do not divide within the red cell, but instead "metamorphose" into *microgametocytes* (male) or *macrogameto-*

cytes (female) . Swallowed by another mosquito with her blood meal, these gametocytes emerge as *gametes* from the digested red cells; union of a *microgamete* and a *macrogamete* results in a motile *ookinete* which bores through the wall of the mosquito stomach, encysts as a *sporablast* on the stomach wall, and undergoes multiple fission to produce large numbers of sporozoites which migrate to the salivary glands of the mosquito where they are available for injection into the vertebrate blood stream to begin the cycle anew in another vertebrate host. *Each of the "stages" in the life-cycle is distinctively different from the others, functionally as well as morphologically, and yet malaria cannot continue to exist without all these separate but interdependent stages.*

How then can plasmodium be viewed as an organism? Atabrine or quinine in the vertebrate blood stream can annihilate trophozoites, merozoites, gametocytes; and hundreds of sporozoites will die with the swatting of one infected mosquito: in either case, is plasmodium dead? Then what *is* dead? It seems equally unsatisfactory to conclude that the organism is any one of the stages in its life-cycle or that it is the repetitive sequence of all the stages. How can we characterize death in such circumstances, even though we face the undeniable fact of its occurrence?

This aspect of the problem need not be restricted to the "easy" level of the protozoa. Consider, for example, the social insects: is each honeybee really an individual member of the species, which is to say (very loosely) a population of taxonomically indistinguishable individuals, or is a honeybee a human concept instead of an organism? When a drone—or a worker or a queen—is killed, is it really a honeybee that has died or is it just one dispensable part of the organism (that is, the "hive" or colony) that has been lost? Despite the beauty of Donne's imagery, if a clod be washed away by the sea, is Europe really the less?

One of the most interesting biological aspects of death to many observers is the fact of the utility, indeed the necessity, of selective or "partial" death for normal development and survival of the individual. Of the innumerable instances of this found throughout the animal kingdom, a few selected for illustrative purposes are as follows:

(1) The surface of the human body comprises perhaps millions of hardened cell corpses without which the skin could scarcely qualify for its characterization as the body's "first line of defense" against infection (as against excessive dehydration by evaporation). Since these dead cells are constantly being lost by sloughing and abrasion, the maintenance of the surface layer depends upon the continuing production of daughter cells by cell division in the underlying layer of the skin and, naturally, upon an adequate death-rate among these daughter cells as they are pushed toward the surface. (The process does not begin in the vertebrate embryo until a rather late stage of development is reached, so the problem of time or aging intrudes itself here as in many places.)

(2) The human body's "second line of defense" consists of those leukocytes ("white" blood cells) which represent about two-thirds of the total white count, the neutrophils. These cells are scavengers by virtue of their propensity for ingesting foreign particles as an amoeba ingests bits of food. They also show the remarkable phenomenon of diapedesis, squirming between capillary cell junctions and thus emerging from the blood stream into the adjacent tissue spaces. Many types of infection elicit a rapid and sizable increase in the number of neutrophils and a striking concentration of these cells at sites of infection. Thus the introduction of bacteria through penetration of the skin, as by a splinter, is followed by the accumulation of neutrophils in enormous numbers about the locus of infection where they ingest the invading particles and subsequently die. Additional protection ensues from the fact that the pus, which is largely the result of this neutrophil "suicide," serves as a mechanical barrier or dam against more extensive invasion by the foreign agent.

(3) The amphibian tadpole, with its large and admirably functional swimming tail, becomes a tailless adult through metamorphic processes which include rapid and complete destruction of tail tissues by the carnivorous activity of specialized cells resembling neutrophils. Without the death of tail tissues

and consequent loss of the tail, it may be questionable whether many of the frog species could survive, and at least there would be no species of tailless amphibians.

(4) In tetrapod development, the limb rudiment first appears as an amorphous bulge from the lateral body wall. As this limb bud enlarges and develops internal differentiations, its distal growing tip is divided into digits by lines of "cell death" which effectively separate the digits from one another. When this selective cell death is incomplete, the webbed condition results (which is normal in the feet of ducks and the "hands" of bats, for example). The wing of the avian embryo, however, shows an additional illustration of selective death: the wing bud at first is free of the body wall only from the elbow outward, while the entire upper arm to the elbow is adherent to the body wall. This upper arm is cut away from the body by the death of cells which, in effect, drives a wedge of death between body wall and upper arm. Failure of these cell deaths to occur would mean flightlessness, of course. (Incidentally, if these doomed cells are removed when the limb bud first appears and transplanted to some other region of the embryo, they will survive nicely in their foreign environment until the appointed time and then die precisely on schedule, near 96 hours of development in the chick.)

While it is true that there can be no death without life, there seems no escape from the conclusion that, conversely, there can be no life (at least in most of its known forms) without death.

Pursuing this consideration from the microscopic to the opposite end of the biological spectrum, it is quite possible to view the history of life on this planet as a panoramic necrology which represents a necessary condition for evolution and survival of the forms of life.

Even the most cursory attention to the fossil record, to comparative morphology, to geographic distribution of organisms, to genetics, and to earth history makes impossible today any reasonable doubt that the history of life on earth is a history of unbroken continuity through the process of biological descent; that it is a history of descent with modification; and that these modifications, differing in degree and kind among different organisms, have represented varying degrees of potential evolutionary success.

The extent to which these potentials can be realized is obviously limited by the extent of their opportunity for expression, and paleontology is replete with indications that new waves of evolutionary success often represent either exploitations by the survivors of opportunities provided only by death or exploitation by their possessors of modifications comprising more efficient (though sometimes less obvious) death-dealing techniques. This is simply to say, of course, that organic evolution is a story of selective survival (and therefore of selective death) in a world where many must die if some are to live.

One of the most dramatic illustrations of this thesis may be found in the fossil record of the Mesozoic era which began with the Appalachian Revolution about 200 million years ago and lasted for some 130 million years until the Rocky Mountain Revolution ushered in the Cenozoic "age of mammals." The Mesozoic is aptly referred to as the "age of reptiles" because, from a tenuous strand of ancestral forms originating in the late Paleozoic, these animals in the Mesozoic achieved such a "bloom" of size, diversification, and numerical strength that by the late Mesozoic they clearly deserved the appellation "ruling reptiles." The closing (Cretaceous) period of the Mesozoic has been referred to as "the age of the great dying," for in this relatively short time the reptiles fell into a catastrophic decline leading almost to the point of extinction. There is no wholly satisfactory explanation for this sudden annihilation of such a surpassingly successful dominant group, but one result of this "great dying" was surely to open the evolutionary door for the mammals which at that time had evolved only so far as tiny, shrewlike creatures with quite unpromising prospects, but who nevertheless proceeded thereafter to inherit the earth.

One of the safest evolutionary generalizations to be drawn from the fossil record is that, while each ensuing geologic period sees the ascendancy of a new dominant group (best adapted, hence most successful, hence "dominant"), this new dominant group stems always from some one of the most generalized (i.e., least specialized and apparently least success-ful) branches of the former dominant group. This is not sur-prising, of course; by definition, in any organism the degree of adaptation to a given environment varies inversely with the degree of adaptability to a different environment—or, blessed are the meek when the environment changes. It follows naturally that evolutionary success or failure in a changed environment cannot be predicted without fore-knowledge of the nature of the new environment; and that, while evolution reflects the survival of the fittest, the fittest can be recognized only in retrospect.

"All flesh is grass," cried the prophet, and every schoolboy learns that biologically this is axiomatic, for life in its known variety of forms could not continue and could not have arisen without the great evolutionary breakthrough called photo-synthesis, the process by which solar energy is converted by the chlorophyll of green plants into the chemical bond energy of carbohydrate molecules. A next necessary step in diversifi-cation was the development of techniques by emerging ani-mal forms for expropriating these stores of energy from the chlorophyll-bearers and for the release of the stored energy in usable form within the body of the predator. These tech-niques involve the familiar sequence of ingestion, digestion, and cellular respiration. Another tremendous biochemical breakthrough was the development of oxidative respiration through glycolysis, the citric-acid cycle, and the respiratory enzyme system, for the much improved efficiency of this method over the older process of anaerobic fermentation yielded a surplus of energy above the level needed for sub-sistence and thus provided the "risk capital" for growth, diversification, and evolutionary experimentation along many lines. And so the web of life became "the great chain of being" which is, in the language of the ecologist, a great "food chain" of photosynthesizers, herbivores, and carnivores—a

hierarchy of killers and killed, eaters and eaten. Thus it is
that, at every biological level above the photosynthetic, every
man's life depends daily upon the regular, orderly, uninterrupted occurrence of death after death after death.

Perhaps this consideration becomes more pointed if it is
framed in terms of current concern over the human "population explosion." The statisticians argue rather persuasively
that if the present world birth-rate–death-rate balance is
maintained, then in short order we can look forward to a
world whose every square foot of land will be occupied by
a human being with at least one other standing on his shoul-
ders—this, of course, because of the fact that the population
increases by geometric progression (as pointed out over a
century ago by Malthus in the economic essay which played
such a significant part in generating the Darwinian hypothesis). The only effective means of modifying this trend would
seem to involve either large-scale prevention or widespread
destruction of human life. In this light, what would have
been the history and present state of Western civilization
if the Black Plague some six hundred years ago had not
destroyed about one quarter of the human population of
Europe?

If death is understood to involve at least an irreversible
cessation of those metabolic processes which biologically distinguish the living from the nonliving, how are we to think
of the Jekyll-Hyde transformations which, undoubtedly, effect such significant change as to comprise the replacement of
one individual by another?

The "transformation" of bacteria represents a dramatic
case in point. The essential functional difference between the
pathogenic and the nonpathogenic pneumococci seems to
derive from the inability of the latter to produce the poly-
saccharide capsules which coat the pathogenic strains, and
this is a species-constant, i.e., genetically "fixed," difference.
Yet when the nonpathogenic strain is cultured in media containing trace amounts of the genetic substance DNA extracted
from pathogenic colonies, this "foreign" DNA is incorporated

into appreciable numbers of the rapidly multiplying bacteria, and these (and their descendants) are thereafter in every respect indistinguishable from the "normal" pathogenic forms. By the same techniques it has been shown that bacteria can be transformed with respect to several dozen other such fundamental traits, including drug resistance and digestive enzyme production.

Bacteriophage accomplishes a similar, though transient (because eventually fatal), result in the bacteria which it parasitizes: the phage nucleic acids penetrate into the bacterial cell where they usurp the place of the bacterial controls, enslaving the bacterial cytoplasm for the completely unbacterial task of manufacturing phage particles.

These and similar phenomena seem to be different only in degree from the radical alterations of the human organism effected by the psychomutagens, by electric and chemical shock, or by surgical procedures such as prefrontal lobotomy. In such cases, a successful outcome clearly seems to represent a "casting out of devils" difficult to interpret as other than the substitution of a new and qualitatively different individual for the old.

Is death involved in the occurrence of such transformations as these? If so, who dies? If not, what has become of the pretransformation individual?

It has been suggested that biologically death must involve at least the irreversible cessation of the metabolic processes which distinguish life, but what of those states in which such cessation, while reversible, is nevertheless for all practical purposes complete?

When amphibian embryos, even in rather advanced stages of development, are transferred to cold chambers held constantly at temperatures below the level of enzyme activity but above that of water crystallization, development is halted, as apparently are all metabolic processes. Return of the embryo to the higher temperature is followed by resumption of development where it left off. (The "time" problem again: how old is an embryo which has completed two days of development sandwiched around two weeks of such inactivation? Is it the same age as an embryo of two days' uninterrupted development?) During the period of cold-inactivation, surely the embryo is not dead—but if alive, it is certainly not engaged in the process of living. If an embryo should be physically disintegrated after such a period of inactivation, at what point can we fix the time of death?

Familiar parallels to this condition are numerous in nature: the inhibitory effect of low temperature on bacterial metabolism; the phenomenon of encystment among the protozoa and some of the metazoa (notably the rotifers) with its obvious survival value; the retention of viability over incredible periods of time by nonmetabolizing spores and seeds. And, granted the differences of degree in metabolic activity, do the same troublesome questions apply at higher levels of life when we consider such states as coma, hypnotic trance, general anesthesia, hibernation—or even normal sleep?

Resuscitation following what would otherwise have been a fatal experience—water inhalation, cardiac failure, barbiturate overdosage, electrical shock, for instance—is of course an all-too-familiar feature of the life of modern man; and how we should understand such a "strange interlude of darkness" in terms of living and dying is no more apparent than it is in the case of sleep, of hibernation, or of anesthesia.

It will be evident, however, that recovery from any of these states represents a biological phenomenon categorically different from that of reconstitution following dissociation. The classic illustration of the latter is provided by experimental work with marine sponges early in this century: the body of the sponge was forced through bolting cloth of such fine mesh that the cells (and, of course, the tissues) of the animal were dissociated as effectively as droplets of fluid at the nozzle of an aerosol spraygun. These separate cells fell into a dish of seawater, apparently uninjured by the treatment, and there proceeded to aggregate into clusters within which each cell-type became properly oriented in relation to other cell types, with the result that the characteristic body of the sponge was restored or reconstituted both structurally and functionally. Similar behavior has been reported in the freshwater coelenterate hydra, whose sack-like body has a wall comprising two distinctively different tissue layers. When the body of hydra was caused to turn inside out by eversion through the open "mouth," the inside and outside tissue layers were of course brought into reverse relationship with one another; and thereupon the cells of each tissue moved in opposite directions, passing through one another like the members of a military drill team, until each tissue had regained its original position with respect to the other.

How cells "recognize" one another, distinguishing likeness and unlikeness as well as degrees of both, and how they "know" their proper spatial relationships with other kinds of cells are questions of fundamental interest in developmental biology, since such behavior is an essential feature of normal morphogenesis. In the present context, though, these questions must be only incidental, for we must obviously consider to be of primary importance the question how we can define such a state of being as organismal dissociation or tissue-reversal. Death? Disorientation? "Suspended animation?" Or what?

The striking nineteenth-century phrase, "the immortal amoeba," was no doubt intended to direct attention as dramatically as possible to the newly enunciated principle of continuity of the germ plasm in sexually reproducing organisms. Nevertheless, it does underline the rather obvious fact of protoplasmic continuity from generation to generation in those forms, notably some of the unicellular organisms, which reproduce only asexually and by the familiar process of cell division. Amoebas die daily, of course, probably in their millions; yet it is clear by definition that no amoeba living today has a single instance of death in its direct line of ancestry back to the beginning two or three billion years ago, since every ancestor of a now-living amoeba must have divided instead of dying. (Is mortality a part of the price we pay for sexuality?)

The same phenomenon can be observed at the multicellular level of organization in the case of those organisms with a high degree of regenerative capacity, such as the common sexually reproducing planarian flatworms. These worms show anteroposterior axial organization, bilateral symmetry, and a variety of structural specializations at the organ-grade as well as the tissue-grade of differentiation. Yet such is the adult's ability to regenerate that when the body is cut transversely into two (or more, up to a dozen or so) parts, each fragment is capable of regenerating (involving both growth and differentiation) to form a complete adult equally capable of regeneration. Here "immortality" depends only upon the regular recurrence of the appropriate injury, it seems.

Within the recent past, biochemical knowledge and medicosurgical techniques have been advanced to the point that the possibility of physical immortality for man can no longer be limited to science fiction (which has the irritating habit of persistently refusing to remain fictional!). The use of heart-lung-kidney machines, of hyperbaric and cryogenic procedures, and most significantly the recent breakthroughs in the theory and practice of transplantation and grafting of tissues and organs—all of these in concert seem to make it clear that in principle only technological refinements are now required to permit the surgical construction of a "mosaic" man: kidneys from one donor, digestive tract from another, heart from a third, brain from a fourth, gonads from a fifth, and so on, with subsequent replacement of parts as required *ad infinitum,* as the antique car buff lovingly maintains his classic model in mint condition, though every original part has been replaced.

Who will this "mosaic" man be? Who will be his offspring, who his ancestors? And, more to the present point, if he should be not the same person as the presurgical patient, will death have occurred in the process of becoming different, or will we view this as a sort of Enochian "translation"?

CONCLUSION

Perhaps I have sufficiently illustrated my contention that it would be foolhardy in our present state of knowledge to attempt (and futile to expect) a simple, precise, adequate definition of death or of life as biological phenomena. It is nevertheless possible to make certain generalizations and to draw some conclusions which may be relevant to consideration of the meaning of death, and it is with this in mind that the following far-from-original suggestions are offered.

The truly distinctive characteristic of life at all levels on this planet seems to be its structural-functional organization; and here the hyphen is obligatory, for in life, as in art, form and function are the inseparable components of entity, the two sides of the coin without either of which it would not exist. At the ultramicroscopic level, this unique structural-functional organization is revealed in the incredibly constant and specific molecular configurations of the "organic" compounds—proteins, carbohydrates, lipids, DNA, RNA, etc.—and in the marvelously precise ordering of their interactions as they engage in those utilizations of energy which comprise metabolism (reproduction, respiration, growth, repair, and the like). At the organismal level, this distinctive organization is illustrated by the unending variety of the forms of life, each with its unique constellation of processes and potentials.

As the forms of life have come into being through the millennia by the evolutionary process of descent with modification, two related and often contemporaneous but significantly different kinds of organizational modifications can be discerned, at least in retrospect:

(a) There are those changes which represent variations *on* an established theme, constituting therefore variations of degree but not of kind. Such "horizontal" variants account for the often extensive diversity found within any given level of being, as for example the several thousand species of free-living protozoa or the several hundred thousand of arthropods. Modifications of this kind represent advantages or disadvantages leading to survival of the fittest as a result of improvement rather than of innovation or "invention" (improved efficiency, that is, at the business of being essentially the same kind of being).

(b) In sharp contrast are the organizational modifications which are variations *from* an established theme, for they represent alterations of kind rather than of degree and open the way to new, and theretofore nonexistent, levels of being. Examples of such radical departures by "vertical" variants from the established norms of biological success would include such innovations among vertebrates as tetrapod limbs, lungs, and amniote eggs which could hardly equip their possessors for more efficient prosecution of the business of being at the level of their aquatic competitors (probably the reverse, in fact), but did undoubtedly provide access, at new levels of being, to the vast new world of terrestrialism. This interpretation of organic evolution as involving an emergent process necessarily views the "hopeful monsters" as representing significantly different kinds of life-forms in which the drastic alterations of structure are inevitably concomitant with the appearance of functional capacities that are entirely new rather than being mere improvements of the old (e.g., as the unique properties of water "emerge" with its formation by reaction of its two gaseous components).

If the result of the evolutionary process to date has been the emergence of forms of life differing not only in degree but more significantly in kind, then it must follow that death may have different meanings at different levels of organization or being, for surely disintegration would put an end to categorically different "lives" when a tapeworm perishes with the death of its human host.

It can no longer be reasonably questioned, of course, that man is part and parcel of the evolutionary process. At the same time, it is intellectually quite "respectable" to consider seriously whether he may be an emergent form whose qualities include some which transcend his quantitatively measurable and physicochemical framework; and, if so, whether death for man may represent a distinctively human experience, qualitatively different from death in any other species. In any such consideration, it would be utter folly not to take full account of those truths about man which have been accumulated through biological investigation. Equally it would be intellectually indefensible to ignore those truths about man which the human mind has come to know by pathways other than the scientific method.

The editor found the selection of an educational psychologist the most difficult of all the contributors to obtain. Numerous calls were made to university professors throughout the country.

"How do you, in the school situation, handle youngsters who have sustained a loss?"

The replies were almost the same: "Frankly, we never thought of it. I guess we leave it to the individual teacher."

"But you give instruction for all the details of academic life. You mean that there is no portion of your curriculum to teachers regarding the crisis situation of death?"

The resounding response: "Yes—we have avoided the subject."

Hella Moller, Ed.D., has made a pioneering effort in handling youngsters who have sustained loss and have returned to a school routine. Dr. Moller is the School Psychologist and Coordinator of Psychological Counseling for the Arlington, Massachusetts schools. She is a contributor to the book, Psychological Evaluation of Children in Schools and Clinics.

CHAPTER VI

Death: Handling the Subject and Affected Students in the Schools

HELLA MOLLER

CHILDREN ARE SUBJECT to two profound fears: the fear of bodily injury and the fear of the loss of loved persons who care for them and whose death would leave them helpless and alone.

The infant begins to respond to human stimuli in the first few days after birth. As early as the age of six months, the infant reacts vehemently to the loss of the mothering adult. He may show his grief in an inert facial expression, a limp posture, or in a lack of motility. If his needs for attention are frustrated, he immediately mobilizes anxiety and anger,[1] and if his state of abandonment continues, he may intensify his protest with refusal of food and finally with complete withdrawal and apathy.

> The need for a relationship to support life points to the helplessness that is characteristic of man in childhood. The child cannot alone relieve his discomfort, nor can he reduce his tension without the fostering or nurturing care of an adult.[2]

As the child becomes older and learns more about his surroundings, his uncertainties about his own role in life become more varied and his relationships to his parents and siblings more complex. Childhood, with its intense feelings of helplessness and its strong needs for dependence on the nurturing adult, holds many serious problems for the latency child—problems which are further complicated by the birth of siblings or the death of a family member.

At the age of four to five the preschool child begins to acquire an image of his own body which he can visualize in his mind and draw on a piece of paper, if ever so crudely. When he has achieved a body image of himself, he has reached the physical, intellectual, and psychological level of maturity appropriate for school attendance.

The nursery school and kindergarten child is particularly anxious that nothing happen to his body integrity and often cries impetuously at the smallest scratch or fall. While he is not yet aware of the integration and organization of the whole body, he is still fearful of part-injuries to his legs, arms, nose, genitals, etc.

Lauretta Bender has pointed out that the child is not primarily concerned with his own death—though, having observed the death of others, he is ready to accept his own as a possibility. The child's concern is with the immediate future and the fear of not being fed or cared for. In children's minds, death is predominantly associated with some form of violence, particularly dismemberment. Since children are aggressive, they visualize death as a violent force. Many cannot understand death by illness, but they can understand death by dismemberment. Also, when they perceive concretely that an animal or a person can no longer move, they accept death as a fact. "Dead people are carried away and buried up, just like fallen leaves."[3]

Death remains basically incomprehensible also to adults, but they have a different attitude towards it: they have *Todesangst*—a terror death—which is unknown to the child. He lives in fear that his mother will not be with him all the time and he cannot understand why she leaves him even for a brief period. Anna Freud has made the observation that the young child, because of his dependency needs, lives in a state of natural egocentricity and therefore fundamentally misperceives his mother's role:

> The mother is perceived not as a person who leads a life of her own, but only as someone who is there to fill the young child's needs and wishes. Her interest in her other children, in the father, or her illnesses or even her death are perceived as rejection and desertion.[4]

In the elementary school years the developmental process revolves around the task of identification, the great problem which begins in middle childhood and throughout adolescence: Who am I? What am I going to be? For the school-age child, identification with the parental figures becomes an organizing force of his personality makeup. In the normal development during this stage of life the child assimilates the image of his parents, thereby constructing his self-image and gaining a sense of personal identity. In a sentence-completion test most healthy six- to ten-year-old boys produce the association: I want to be like . . . "my father," and most girls want to be like their mother at this age. Children who internalize the image of their parents in this way gain a sense of security and are stronger when a loss occurs.

Teachers and parents subscribe to the adult idea—at least theoretically—that death is part of life. But when a situation arises which makes it imperative to discuss the end of life in general or to reflect upon the death of a family member, they often avoid the issue. They themselves may not wish to think about it, and, hoping to spare children what they sincerely believe are adult pains, they frequently say, "Children under ten are too young to understand," or "It only makes children unhappy to talk about this; it is better if they are allowed quietly to forget it," or "Why burden children with worries and depressive feelings in their childhood?"

In reality, children worry a great deal about the beginning and end of life, especially when grieving adults are observed with tears in their eyes, or when bereaved parents are so dejected over the loss of their own parents or brothers and sisters that they seem temporarily to forget and neglect their children. A child is part of the family and should share in the mourning experience by expressing his own upsurge of sadness with the loved adults that still remain with him. A child may be emotionally too immature or he may scarcely have known the distant relative for whom the family is grieving, but if he sees his mother weeping, he feels the need to cry in sympathy. If he is sent away to friends in order to spare him the family's sadness, he may show serious disturbance later on. Very young children, it is true, should participate in the mourning process only for a short time, but for the school-age child it is important to witness the grief experience of the adults more fully, and to participate in it. In this way, the actual grief of the child is worked through and, rather than being disturbed, the child gains an emotional experience by which he learns how to live through an extreme situation of the human condition.

The psychiatrist, Norman Paul, who is working especially with schizophrenic families in "conjoint family therapy," found that unresolved and uncompleted mourning for lost family members greatly contributes to the disturbance of the family's emotional climate. In his experience, mourning later has to be induced by the therapist in order to initiate and catalyze the experience.[5]

Most children are exposed to frequent views of violence on the television screen and in films. Visual evidence of death is almost a part of their daily diet. It is surprising that many children accept heavy doses of lethal brutality apparently without any great mental agitation. In every elementary school, however, a few sensitive children can be found who have nightmares and show signs of emotional upset after programs that are replete with violence or death (a not insignificant minority of school children, incidentally, shun shows of this type). Fortunately most of the TV dramas have happy endings to relieve pent-up anxieties.

The need for the "happy ending" in fairy tales and children's stories gives evidence of this timeless fear of loneliness and bereavement. It expresses a need to deny the reality of death. Usually the heroes and the "good guys," with whom the youthful viewer identifies, are rewarded and "live happily ever after"; the evildoers are punished with death, in fulfillment of the need for retribution and revenge. The wicked queen in Cinderella has to dance in red-hot slippers until she dies, because she was so cruel. The good grandmother in Little Red Riding Hood steps out of the stomach of the wolf, hale and hearty, representing complete denial of death. Hansel and Gretel, though abandoned by their cruel mother and their weak father, return home laden with many treasures taken from the wicked witch, whom they killed; they live harmoniously with the same parents who a short while ago deserted them in the woods. Stories of death and abandonment serve the function of learning, on the fantasy level, to cope with one's fears and at the same time to reassure oneself of the unreality of these fantasied terrors. Emotionally disturbed children greatly dislike stories which have a sad ending.

In real life, however, bereaved children can become extremely depressed and anxious, unable to concentrate on their schoolwork, uninterested in play, and too preoccupied to join other children in activities. In spite of their suffering, children often suppress their feelings of sadness or their apprehension of additional loss. Also, their state of depression is often interrupted by more carefree moods; they vacillate greatly. Children in the early latency period—between the ages of six to nine—can at times admit verbally that they are unhappy; but nine- to twelve-year-olds hardly ever do so, unless they are in the midst of an acute crisis. Although the defense mechanism of denial is of some assistance in avoiding depression, its use does not solve the underlying feeling of loss and only magnifies the anxiety.

Sometimes the grief reaction after the death of a family member is resolved so well in the home that the child readjusts to his loss without protracted complications in the school situation. In many cases, however, the children suffer for a considerable time from the aftereffects of the shock; their behavior and school performance are noticeably affected, and the attention of a school psychologist or school social worker is called for.

The children who are described in the following four case histories did not have family members or close friends who were able to sustain them effectively in their time of crisis and dejection; therefore the school psychologist tried to help them to overcome the unhappiness their loss had caused them.

Case 1

The impact of the death of a parent on a child is often not appreciated in all its importance by school personnel. In addition there is usually a shortage of professionals to detect and treat all the children who could benefit. Paul was brought to the attention of the school's counseling department when he was in the fourth grade—fully three years after the death of his mother.

Paul's kindergarten adjustment had been good, except that he used to cry easily when he was corrected. Both his first grade teacher and his mother had been concerned about his shyness. Whenever a stranger or a special teacher entered the classroom, he would hide underneath his desk. When he was still in the first grade, his mother unexpectedly died. From then on Paul was described by all his teachers as a habitual daydreamer who stared out of the window. He paid hardly any attention to his teacher. He often looked as if he were on the verge of tears, and his personal appearance became untidy. Strangely, he learned to read well and seemed to know his arithmetic, even though he rarely did his homework.

Paul was the second of four children in a family of three boys and one girl. His two-year older brother as well as his younger brother and sister seemed to accept their mother's loss with less disturbance. Paul's father had been happily married to his first wife and her death had been a great shock to him. She had developed pneumonia on the way to the hospital to have labor induced expecting her fifth child. She had spent much time with her children, especially with Paul, who seemed to require more attention. They used to have tea together every day after school, while he told her about the day's activities. All the children had been very upset by their mother's death, but Paul had taken it the hardest, refusing to believe it and continuing to call for her by name after school. He became so depressed that he no longer played with the neighborhood children, but sat by himself on the curb. A few months after the death of his mother, the paternal grandmother, who had been taking care of the children, also died. Paul became even more upset after this event and asked his father when he would die and leave him all alone. The father also took his mother's death very much to heart; he felt guilty that she had had to work hard caring for his children.

Paul's father was a skilled workman who made every effort to keep his family together. Unfortunately, the several housekeepers whom he employed favored the two younger children, to the neglect of the two older, more sullen, boys. The father became so depressed himself that the household disintegrated, order and discipline were no longer maintained, the house became untidy, and the children got out of control. On one occasion they built a fire in the cellar to roast marshmallows, nearly setting the house on fire. The father then decided to place his children in various homes. Paul and his older brother were sent to a farm with a family who had two boys of their ages, and for one year Paul seemed to adjust quite well.

It happened that the younger children were not happy in their new home, and the father decided to bring the family together again. He hastily married a divorced woman with three daughters. This second marriage did not work out well, and the couple, burdened with seven children, fought continuously. The new mother did not understand the needs of the four bereaved children of her husband, and she alienated them from the start by trying to discipline them. The father felt that she was angry with him but took her resentment out on the children, sending them to school dirty and without adequate lunches. The children were unhappy and hated her. Paul stopped doing any work, would not even answer when called upon, and became practically mute. It was during this period that the school psychologist became involved in the family crisis. The other children had gotten on rather well in school; Paul was the only one who could not overcome his grief. He had a sullen look every time he came to see his psychologist and it was a long and slow process to build a relationship with this depressed boy.

At first, the idea suggested itself that Paul's depression was caused by the attitude of his stepmother; but later developments showed that the basic reason for his abiding sadness was the grief over the loss of his mother that had never been worked through.

In the first few therapy sessions Paul scarcely spoke at all. After the Christmas vacation he began to talk about things he enjoyed doing, such as the way he made a touchdown in football or built an airplane model. When he played checkers, and other games, with the school psychologist, he became more spontaneous, but soon again he became mute and motionless. Whenever he was asked about his schoolwork or his parents, his eyes welled up with tears and he ceased to talk. When the psychologist went to see his stepmother, trying to help her to become more giving to the children, especially to Paul, he became withdrawn again, refused to speak at all and spent most of the session turning his back towards her. At that time, he even refused to play games or tried deliberately to lose. Although Paul did not converse, the psychologist took up various subjects, assuring him of her concern for him and confronting him with his feelings toward his stepmother.

His parent conveyed the information that Paul feared he was seeing the school psychologist because he was "crazy" and this was also discussed with him. The psychologist gave candy and other food to him—therapeutic feeding—to assure him of her concern. One morning, after many sessions of "giving" without getting any response, she fixed some hot chocolate for him; he first refused it, but then somehow the hot chocolate seemed to reach him, and he finally broke the long silence with an inappropriate silly laugh; then he started to make paper airplanes (which he had learned to construct in a previous session). Slowly the relationship was built up again to its earlier level of confidence, and he began to talk about the little things in life and also about the negative feelings he had about school and his stepmother. His school-work improved; he passed the fifth grade, thus avoiding repeating twice in succession, as he had already repeated the fourth grade. He began to do quite well academically with little effort, being an intelligent boy with an I.Q. of 115, which would have been even higher if he had not been so depressed. His teacher and parents now thought he liked to see his therapist, although he would not admit it.

Paul's father was truly concerned about him—as well as his other children—and admitted that he did not have enough time to spend with them because of his long hours of work. He made an effort to converse with Paul and to have more activities with all his children. The psychologist tried to help both parents to communicate better with each other and not to bear silent grudges. She also induced them to present a united front to the children when discipline was necessary. Slowly the family began to work their ordeal through, and the stepmother began to give more love and show more attention to Paul, who in turn began to like her. Indeed, she wanted to be accepted by her stepchildren.

At home Paul emerged from the depressed state and began to interact normally again. He made satisfactory school grades, but he had still great difficulties in establishing good relationships with children and unfamiliar adults.

In Paul's case, a severe grief reaction extended over several years, because he lost a mother on whom he had been more dependent than his brothers and sisters, and because no effective mother substitute was found. No one, not even his father, could fulfill his emotional needs. After more than four years a psychological diagnosis of Paul's unexpressed grief reaction, aggravated by a complex family situation, became the starting point of individual child- and parent-counseling within the limits of the psychological services of a public school. The academic adjustment of Paul and his greatly improved home situation were definite evidence of his

emotional recovery, though there is no denying that this
vulnerable child had experienced a damaging trauma that is
likely to leave permanent traces.

Case 2

In the following case, the child became severely disturbed
not by bereavement in his own family but by accidents to
his friend's parents.

Robert, a six-year-old boy, who for an entire year had
gone to kindergarten, suddenly refused to go to school after
summer vacation. He wept bitterly and was so unhappy that
his teacher, who had two other phobic children in her class,
referred him to the school psychologist. Robert refused to
leave his parents and insisted that one of them stay with him
in school.

An interview with the parents revealed certain traumic
events which Robert had experienced in the past six months.
First, a friend of his father had accidentally drowned while
swimming in a pond. Then the parents of neighborhood
children, whom Robert knew superficially, died in an airplane accident; and finally a close friend of the family died
following a kidney operation and his wife was badly injured
in a severe car accident a month later. Her three children,
who were in the car with her, were severely shocked but un-
harmed. Robert's parents took in the oldest boy, Billy, age
9; and other friends gave shelter to the other two children.
While Billy was at Robert's house he felt the need to relate
the minutest details of the accident. Two days later the new
school year started. When the mother drove Robert to school,
he cried bitterly when his mother let him out of the car.
He did not want to go to school; but because Mother had to
drive Billy to his school in a nearby suburb, she could not go
out of the car with Robert, who walked forlornly to the new
classroom and to an unknown teacher. When he saw two
other children crying, Robert also was overcome with despair
and started crying. As no one paid any special attention to
him, he ran home after some time, unnoticed in the con-

fusion of the first school day in grade one. (As minor pathetic details, it might be added that the teacher happened to suffer from phlebitis, and that the principal who meant to come to the rescue in this harrowing situation was herself a phobic person who in the face of these despairing children became defensive and ineffective.)

Thereafter, Robert refused to leave his home except for short periods of play, during which he would run into the house every few minutes. He even refused to stay with his grandparents, who came to baby-sit when the parents went out for a few hours. When the mother became aware of the seriousness of Robert's anxiety, she accompanied him to school and remained outside the door so that he could see her. As soon as she attempted to leave, Robert began to scream and refused to stay. When the father brought him to school and took a much firmer stand, even spanked him, the result was no better.

When the case was referred to the school psychologist, she visited the home and came to know the parents and the three children. As she assembled the details of his case history, it became apparent that Robert's school phobia was brought on by the impact of several deaths in the family's immediate environment. The psychologist asked Robert to show her his room which he now had to himself again, because his friend Billy had gone home after the recovery of his mother. The psychologist made friends with Robert and asked him to come with his mother to visit her at school where she promised to play some interesting games with him. It took three meetings for him to relinquish his mother's reassuring presence in school. In the treatment of any phobia it is important not to exert much pressure, in order to make it possible for the child to regain his feeling of basic security and to repair the trust in adults which the phobic child has lost. He finally began to trust the school psychologist and believed her promise to drive him home when he became fearful in school. He began to talk to her about his nightmares, which were fraught with accidents. The accidents always happened to his parents, never to him, and he was panic-stricken from fear of losing them. In therapy he played with toy cars and a doll family. The imaginary family was forced to act out some violent automobile collisions. They were also sent off to swim and then made to drown.

When he had learned thus to express his fears and feelings, he became more relaxed, slept better at night, and played outside the home for longer periods of time. When the psychologist brought up the question of going back to his classroom, he became uneasy again, but he finally relented and agreed to go provided she would stay with him. At first he only looked through the door but refused to enter, although his teacher invited him in, as she had done several times previously. Next time he visited for about ten minutes, testing the psychologist two or three times to determine whether she would really take him home when he wanted to go—which she always did.

Since Robert's trust in adults had been impaired (his mother had tried to run away when he was not looking, and his father, unaware of Robert's state of anxiety, had spanked him), the psychologist had to win the child's confidence, even though the teacher felt that Robert was being coddled and should be forced to attend school no matter whether he cried or not. If forced in this manner, the child's "stubbornness" might finally have been broken, but the damage to his personality instead of being healed would have been replaced by another phobia. In the case of this frightened and highly sensitive boy, it took over half a year to induce him to stay in school unaided, without running home. And it took another half year of play therapy and consultation with the parents and the teacher to help Robert to overcome the traumatic fear of losing his parents.

The question might be raised why Robert's siblings did not react with the same exaggerated panic. It is true that the dissimilar behavior of children who have been raised in the same family cannot always be accounted for. In this case it could be pointed out that Robert was subjected to the much stronger impact of the detailed description of the auto accident that his friend Billy gave him in order to release his own shock. Furthermore, Robert had always been an oversensitive child with problems of feeding and toilet training. Children like Robert, who have never been left alone with a baby-sitter except his grandparents, are prone to be overdependent on primary family members. Lastly, it might be considered that Robert's position as the oldest child in the family may have rendered him especially vulnerable to fears of deprivation of parental support, because he had once been dethroned from his foremost position by the arrival of his brother and sister.

Case 3

In schools, children are often referred for maladjustments that are not known to be connected with disturbances of the family situation, and it can take considerable detective work to unravel the etiology of the child's predicament.

Nicky was referred by his teacher who wrote in her referral to the school psychologist: "He is a nine-and-a-half-year-old boy in the fourth grade. His mother says that he is so belligerent at home that she does not know how to control him. His schoolwork is below grade, and he may have to repeat the year. He is a severe stutterer; he has innumerable fights with the boys in the street, and the neighbors fear him because of his destructiveness."

The request for help came from both his teacher and his mother. Nicky's mother was a depressed woman, whose husband had deserted her eight years before, leaving her with two small boys. In her first interview with the school psychologist she broke into tears as she talked about her sad past. It seemed that she had spoken to scarcely anyone about the loss of her husband; the conclusion was inescapable that she had never worked her grief through. She had told her two sons, Nicky now aged nine and a half, and Albert, aged twelve, that their father was a sailor and would soon come to see them. In reality, the father lived in Los Angeles. He had sent money home irregularly, but the boys had never seen him again. The older brother, who was four when his father left, seemed to have made a better adjustment than Nicky—then one and a half years old—who asserted vehemently that he had a father, just as his mother wanted to believe, with whom he strongly identified.

In his sentence-completion test he used the defense mechanism of denial. Some of his completions were:

> *I remember best . . . "my mother and father."*
> *Sometimes I wish my father . . . "was nice to me; sometimes he is not."*
> *Children should have . . . "mother and father."*
> *My mother sometimes . . . "hits me."*
> *I worry most about . . . "my mother. If she gets killed who will take care of me? One time she went away and did not come home for a long time."*

Nicky was obviously afraid of also being abandoned by his mother. It became clear in further interviews with the mother that since she had become absorbed in her grief, she had given only the most perfunctory care to her children. She had never inquired about Nicky's schoolwork nor about where he spent his afternoons. Nicky's mother had remained attached to the memory of her separated husband and had never even thought of remarriage. In play- and interview-sessions with Nicky it became clear that he idolized his father but at the same time hated him for having deserted him and his mother. As Nicky had never been told the true version of his father's desertion, he had fantasies about the parents' relationships which he revealed in response to a thematic-apperception test picture:

> *This man is talking to his wife. She does not like the man because he did something wrong. (What did he do?) He opened the door and hit her in the face. Now she does not want to talk to the man any more, but he wants to apologize.*

If mother would let the man apologize, Nicky thinks, he would have a father again. In this story Nicky implies clearly that he feels that his mother is to blame for the loss of the father.

In a series of interviews, the mother was helped to realize that it was not good for her to be always alone and to shun the world. She had to face the fact that her husband would not come back and that she had to tell her sons the truth. After eight weeks she was able to do so, and the psychologist could then take up this subject with Nicky. Several months after his mother had come to accept her real situation and—when she was able to give more time, love, and attention to Nicky—the boy began to make a striking adjustment. The teacher and principal had known that Nicky had no father, but they were not aware of the devastating effect a divorce of eight years' standing can have on a child. Nicky went to camps for two months; it was the first time he was able to leave his mother. Back in school, he talked much more freely with the psychologist. In one of his play therapy sessions he had a cat-puppet say: "I am very old and must die soon. I am 11 years old. I am losing all my hair and feel ill. I will die in two months." Then Nicky took the mother puppet and made her say: "I am an old lady, too, but I will not yet die. I have lots of work to do. I must live and cook for my son. I am only 70, and I will not die till I am 99 years old; he needs me." Nicky had perceived the change in his mother and so he could also change.

His teacher, who had been kept informed about Nicky's development and who had learned that this boy had some serious conflicts to work out, was surprised to see him so much happier when he returned from summer camp. She observed that he appeared more animated, that his work had improved, and that he was no longer aggressive toward other children. Along with his better adjustment his stutter diminished notably since he now had fewer hostile thoughts to repress.

The case exemplifies the dependence of young children on the thoughts and attitudes of their parents: It was not possible for the mother to hide her grief and anger over the

desertion of her husband. When Nicky learned that his father
had another wife and family, he lost all interest in him.
Mother, however, was able to fulfill her maternal role more
competently, with additional help from a social worker to
whom she was later referred. Though Nicky had been referred for poor behavior and low academic achievement, the
underlying cause of his difficulties was unconscious grief
over the loss of a parent.

Case 4

Fear of death may be only one of several factors contribut-
ing to a child's problem in school, and yet its terror is likely
to hold a paramount place in its causation.

Jack, age seven, was referred by his second grade teacher
as a daydreamer who at times spoke out in class and brought
up matters entirely foreign to the lesson. Once he spoke about
President Kennedy's funeral, when this was in no way related
to the subject treated in class. He was shy and withdrawn and
failed to participate in group activities. Often he refused to
do his written work and just sat quietly in his place, or he
had tears in his eyes. The first grade teacher had thought him
unintelligent and stubborn because he did not work unless
he "felt like it." He also had severe articulation difficulties.

Jack's mother reported that he often did not want to go
to school, and that he had also felt unhappy in the preceding
year. At the time of the referral, the mother was pregnant
with her fourth child, often felt sick, and could spend only
very little time with Jack. He cried so much at home without
apparent reason that his mother asked for help from the
counseling department of the school. The psychologist found
that Jack's fears centered around his awareness of death. Jack
had his first encounter with death when President Kennedy
was assassinated. During that agonizing weekend he had been
glued to the television screen and had suffered from stomachaches and diarrhea. It happened that within the course of
the next year and a half two uncles of his mother died. The
entire family was greatly upset, especially the mother who

was haunted by the knowledge that cancer ran in her family. More recently, Jack's grandfather, to whom he was very much attached, had also passed away, and soon thereafter Jack and his brother Howard were sent alone to the cemetery to put flowers on the grave. Jack had never seen a cemetery before. When home again, he asked why grandfather had to die; this subject apparently had never been sufficiently discussed with him. Jack's father worked 12 to 14 hours a day, and most of the responsibility of handling the four boys (nine, seven, and four years old, and the baby of four months) was in the mother's hands, who was not feeling well and was often tense and quite stern.

Jack was a bright and alert youngster with a Wechsler Intelligence Scale for Children I.Q. of 130; quite obviously he did not have sufficient opportunity to air his problems. When he was praised by the psychologist for his answers to test questions, he replied, "My mother says I talk too much, I should only speak when I am spoken to"; an overt discouragement against discussing his problems at home, or simply to chatter childishly, may well have contributed to his withdrawn behavior. When assembling puzzles and block designs he was too slow, because his fear of making mistakes interfered with his ability to concentrate, which is a definite indicator of anxiety.

Soon Jack revealed that he had "bad dreams," especially one in which his older brother Howard was dying. He initiated many questions regarding the subject of death, as he realized that the psychologist did not shut him off but answered his questions and encouraged him to talk about the things he was concerned about. "What happens to people who die?" When this question was reflected, he answered, he did not really know but thought that when his grandpa died, part of him came back as a baby. His baby brother was born three weeks after grandfather's death. When asked who had told him so, he replied that he had figured it out by himself. He thought whenever a baby is born someone had to die. He also volunteered the idea that it is safest not to go out, but to stay at home so that no cars can run you over and robbers cannot kill you. Even policemen make mistakes sometimes, and it was therefore best not to put trust in them and be out on the street. He remembered that his mother had said that the world was not big enough and that some people had to die to make room for new ones. When the psychologist replied that many people became very old these days because doctors know so much and can help many children and adults to live until they are very old, he replied that he would like to become a doctor and help people not to die. He also inquired whether it hurt when people died. In a later session, Jack said that he "could kill Adam and Eve." If Adam and Eve had not sinned, we would still be in Paradise and would not have to die. When the psychologist expressed skepticism about this, he replied that the nun in Sunday School had talked as if she really meant it. A child preoccupied with the fear of death will find innumerable occasions to reinforce his feeling intellectually.

It is commonly found that a child who is intensely preoccupied with fears of death has additional intrapsychic problems. Jack felt uncertain whether he wanted to be a boy or a girl and whether it was preferable to grow up or stay a child. After eighteen sessions with the school psychologist he had regained sufficient energy to concentrate on his schoolwork and to improve academically. His nightmares and stomachaches diminished considerably but he remained emotionally fragile.

In this case, the question arises why only Jack was so affected by the deaths in the family and why not the other boys. The two other boys also showed some symptoms of anxiety; both were enuretic, and the mother was quite worried about it. Jack had unconsciously chosen another symptom, since he was probably the most sensitive child in the family and since he strongly identified with his mother who was herself preoccupied with thoughts of death. In fact, the mother said, she had been just as fearful as Jack when she was a child. It also appeared likely that she unconsciously would have preferred it if Jack had been a girl to whom she could have felt closer than to her boys.

The sample cases presented above—in combination with various research studies—permit certain observations on grief reactions in elementary school children. Nearly all children of this age group who suffer a loss do not show their grief verbally—as most adults do—but use displacement on an external situation in order not to deal directly with the internal conflict. Since the school is their natural habitat outside the home, the school situation usually becomes the main focus of this displacement. Most of the bereaved children cannot concentrate on their schoolwork and do poorly, even if they have average intelligence. The bereaved children observed in the study started to daydream and became withdrawn. They had no more desire to play with their friends. They hovered near their homes, and some even refused to go out at all. The reason for their depression lies not so much in their sorrow, as in a fear that the remaining parent may be lost. Quite suddenly their unsuspecting trust in the security of family life is broken. Overcome by shock and apathy, they lapse into a long period of apprehensiveness.

It is imperative to give bereaved children an opportunity to talk about their bafflement. Well-meaning adults often shower them with verbal reassurance, giving them no time to express their own thoughts. In school, psychologists, social workers, guidance counselors, or teachers should try to stimulate discussions on the subject to help the child work through his grief. Children have a whole range of theories about death; like Jack, who believed that someone had to die to make room for every new baby. Other children, believing that God can take away anyone who is bad, suspect that the deceased person must have "sinned" somehow. The loss of well-known public figures can be made a theme for a general discussion about the inevitability of death and for placing the end of life in the context of a person's growth and accomplishments. Parents and teachers often do not talk about sensitive subjects such as death or the facts of life when children are in greatest need for helpful explanations of these puzzling questions. The well-intentioned desire of adults to avoid discussions of sad or embarrassing events such as death and suicide can create the feeling that knowledge is useless or necessarily secret or even dangerous. In this way, repressed sorrow or hidden curiosity can play a major part in withdrawal, learning disability, pseudostupidity, and inhibition of speech.[6]

Bereaved children also feel that it is of no use to make any effort to learn in school. For whom should they work hard? Who would reward them for their achievement? Young children do not learn for the sake of knowledge. Their motivation is based almost solely on the approval and recognition of parents and teachers.

A study conducted in the Arlington Public Schools on 49 bereaved elementary school children[7] found that nearly all of them showed a decline in grades. The children also became passive and withdrawn from relationships in general. However, with good support from the home, one third of the group recovered from their traumatic events at the end of the first year. A major finding of the research study ascertained that loss of the parent of the same sex lowered school grades more than loss of the parent of the opposite sex, which shows the importance of the same-sex identification figure for the child. Another correlation of the same study found that the loss of the mother depressed grades twice as much as the loss of the father. Consequently girls who lost their mother had a steeper drop in grades than boys who lost their mother. Academic functioning changed more drastically for younger children, of ages six to nine, than for older children, of ages nine to twelve. For each age group the schoolwork of girls deteriorated more. Also, boys regained their former academic level quicker than girls did.

Regarding peer relationships, the reversed pattern evolved. Children who lost parents of the opposite sex showed greater change in peer relationships than did children who lost a parent of the same sex, i.e., boys who lost a mother became more withdrawn from their peers than boys who lost a father. The etiology of these behavior patterns is mostly speculative, but changes in the parent-child relationship at the various stages of the child's psychosocial development seem to be a vital factor.

About half of the bereaved children tried to receive a great deal of attention from their teachers and felt a need to relate many incidents that happened at home. Teachers found that personality traits that were prominent before the loss of the parent tended to be exaggerated afterwards. The shy child became more withdrawn and the antagonistic child more aggressive. This change, however, was less drastic in those who were well-adjusted before the loss. Teachers were usually kind and understanding during the first year of the loss and often gave better grades than the child had earned—so-called "courtesy grades." But lack of time and a lack of deeper understanding in approaching these withdrawn children left the therapeutic interference mostly to the psychological staff. Teachers found it hard to accept the fact that, even two or three years after the original deprivation, a child could still be uninterested in classroom subjects, fail to pay attention, and not work up to his capacity.

An article by Cain and Fast on children's emotional perception to the suicide of a parent indicates the serious guilt feelings under which some children suffer as a result of a parent's suicide. They are convinced that their parent's death was to a large extent caused by their disobedience and misbehavior. "Coming home late from the playground, a bad report card, another fight with the boy next door, and even getting another bad cold were all stated as causes of the parent's committing suicide."[6] One child remembers the financial trouble and all the arguments his parents had, and others feel, in their naïveté, that they were "costing too much money." The authors point to the two areas that need to be discussed with the bereaved child: his guilt feelings and his distorted perception of the true cause of the parent's death.

These subjects have to be taken up by an understanding adult at home, in the school, or in a child guidance clinic.

A school psychologist who is counseling a bereaved child has to be very much aware of the role of irrational guilt feelings. Unreasonable as they are, it is easy to account for them. In his socialization process, the child becomes angry at times at his parents when they have to punish him or frustrate his wishes. In these situations, which naturally arise in the home, the child experiences surging feelings of anger and even hatred against his parents. He usually is not fully aware of his hostility, because repression sets in quickly. Then, if a death occurs in the family, guilt feelings come to the fore and cause severe anxiety since he feels that his anger and fury have indeed led to his parent's death. Children who have had a conflict-laden relationship with their mother or father will undoubtedly suffer more guilt feelings than do those children whose homelife was less agitating. In the long run, emotionally healthy children have a greater sense of security and therefore they suffer less damage to their personality after a loss.

John Bowlby[8] believes that anger is an integral part of a grief reaction in children and in adults, including anger with the lost person for leaving them. The ability to express overtly one's anger by protest, despair, and detachment for a certain time leads to a healthy outcome. Bowlby calls this three-stage experience the mourning work, and adults and children alike who have lost a loved person will have to go through these periods to overcome their depression. Healthy mourning takes place right away so that the emotions do not undergo repression. If the grief is not worked through by the bereaved child, he may withdraw into habitual affect-lessness, because he has learned from his bitter experience that to love someone will end in being hurt.

As the death or departure of a loved person cannot be hidden from a child and cannot be made painless for him it is important for relatives and friends not only to give the child answers to his questions, but also to help him to participate in activities and actions which are part of the elementary school child's way of expressing himself and resolving a situation. His activities often reveal symbolically how he feels. A boy who may choose aggressive gun play when he is angry may not be able to find anything to do when he is depressed. He needs to be reassured that the adults around him have not forgotten him and that in due time they will recover from their preoccupation with memories of the deceased, will smile again, and will have time to be affectionate and have fun with him again.

No doubt, the ideal solution for a bereaved child is reached when he finds a new parent to love and to attach himself to, after his grief has been overcome. A school psychologist or social worker can become an important source of strength during a crisis situation and can help the bereaved child to overcome his fear of abandonment and to vent his despair over the loss of a loved person.

In the Rev. Edgar N. Jackson's books, one finds the most integrated study of the theological, psychological, and philosophical dimensions of bereavement. He brings the insights of his ministry, as former pastor of the Mamaroneck (New York) Methodist Church, together with a fine blending of his own psychiatric research.

Educated at Ohio Wesleyan, Yale, Union, Drew, and the Postgraduate Center for Psychotherapy, Dr. Jackson has served as head of a psychiatric clinic for children at New Rochelle, New York, and has lectured widely at colleges, universities, seminaries, medical schools, and professional conferences in the United States and Canada.

Edgar N. Jackson is the author of twelve books concerned with pastoral care, including Understanding Grief, Facing Ourselves, The Pastor and His People, How to Preach to People's Needs, Telling a Child About Death, A Psychology for Preaching, *and* The Christian Funeral.

The Theological, Psychological, and Philosophical Dimensions of Death in Protestantism

EDGAR N. JACKSON

INTRODUCTION

IN ANY RAPIDLY CHANGING culture it is possible for important resources for living to be lost, not so much by deliberate design as by the accidents of rapid change. This is true of the traditional therapeutic methods employed by the social group in coping with the sharp evidence of man's mortality in the fact of death.

Education employs a selective process so that those things that are considered important and profitable are passed on to the next generation, and the things that are a threat to values and a social and psychological hazard are quietly ignored until they tend to disappear.

We should all be well aware of the fact that we stand always just a generation away from barbarism. If the resources for education and communication break down for any reason, the great body of accumulated fact and feeling that we think of as our cultural endowment may be lost.

The trend now seems to be apparent in the matter of the transmitting of ideas and cultural patterns in coping with death. Geoffrey Gorer, the English anthropologist, tells us what is happening in England as parents and other adults transmit their thoughts and feelings about death to their children.[1]

Gorer points out that increasingly adults become anxious about death, and their anxiety leads them to irrational acts. These acts include the destruction of the traditional methods employed in coping with death plus a breakdown of the significant communication with their children about the event and its meaning. In the survey he conducted, 44 percent of parents said nothing to their children about a death that occurred in the family. As Gorer observes this is quite the opposite condition from a couple of generations ago when parents could not talk about the beginnings of life but could confront its end honestly. Now parents talk openly with their children about sex, childbirth, and the biological processes surrounding the beginnings of life, but are strangely confounded when they try to speak of death, dying, or the emotions relating to these evidences of the end of the life cycle.

This means that instead of transmitting information and the capacity to cope with crises in competence, adults tend to pass on mainly their anxiety and other negative attitudes about death. This means that the open and honest inquiry so natural with children is doubly thwarted, for in response to their questions they get not only a denial of information but also the hazard of anxiety which tends to be cumulative with the years. So the children accumulate and pass on their unwise attitudes toward death and dying in compounded form.

We begin to see what the dimensions of this problem are when we look at the rapidly growing role of children and young adults in the emergence of cultural patterns. In the year 1970 one half of the population of the United States will be twenty-five years of age or younger. At the present time the incidence of death is greatest in the over-65 age group, next in the one to four age group, and third in the 19 to 25 age group. This means that in determining the attitudes and practices toward death and the events surrounding it this group of one hundred million children and youth will have the most prominent role. They will be arranging for the activities surrounding the deaths of their parents and other adults in the over-65 group, experiencing the deaths of young children in the one to four age group, and in that group that has the most accidental and military deaths, the 19- to 25-year-olds will be the active participants. This means that they will be in a strategic position to determine, perhaps for generations to come, the attitudes and patterns of our culture toward death.

It is quite clear, then, that if these attitudes are the product of anxiety, they will not be healthy. Rather, they will tend to show the inadequate values of the culture from which they grow. The values that are emphasized most in our social structure are youth, vigor, health, and beauty. The ugly, painful, and aged are brushed aside. Sociologists[2] speak of the result as a death-denying, death-defying mood. Part of the mood is the frenzied effort to try to obliterate those processes that focus on the reality of death even though these processes represent a more healthful way of coping with death, dying, and the emotions that accompany these human experiences.

Here again Gorer gives useful insight. He found that where persons engaged in traditional practices surrounding death, they emerged from the experience more rapidly and with more basic health of personality. But when the traditional practices were denied or ignored, there were neurotic symptoms, long and unresolved periods of maladaptive behavior, and a loss of the capacity to feel concern or express love. Human relations were increasingly reduced to a use of other people for selfish purposes rather than a feeling with other people in mutual fulfillment.

Gorer made it quite clear that the more group activity of a structured, ritualized, and ceremonial form there is at the time of emotional crisis, the more the total personality is engaged in the healthful processes of acting out the deep feelings. When these are denied, the feelings are repressed and find expression through unhealthy detours such as physical illness, self-destructive behavior, and unfortunate personality changes.

This judgment of Gorer's is supported by the research of Erich Lindemann,[3] former professor of psychiatry at Harvard, who has examined grief reactions as a form of illness which engages the total organism in its effort to resolve the powerful emotions that have been repressed. James A. Knight,[4] professor of psychiatry at Tulane, has also pointed out that the major area of psychosomatic research at the present time centers about the unwise management of acute deprivation experiences of which the most traumatic is the experience of loss through death.

THE COMPOUNDED PROBLEM IN OUR CHILDREN AND YOUTH

These insights make it quite clear to us that we are now faced with a crucial period as far as the education of our youth and children is concerned in regard to bereavement, grief, and mourning. But if we assume that there is no education going on, we need to look closely at the more prevalent forms of indirect education that are continually bombarding the consciousness of our children.

The mass media do not ignore death as a part of their programs of entertainment, but they present death in a two-dimensional aspect that tends to make it unreal and devoid of significant emotions. In the two major forms of television programs, the western and the crime or espionage stories, death is a common thing, but common in the sense that it is treated with disregard. Dozens of persons will be shot in an hour's episode with no real concern for a sacred being, made in the image of God, who has just completed his personal history. Everyone watching the program knows that the same people will be acting out their parts next week as if death were not permanent and did not really hurt or amount to much. This tends to erode the value of life and the reality sense that is essential in coping with major human crises, and further tends to make any important emotions seem irrelevant and out of place.

The basic anxiety that is incident to this type of denial of man's mortal nature shows up in the behavior of young people. Games such as "chicken" where youths race their cars toward each other to see who will pull out first and be called "chicken" are efforts to cope with the anxiety that surrounds the fact of death. While the youths themselves would say, "Look, folks, we are not afraid of death for we even make a plaything out of it," those who are discerning see the real meaning of the behavior, for they know it really says, "Look, folks, we are so filled with anxiety about death that we are even willing to make a plaything of life in order to try to allay it." And this is real tragedy when life is traded for a bit of inner security so important to the anxiety-ridden.

Any student of the folk songs that are so popular among children and youth soon becomes aware that these songs with their epic character are often burdened with thoughts of the gruesome, the tragic, and the death-centered. It is as if the emotional need produced by the anxiety were to be satisfied by preoccupation with the vicarious emotions felt in substituted relationships. The implications of this for the discerning student of human behavior are rather distressing. For in this trend of substituting imagined feelings for the real ones that are denied by acute anxiety, we could well produce a generation of persons who have lost the capacity for real feelings for each other.

Signs of this are already too common. The dances of the present are marked by rhythm and unrelatedness. The emphasis in magazines for men is upon two-dimensional sex which promises satisfaction without relationship. The complaint is not that the emphasis is too sexy but rather that it is not truly sexual at all. It moves at the merely visual and glandular level with no opportunity for the real engagement of the emotions in true feeling with and for another. All of these escapes from the reality of human relationships may be traced to a breakdown of a philosophy of life that speaks directly to all human needs, even of life and of death. It increasingly cramps life into an experience of the now with the urge to satisfy its immediate needs with little thought of what has been learned in the past, or what can be assumed about the future. Such living is increasingly denied the perspective that has traditionally characterized the human consciousness, and tends to reduce living more and more to the concern for material things and the satisfaction of appetites.

Yet traditionally the adolescent and youth busily engaged

in building his philosophy of life has been most courageous
in coming to terms with death as an essential prerequisite for
coming to terms with life. Yet he has sought to come to grips
with real life, not an illusion. So it is that Bryant wrote
"Thanatopsis," Edna St. Vincent Millay wrote "Renascence,"
and Franz Schubert wrote his *lieder* of death, all while they
were teen-agers.

Any true theology or philosophy has its strength at the
point where it helps people cope with all there is of reality,
and not merely the illusions. Actually, religious faith becomes strangely irrelevant in dealing with illusions, for it
seeks to look at all of life honestly and boldly. Our modern
problem is that the effort to escape from the burdens of our
mortal nature through denial tends to make many of our
traditional resources for coping with crises appear to be
without meaning.

BASIC CAUSES OF THE PROBLEM

Lest we be misunderstood, we make no effort to place blame
on anyone for the conditions that now exist. They are clearly
the result of cultural forces that were unplanned and social
accidents that came with specialization and change in the
family structure. Where death used to be a part of homelife
and could be met openly and honestly, now due to different
modes of living it comes in the hospital, the nursing home,
the highway, and the battlefield. The specialists who participate in death are skilled technically but largely uninvolved
emotionally. And the emotionally involved are remote from
the events and so are not able to cope with them realistically.

Youth growing up in the typical family of today are subject to a type of circumstantial anxiety that did not exist so
markedly in the past. Until quite recently the family tended
to be multigenerational, with parents, children, grandparents,
and other assorted relatives nearby. When death occurred
in that setting it was possible for the emotions to be diffused
with a variety of people to talk with. While the experience

of death might not have been pleasant, it was not remote and could be dealt with realistically, in both the event and the feelings that went with it. The things feared were met directly and openly. There was little pretense or illusion about the major events of life.

Now that pattern of family living is largely outmoded. The old folk take their social security and move to a retirement village or a part of the country populated largely by those in the 65-and-over age group. The basic family unit tends to be a father, a mother, and two or three children. The family, as such, begins with marriage and ends with or is broken by the death of one of the parents. This threat hangs so heavily over all the members of the small family unit that they face it only with difficulty. Instead, they spend time and effort creating illusions and pretending that it could never happen to them. Even the insurance men who make a living penetrating the pretense, do it with euphemisms such as "estate planning," "life insurance," and "security against the unexpected eventualities of life."

When effective communication breaks down, the end result is depression, undiffused anxiety, and the creating of illusions. None of these helps a person meet a real crisis. Rather, they make the person particularly vulnerable to the one thing that marks man as mortal, the need to contend openly and honestly with the fact of his own and other people's death.

The emotions are so intensified that they cannot be faced. Free-floating anxiety takes their place and is passed on to children who have little or no protection against it. The fear of death that once through open confrontation led to medical research, agricultural advancement, and architectural improvement, now seems often to be replaced by a nameless, faceless anxiety about death that constricts the creative processes of research. Even in medical circles death and dying are evaded as essential aspects of human existence, and the causes of death are identified not as normal but as accidental. So medical language is weighted by terms like "cerebral accident," "cardiovascular accident," and "circulatory accident."

This, then, is the cultural state in which we must begin to think of the role of the pastor with those young lives for whom he assumes responsibility when facing the fact of death. We have taken considerable time in preparing the social and cultural setting for this consideration, for to do otherwise would be merely compounding the illusion. We are at a critical juncture in social history, and we have to decide whether or not we will be a part of the problem or a part of the solution.

Some well-intentioned but imperceptive clergymen have already indicated their intention of making their religion an ally of the death-denying, death-defying forces at work by largely ignoring death, grief, and the process of dying. In their practice of pastoral care they have given religious support to the process that would reduce, limit, or destroy the rites, rituals, and ceremonials that surround death without making any effort to understand their importance in the emotional lives of their people. Too often they have removed any constructive facing of death in their educational or preaching program, or have felt it was sufficient to make an occasional assault on the one sure remaining social symbol of real death, the funeral director, as if he were the cause of death and therefore the enemy of life itself. It is increasingly apparent that these approaches are not good enough to cope with the major problem that now faces us. To be sure reform may be needed, but it should be psychologically and spiritually perceptive and not an ally of unhealthy trends.

What then must we do?

Toward Some Solutions

No one knows better than I the hazards of sweeping generalizations when speaking of Protestant thought and action. However, there are some basic ideas that we can probably agree on as a starting point. Within the past two generations it has been almost universal among Protestant groups to make a major emphasis on the education of its children and youth. Large amounts of money, time, and energy have been invested in school buildings, lesson materials, and teaching programs. So the basic equipment already exists for a discerning and psychologically sound educational approach to death, dying, and the emotions that are related to these events. Also, most pastors have some training in basic psychology and in understanding the importance of the emotions. More than twelve thousand ministers have received clinical training under supervision.

But this does not preclude blind spots, for some of the best trained have such fear of death that they distort their thinking in relation to it. The general lack of clearly defined traditions in Protestantism makes it easy to encourage rapid change without appreciation of the social and psychological meaning of the ways for acting out the deeper feelings that have been provided by tradition to meet the deeper subconscious needs of people. The unexamined response to generally accepted social trends may often ensnare the minister in the prevalent mood of the community at the time when he should be exerting an influence contrary to that which tends to be dominant. Some of this has happened in the teaching of seminary professors, who have had little experience in the parish with real people, but yet presume to ridicule and downgrade the traditional processes they apparently do not understand or properly evaluate.

We can wisely encourage some constructive trends that have been emerging in recent years. Much of the study of the impact of emotional crisis on personality has come from the personality sciences. The pastor can become familiar with this experimental and interpretive material and try to relate it to the needs of his people. He can encourage serious discussion of these subjects in church publications, in seminars provided by psychiatric clinics, hospitals, funeral director groups, and other serious students of death in our culture, and he can keep an open mind so that in rapidly

changing times he can continually reexamine his own attitudes.

Also it is important to take a good long look at the traditional teaching of the church and church school as it per-
tains to death. Too often the things that have been passed
on from one generation to the next are not only intellectually not worthy of respect, but they are completely at vari-
ance with the cosmology, psychology, and theology that make
up the body of knowledge children acquire in growing up
in our day. This tends to make religion not only nonrational
in its loyalties, but if any loyalty remains it is apt to be
among the segment of the community that has lost intellectual curiosity or the ability to coordinate what is learned.
In either case, the cause of true religion suffers.

No answer to an honest question asked by a child should
ever be given that causes the answerer to deny his own ideas
or distort the truth he knows. Gorer pointed out that when
parents in England did try to answer questions about death
they told children things they did not believe usually because
they couldn't think of anything else to say. This is not good
enough for the children of today. The talk about heaven
and hell is as outmoded as the moon of green cheese in an
age of astronauts who are prepared to colonize the moon.
The ideas of God "up there" or "out there" are as unrelated
to the modern cosmology as the flat earth theory is to modern
geography. The effort to reassure a child by falsehood is
doubly damaging because when he finds that he has been
deceived he feels anxiety not only about the deception itself,
but also about the person who is so insecure that he can no
longer be trusted to serve as a dependable source of information about the important questions of life.

THE NEED FOR REASSESSMENT

In view of the changed social and cultural conditions surrounding our attitudes toward death, it seems important for
us to reassess our educational processes, our theological as-

sumptions, and our religious and social ceremonies so that all three may more nearly meet the needs of our current set of circumstances.

Because the basic problems of communication we are considering are emotional rather than informational, and the chief transmitters of emotion are parents and other adults, it is important for us to start any consideration of what can and should be done with an examination of the adult educational program of Protestantism. As Walter Holcomb, professor of Christian education at Boston University School of Theology, has observed, the Sunday school is the best institution ever designed for the preservation and communication of falsehood and folly. The church as an institution has been slow to challenge outmoded ideas. It has been content to use old words that have little contemporary meaning. It has tried to adjust religious teachings to a new psychology and cosmology without admitting their basic irrelevance. It has compromised its standards partly because of disinclination to accept the challenge, but also because it recognizes the limitations of those to whom it ministers. As one who has written lesson material for adults it has always been distressing to face the fact that the materials must be adapted to the twelve-year-old mental capacity.

Focus on Parent Education

In view of the importance of the task and the inadequacies of the present efforts, it seems obvious that some better use could be made of the educational facilities of the church. These conditions make it wise for us to reconsider the importance of parents as teachers and the early years in the home as the most significant classroom. For it is here that the emotional attitudes toward life and death are learned.

The theoretical base for this reconsideration is found in the thought and writing of four psychological innovators, Freud, Rank, Fodor, and Piaget.

It was Freud's theory[5] that the emotional life of an individual was largely colored by the early life experiences. In his exploration of the lower levels of consciousness he discovered that practically all of the experiences of the first three or four years of life were stored in the unconscious. Very little of this early experience can be recalled. But all that happened in these years had its impact on the personality and its function. These ideas have led us at the very least to pay more attention to what is said and done to children in their preverbal years. Such early experience as the deprivation that comes with weaning, the insecurity that comes with separation from parents, the threat to love that comes with younger brothers and sisters, all produce strong emotional responses. The behavior of young children is the acting out of their feelings. Rarely can a person explain how his feelings develop, but the processes by which feelings are shaped are so important that those who assume a professional interest in children cannot ignore the impact of these early years. As these years are usually preschool and pre-church school, the importance of parent education as the major resource for understanding and guiding the emotional development that takes place during this period must be emphasized.

Otto Rank,[6] a student of Freud's, differed from his teacher at some points. He felt that sex itself was not sufficient motivation for understanding what happens in the developmental processes of life. He believed that man's basic nature and his initial experience in life, birth itself, were so important in explaining the development of personality that they could not be overlooked. His thesis was that birth is the critical emotional experience of life. Before birth the child lives in a safe, secure, perfectly contained, and blissful world, where every need is satisfied and where there is no hazard except the growth process itself. Growth makes the little world too small to contain the growing life. In the act of emerging from the cozy and comfortable womb into the cold and threatening world, the baby endures an experience that may be exceedingly painful and can actually be fatal. The first act of life is often a bellow of anger and rage. Being deprived of all that has sustained life in the past is a threatening event. Rank felt the trauma associated with this event was a major factor in determining the way a personality developed. His study correlates the serene emotional nature of children with easy births or of Caesarian sections with the emotionally disturbed patterns shown by those who had unusually difficult births. While his findings may be more specifically relevant for the therapist than the religious educator, it is important to understand that this experience can be a factor in personality development and therefore significant for adult behavior. Education for understanding and adequate compensation for such traumatic events may well be a basic part of parent education.

Nandor Fodor,[7] a Hungarian psychoanalyst, has carried the idea of parental influence one step further. In two major works he developed the idea that the psychic sensitivity that exists between mother and unborn child may be a significant factor in determining the emotional development of the personality. On the basis of studies of telepathy and the direct communication of emotion from subconscious mind to subconscious mind, he postulates that no relationship is closer than that which binds mother and unborn child. So the attitude of the mother toward the fetal being may determine how the child feels about himself in later life. In the analytic process he found again and again material that did not seem to be related to the life experience of the individual. By correlating this material with the attitude of the mother toward the unborn child, he thought he found a clue to its reasonable explanation. For instance, a child who was unwanted, and toward whom the mother had harbored persistent resentment and hatred with even the thought or attempt at abortion, carried through life a reservoir of low self-esteem and self-destructive hatred. On the other hand, the child that was planned for and eagerly and lovingly awaited, appeared to have a backlog of self-acceptance and assurance upon which the healthy growth of the personality could be

built. Whether this theory is acceptable psychologically is not
for us to determine here, but surely it can deepen our understanding of the potential importance of the early influence
of parents upon their children, and emphasize the significance of parent education.

Jean Piaget,[8] in ten important books has examined in
depth the life, behavior, and experience of children to understand what takes place in the emergence of intelligence, personality, consciousness, conscience, language, thought, reasoning, judgment, and the construction of reality. After careful
observation of large numbers of children, he has concluded
that the significant patterns of personality that persist through
life are well established before the child is five years old.

PASTORAL RESPONSIBILITY

These insights from careful studies of child development
imply that traditional programs for child education in the
church come along with too little, too late. They make it
clear that the basic assumptions about life are not the product of formal education but of those important earlier relationships that strongly affect the emotional quality of life
itself.

In dealing with as emotionally charged a subject as death
it becomes doubly clear that the important attitudes for good
or ill are established in response to the emotions of others
early in life. The pastor's more effective role then will appear
to be in parent education. This may well include premarital
education and counseling. It would certainly assume responsibility for family planning, not in the merely biological
sense but in terms of the attitudes, motives, and adequate
preparation of parents for the privileges and responsibilities
to be assumed. Just as much of the damage done to the emerging personality is done through ignorance and lack of understanding of these early years, so also the important challenges
to an improved state of religious education cannot ignore

the new insight into the relationship of parent and child emotionally as the base from which any sound educational process will be achieved.

If the theoretical insights that have developed in recent years are to be significantly employed in the wise education of children and youth, we must look closely at the existing methods, materials, and motivations. From the point of view of the personality development of the child, it appears that the methods now employed in religious education are not only inadequate, but may well be destructive of the goals that are set. The efforts to present illusion-creating concepts within an atmosphere of irrelevance tend to make religion itself meaningless for life rather than the source of life's meaning. The contrast between the teaching methods and equipment of the secular school and the religious school becomes a source of teaching itself, for its says that religion and its ideas are unimportant, not interesting, and perhaps not valid. The indirect and subconscious implications of the methods employed may be so large that the credit balance of religious education is overweighted by its inadequacies and basic destructiveness of real values.

As long as religious teaching is subject centered, Bible oriented, and tradition dominated it will tend to treat living people and their needs as incidental. It will by implication express a pessimistic view of human nature, with no real confidence in man's inner resources for self-realization and self-fulfillment. It will in effect be the organized effort to deny to mankind the very resources it claims to represent.

But this need not be so. Psychological innovators in our time provide the insight and understanding of human needs adequate for a sound basis of understanding of the relationship of life and death and a responsible attitude toward both. The insight of Carl Rogers[9] concerning inner resources for discovering emotional truth, and the studies of the emotionally healthy individual by Abraham Maslow,[10] give a clear direction for educational movement. The method can be person centered, need oriented, and reality related. When this determines the basis for communication of both thought and feeling, a more healthful attitude toward the experience of and meaning for death will be achieved.

This of course brings us face to face with the materials that will be employed in a modified methodology. Instead of using Bible oriented, subject related, and tradition dominated materials for teaching, the focus would become the persons who are engaged in the process of exploration and growth. The needs and experiences of the individual would become paramount, and all resources and materials would be employed to fill the experience with meaning that is adequate to the emotional needs of the individual.

This could even create a new possibility for pastoral counseling. Traditionally, counseling has been primarily a relationship with adults. Experimentally, I have found that a period of time set aside for children and youth produced some interesting results. The periods were shorter, the encounter more direct, and the movement more rapid. I have had children as young as five come with their questions, and it appeared to serve a useful purpose for they told others that they could talk with their pastor about anything. The discussion often centered about emotionally charged subjects like death, their parents, God, and science.

When the experience of death is faced, the child would not be introduced to philosophical considerations concerning death as the primary answer. He would not be subjected to theological assumptions having to do with revenge and punishment, heaven or hell, or the scapegoat theory of God as one upon whom cosmic blame can be placed. Rather, the experience would be explored in terms of its emotional meaning for the individual who encounters it. The concern would be primarily to gain understanding of the experience in all of its dimensions as a basis for developing the inner strength to cope with it.

THEOLOGICAL ASSUMPTIONS

Traditionally, the ideas about death prevalent in Protestant thought have not been designed for children or their capacity for understanding. They have been a restatement of the adult ideas in simpler language but without a consideration of the child's capacity to cope with tertiary abstractions. This, of course, only compounds the dilemma of the child. These traditional ideas have included the Resurrection with the promise of the restoration of the physical organism of the faithful at some future date when the trumpet shall sound. It also uses the idea of the immortality of the soul and its continued life in a place of reward or punishment depending on the behavior of the individual in life. The score of each individual is supposedly kept by a cosmic bookkeeper who is able to see and hear all things. The comfort of the bereaved is centered about the promises implicit in the concept of immortality or the doctrine of the Resurrection. The prevalent Christology is geared to these ideas of death, Resurrection, and immortality, for the Christ is the savior from sin and death and the personal guarantor of the hopes of the righteous. Unquestioned and abject surrender to the way of Christ is all that is needed to overcome death and gain the privileges of the life everlasting. In fact it seems that the benefits of immortality can be achieved without tasting of death. James Snowden in *What Do Present Day Christians Believe* gives whole chapters to immortality and the Resurrection and does so without even mentioning the words death or mortality. In fact, examination of a number of books on Christian theology show little or no reference to death or man's mortal nature, but considerable concern about immortality and the Resurrection. When death is mentioned in current theological discussion it is more apt to be the death of God than the death of man. On the other hand, books on anthropology, psychiatry, and psychology give increasing attention to a consideration of death and its impact on the life of man.

This, then, would call for a reexamination of the theological assumptions used in teaching. The basic concern would be the search for meaning for life and personal adequacy in meeting its experiences. The resources would then be understood as intrapersonal relationships strengthened by a firm grip on reality. These would be amplified by interpersonal relationships that make it possible for identification as a psychological resource to be understood and employed. Then the emotional capital invested in a lost love object can be more readily withdrawn and reinvested where it can produce healthful response in life. This would make it possible for the more basic relationships with a cosmic dimension to be understood and accepted. God would then no longer be the cosmic scapegoat blamed for the tragedies and deprivations that afflict man, but would be the source of ordered processes that can be depended upon as well as the source of the underlying meaning for life experience, whatever that experience may be.

It then becomes obvious that it would be wiser with young children to avoid the abstractions that tend to be meaningless to them. It would call for a new and practical view of that basic theological concern in the nature of man, for it would be extended to a concern for the nature of children. Then instead of weighting the consciousness with concepts so distorted that they have to be abandoned before a framework of maturity and competence will be achieved, the emphasis at every point would be on the things that do not have to be unlearned or insulated from developing rational judgments.

In coping with the experience of death it becomes quite clear that the resources must be geared to the capacity for comprehension. A young child, under three or four, has little or no sense of time or space and thus can have little idea of the meaning of death. His feeling of deprivation would be met at the point where he experiences it by filling the emotional vacuum with care, concern, interest, emotional warmth, and the structure of experience that tends to restore fractured relationships. For how better could we teach that God is love?

From four to seven years of age a child's interests in death would be primarily biological as he tries to understand what has happened in relation to himself. At this age philosophical or theological interpretations would be largely meaningless, but simple answers to direct questions would give reassurance and a sound basis upon which to build his later questions. The body-oriented interests would give a chance to interpret the wonders and mysteries of the human body and the wisdom of caring for it wisely and well. For how better could we let him know that it is the sacred residence of the Most High?

From eight to eleven or twelve the interests in death are centered about its social meaning. Questions would have to do with human interdependence and the breakdown of these relationships when death intervenes. Questions would tend to be economic and familial and would indicate an emerging awareness of the need for social stability and mutual responsibility. These interests would be met where they arise and would be interpreted as an opportunity to explore the basic ideas about true brotherhood and individual responsibility.

With the teen-ager there would be increased interest in abstractions and the meanings that are found in philosophical and theological relationships. There would, of course, tend to be an accumulation of earlier modes of thought and types of interest, but they would be subordinated to the experimental use of abstractions in thinking. The death experience would usually be interpreted subjectively as if it were happening to the grieving individual. As he explores new frontiers of emotional experience, he seeks new resources for interpreting them. This is where the mature concept of death begins to form. But they would have to be concepts related to the world the adolescent knows. To interpret current experience in terms of outmoded science or religion would usually be interpreted as an expression of anxiety rather than as reassurance. For it is in making the audacious assumptions about the nature of man and his place in the universe that a person begins to understand the true meaning of faith.

MOTIVATIONS IN WORK WITH CHILDREN

This would bring us face to face with the problems of conscious and unconscious motivations in education. As we mentioned earlier, education tends to be selective in what is communicated. Sometimes this is defensive. Sometimes it is an offense depending on the stance of the individual or institution that does the communicating. Much of the content of religious tradition has been the effort to cope with existential anxiety concerning death and to relieve the neurotic or existential guilt that accompanies the anxiety. It has been only recently, as a by-product of psychological research, that we have been able to perceive more clearly this basic motivation. Once having that perception it would be irresponsible to act as if it had not occurred. It would make more sense to develop educational approaches that could allay the anxiety rather than to continue the process of first creating the anxiety and then employing the traditional resources for meeting it.

In a predominantly death-denying, death-defying culture our values tend to support our consciously or unconsciously accepted cultural needs. Our two-dimensional view of life and death expresses itself in the enhancing of the practices that support it and in the denial or destruction of the practices and attitudes that challenge it. This shows itself in our forms of amusement which make a large place for unreal death, the prevalence of killings with no apparent awareness of the significance of the event for the person who dies or for the one who is the agent of death. This death without emotion, this two-dimensional approach to death, is poor preparation for the real thing, but most of the indirect education of our children shares this inadequacy.

What is more difficult to understand is that the church in some instances willingly cooperates in creating the attitude of illusion and unreality about death. It might well be that we have lost faith in the spiritual meaning of life and have been overwhelmed with the materialistic attitude which sees nothing beyond the merely physical. Rather than face the fact of weakened faith, we would rather eliminate that basic fact which most obviously threatens the exposure of the withering away of inner resources to cope with any reality. The gradual elimination of committal services, family visitations, and the effort to remove the physical evidence that death has occurred is all part of the effort to remove death from the context of living. It is only natural that children brought up in this mood of defensiveness and this uneasiness with basic reality may be subjected to compounded anxiety through the process.

MEANING FOR LIFE

The church should put a high value on people in life and in death. It should provide the resources to cope significantly with the facts and the emotions that accompany death. When it fails to do this, it tends to downgrade life itself. How does this come about?

With children it can work in two ways. Children employ large amounts of magical thinking. In effect, they are apt to believe that thinking the thought is equivalent to doing the deed. In their quest for independence and restiveness under discipline they often think murderous thoughts against the authorities in their lives. They sometimes say with a limited idea of what it means, "I wish you were dead" or "Drop dead, will you?" When real death comes they may in their own minds feel that in some way they were the agents. When they feel this, the burden of guilt may be intolerable. When they do not have ways of talking it out or asking pertinent questions, their anxious guilt is cumulative. This will show itself in excessive fear of death and in various other forms of disturbed behavior. The traditional ceremonial events surrounding death give a child a chance to ask questions, make comments, express his own thoughts experimentally to see what the effect is upon others, and in other ways to act out his real feelings. Children have a natural affinity for ceremonials for they are forms of communication that are not dependent on words. To deny children the chance to participate in important family events is to deny them important opportunities for therapeutic communication. And the questions that are unanswered become the gathering points for further apprehension and concern.

In a second form of expression, the child identifies with the process and the event of death, and tries to understand what it would mean if it happened to him. He may even play games through which he tries to come to terms with the thoughts and feelings. When a sibling dies and quick disposal with no ceremony takes place, the conclusion of the child is, "If I should die it wouldn't make any difference to anyone, they wouldn't care, so I guess they don't really love me." Insecurity is increased and not only is the real grief of the child ignored, but the implications of adult attitudes make it difficult or impossible to regain self-esteem and personal competence in the face of the fact of death and his fear of it.

Studies of professional persons who cope with death— ministers, physicians, and funeral directors—show that often the vocational choice is consciously or unconsciously motivated by the deep inner needs of the person to gain some competence in coping with death and the profound emotions that are stimulated in confronting it.

It would seem then that one of the significant educational resources of the church would be its rites, rituals, and ceremonials, for it is in these that people work through their feelings. So, rather than reducing the kind and number of these ceremonial events, it would seem wise to use our best psychological insight to invent and increase the number and types of events afforded for these purposes. While no child should ever be forced to participate, it would be wise to offer the opportunities that would be relevant to his needs. For instance, it might be wise to permit him to visit the funeral home with a mature and competent adult who could answer his questions without anxiety. In this way he could come to terms with the death that is a part of his context of life without undue fear but with reasonable understanding of what is involved physically and emotionally. Children are so responsive to feelings that the denial of appropriate feelings becomes a devastating form of communication.

Not All Death Is the Same

It is wise to present children with a discriminating concept of death. When any concept is presented with an underlying stratum of anxiety, the powerful emotion reduces the capacity to be discriminating. Some of the fear related to death can be reduced when it can be clearly seen that all death is not the same. The tragic and untimely death of a person in the full vigor of life and creativity is quite different from that of the aged person who has completed the cycle of life and actually welcomes death as a friend. The execution of a criminal, the suicide of a student, the death caused by an accident, or the casualty of a person in the armed services may all be tragic in their own way, but the different nature of the events calls for the attributing of a meaning clearly related to the event itself, and not primarily related to a generalized anxiety produced by the thought of death. For it is only with discriminating judgment that cause-effect relationships can be discerned and man's responsibility for the tragic events that befall him can be properly fixed. One of the difficulties with children and young people in our day is that the apprehension and anxiety about death is so acute that the discriminating approach to the physical event is largely obliterated in the minds and emotions of a whole generation. To the extent that this is true it is quite obvious that the opportunity to learn wise and careful living from these tragic events is lost in the generalized emotion that is related to death in general rather than to a death in particular.

This unfortunate loss of discrimination with its marked increase in unhealthy and generalized emotions is apt to show itself in irrational efforts to control death. One of the explanations for the fact that the third largest group of suicides is among teen-agers and the second largest is in the student body of colleges is that the anxiety about the fact of death and the meaning of life is so generalized that the effort to bring it into focus may be sought even at the price of self-destruction. In the effort to control his irrational feelings and conquer his despair about them the student may feel that if he can control its time and place he has at least reduced his utter helplessness before a certain fate.

It is at this point that the insights of Viktor Frankl[11] may have special relevance. He would urge that persons seek first an adequate meaning for life, and then all of the other things will be added unto them. It would seem essential, then, that the teaching of children and young people would be aimed at their need to find adequate meaning for their own lives at the time they are obliged to live them. This means that religious instruction would be not so much about religion as it would be a personal discovery of the meaning of life through religious insight and understanding. It would be a basic process by which human needs and the answers of religion would be brought into a vital relationship in the life of the child or youth. For it is only by the process of enlightened confrontation that the deep anxiety about life and death can be resolved and the maturing individual can achieve the self-understanding and the self-realization that provide him with a working philosophy of life that is competent to face all there is of life, even its mark of mortality.

SUMMARY

It is quite clear that we have not tried to interpret a body of generally accepted truth presented by Protestant thought concerning death, for to do so in the midst of so much variety of thought and teaching would be misleading if not presumptive. However, we have tried to present the current setting within which we must face the problems incident to teaching children and youth about the meaning of life and death. Then we have tried to present the inadequacies of past motives, materials, and methods for meeting the crisis by our cultural mood of denial. Then we have sought to indicate some constructive directions in which we can move in trying not only to resolve the problem but also to compensate for the limitations placed upon us culturally by the increased denial of reality in relation to death. This may, perhaps, alert us to the dimensions of the problem we face in education and communication, and may help us to employ our own imagination, sound judgment, and essential concern for meeting the problem constructively.

"The Catholic child is not isolated from the reality of death," writes Bishop Thomas Joseph Riley. "Much stress is laid on the continuity between man's life on earth and his life for eternity."

What is the Catholic philosophy of life? Of family? Of death? What are the teachings that aid the Catholic child to adjust to the reality of tragedy?

The Most Reverend Bishop Thomas Joseph Riley, D.D., Ph.D., is Auxiliary Bishop to the Archbishop of Boston. He is widely known in academic circles and is the former Rector of St. John's Seminary in Brighton, Massachusetts.

CHAPTER VIII

Catholic Teachings, the Child, and a Philosophy for Life and Death

THOMAS JOSEPH RILEY

THE PROBLEM OF DEATH is inseparably bound up with the problem of the nature and purposes of life. As we find it in human beings, life is not something of merely passing importance in a general system of evolution. Life belongs to individual men. It is the sum total of the qualities which constitute the human personality. It is not a commodity to be bought and sold for a price; it is the inalienable possession of someone who claims personal independence as a member of human society.

In this series of studies attention is focused on the termination of human life which is brought about by death. It will be necessary, therefore, in this particular article to speak somewhat at length about the Catholic philosophy of life. And since the problem at hand relates in a special way to children, we must consider the child's position in the family, of which he is naturally a member, and indicate the general directions in which the family is expected to contribute to the formation of the child's character and to prepare him for the responsibilities and struggles of adult maturity.

The child's attitude toward death will be an integral part of his philosophy of life. Within the framework of his religious beliefs as he learns them and follows up their implications for his free activity, the child will be moved gradually to look beyond his immediate experiences for indications of the meaning of life. As he becomes aware of the inevitable reality of death he will look forward vaguely, and perhaps reluctantly, to the moment of his own death. It will be one of the responsibilities of those who instruct him and guide him to bring death into relation with life. The important forces in this process of orientation will be the naturally based truths of philosophical reflection and the divinely revealed teachings of the Catholic faith.

The Catholic child is not isolated from the reality of death. Neither is he presented with a point of view on death which would sadden him unduly, or render him insensitive to the joys of living. For the Catholic, death is not to be feared, but to be prepared for intelligently, prayerfully, and hopefully. To this end he must look beyond passing events and seek the ultimate fulfillment of his desire for happiness and peace in a reality which transcends the pleasures which he now enjoys.

The chapter will be divided into four parts:

A. THE CATHOLIC PHILOSOPHY OF LIFE
B. THE CATHOLIC PHILOSOPHY OF THE FAMILY
C. THE CATHOLIC TEACHING ON DEATH
D. DEATH AND LIFE IN THE CATHOLIC PRACTICE OF RELIGION

A. THE CATHOLIC PHILOSOPHY OF LIFE

I. *The Primacy of God*

No point of Catholic teaching can be understood until it is placed in proper relation with the reality of God, as it is discoverable through reasonable reflection. The truths of divine revelation are meaningful only if it be established on reasonable grounds that God exists and that men, His creatures, are dependent on Him. The starting point of our examination of the truths of faith must be a critical evaluation of the facts of immediate experience as they present themselves to all men, regardless of their religious beliefs.

Two basic problems thus emerge: 1) What is the origin of immediate experience? 2) What is the purpose of the succession of experiences which make up what we call a person's life?

It would be impossible in a chapter such as this to cover the details of the philosophical examination in which these problems are pursued. Suffice it to say that the examination establishes first of all the objective reality of a universe which lies beyond the experience of individual men; and, secondly, that this objectively real universe requires as its ultimate explanation the existence of a Supreme Being who is responsible for its existing reality, and who alone can be the last end toward which its activity is directed. To search for a cause; to find the cause beyond the experience of that which is caused; to acknowledge the Cause as the Supreme Being on whom we depend as His creatures; to seek in God the complete explanation of all else; to interpret the desire for happiness as the expression, in the limited circumstances of our present existence, of our desire for the eternal possession of God—these are the fundamental philosophical truths on which the superstructure of the Catholic faith is erected.

For the Christian, the primacy of God is the truth which makes everything else reasonable. From his earliest days the child of Catholic parents is taught to thank God because He is God—"because of His great glory." The truth of God's existence is presented to him as beyond reasonable doubt, even though it requires the clarification and metaphysical structuring that open up for mature minds the depths of its meaning.

The strength of the child's conviction on this point depends greatly on his early environment. Doubts which arise subsequently about the existence of God are not likely to become practically significant if the child's early years are spent in circumstances which are truly God-centered. The critical examination which affords justification for the idea of God cannot be made by children. Children, however, derive great benefit from the protection which the reality of God's Being affords for those who accept it as a reasonable implication of every conscious act.

II. *The Dignity of Man*

In the Christian philosophy of life, the primacy of God is the ultimate explanation of the achievements of men as they are recorded in human history. The very existence of human history is a fact to be explained. We find nothing comparable to it in the lower strata of observable reality. No beings lower than man have left written records containing ideas which suggest their past impressions and experiences.

Out of the record of human history emerges the truth of human dignity. The Catholic philosophy of life explains human dignity as the consequence of the union in each man of his material body with an immaterial, immortal soul. The concept of the soul has no meaning for those who seek to explain human activity entirely in terms of observable reactions. What we call the soul is beyond what we can find out about man through any process of scientific exploration. It is precisely because science cannot afford a complete explanation of man that the conviction has persisted, even to the present day, that man's true nature involves an invisible reality.

The nature of this invisible reality is a subject of metaphysical inquiry. The Catholic religion assumes the doctrine of the human soul without commitment to any particular theory about its nature, or the manner of its union with the body. The child of Catholic parents is taught that the soul is the reason why he is able to think and to communicate his ideas to other persons. He is taught to look for the source of his dignity as a human person not in the experience of bodily pleasure, or in the comeliness of bodily form, or in the expenditure of physical energy. The source of human dignity is the soul, which is the reason why pleasure becomes a human experience, comeliness a human quality, and energy a resource for the development of human capacities.

Because each man has a soul which will survive its separation from the body, death loses its terminal character and opens up into a new life in which the hope that springs eternal will find fulfillment. It is in the hope of a future life that the dignity that man claims as the noblest creature of the universe finds its only possible justification. Those who look on death as the end of man are driven sooner or later to look on life as empty and without meaning. From this point of view there can be no consciousness of true human dignity. There can be only the questionable dignity that arises in the possession of power and in the victory of competitive achievement. Whatever sense of personal worth may be experienced in these sources quickly vanishes as the weakening of bodily powers foretells the approach of death. In a genuinely Catholic environment the child finds constant reminders of the eternal existence in which the hopes of this life will find complete realization and the fears which now beset him will be forever dispelled.

III. *The Relation of Nature to the Supernatural*

The distinguishing feature of the Catholic philosophy of life is that it acknowledges its insufficiency and its inability to afford completely satisfying answers to the perennial problems of man's nature, origin, and destiny. By itself reason can conceive high ideals, but it cannot bring them to consistent and sustained application. Reason suffers from the long and laborious processes in which it must engage in order to reach the truth and retain the truth as a continuing influence.

Reason suffers too in the very fact of its multiplication in distinct individuals, each of whom seeks to exercise it independently and to challenge the conclusions of other men. The effort to live by reason alone has always met the obstacles of ignorance and weakness. The most learned and brilliant of men must confess their helplessness before the vast expanses of truth which open up to their investigation. The most noble and dedicated of men find it difficult to overcome periods of depression during which baser impulses become overassertive and the attractiveness of high ideals is lost in clouds of emotion and passion.

The Catholic's remedy against ignorance is the revealed word of God. The Catholic's strength in moments of weakness is the grace of God which follows upon humble and faithful acceptance of the teachings of Christ. Over the long centuries of human history men have turned to God for the enlightenment and help which their own resources have failed to afford. In the beginning God spoke through the prophets; in the fullness of time God sent Christ to complete the teachings of those who foretold His coming, and to fulfill the promise of salvation for those who would believe in Him.

For thousands of Catholics who are overcome by the burden of daily living, the Catholic revelation is a source of enlightenment as reason struggles to rise from the confusion of doubt and despondency. The knowledge of God which reason can gain is clarified and broadened by the teachings of faith. The movements of divine grace, active in those who believe confidently and acknowledge their personal weakness, make certain the influence of the truth on the lives of those whom it is meant to save.

The most discouraging moments of any man's existence are those in which he feels completely alone. At such moments doubts become magnified to the proportions of unbelief, and unbelief opens the way to despair. For the great multitude who cannot look deeply into the reasonable foundations of truth, and develop for themselves compensations against emotional instability, divine revelation affords a certainty which rests on the authority of God, and a confidence which resists the inevitable reverses of life. The assurance of divine help, made available especially through the ministrations of the Church, brings to the Catholic child a sense of supernatural security for his lack of understanding of the deeper meaning of life, and God's promise of victory over the seeming defeat which comes at death.

IV. *The Purpose of Life, Sanctified by Divine Grace*

Regardless of what philosophers say about the inadequacy of the concept of causality, all men ask themselves, in one way or another, why they are living, and what they must do to achieve the purposes of life. Many answers to these problems are suggested. None of them, for the Catholic, can be complete unless they are referred to God. However we elaborate the teaching, it is God who is the purpose of man's life. It is for God who made us that our every thought and deed must be performed.

The relation of the problem of death with that of the purposes of life is quite evident. Within a Catholic environment the meaning of life is gradually unfolded as the child is taught to pray and to assist actively at the Church's liturgical services. The reality of sin becomes an obstacle to be overcome, not merely a burden to be borne, as the child gains benefit from the sacrament of Penance. The effort to achieve success, so necessary for temporal happiness, takes on a higher meaning for the child as it becomes integrated with the acquisition of virtuous habits.

Within the Catholic community it is the grace of God which lightens the burdens of daily living. There can be no sense of frustration when failure is placed in the line of progress toward eternity. There can be no feeling among young people that their older brethren are useless simply because they have fought the good fight and are nearing the term of their earthly pilgrimage.

For older people who tend to be suspicious of the inexperienced efforts of those who are beginning their careers, even the mistakes that are often the consequence of misdirected youthful effort are important in the fulfillment of the purposes of life. Divine grace, by intensifying the impulses of charity and by reinforcing the structure of the natural virtues, brings young and old together as members of the Church and as sharers in the common destiny that awaits the moment of death and judgment.

It should be remarked that, especially today, many Catholics seem to be putting thmselves beyond the power of God's grace to clarify for them the purposes of life. Many too, losing awareness of their solidarity with one another, overlook the obligations of universal charity in their zeal for the promotion of particular good causes. Of its nature, however, the grace of God draws those who live by it toward one another. True holiness during life is a necessary preparation for death. The child learns to live and to prepire for death, as he follows in the paths of virtue which lead to eternal union with God.

B. The Catholic Philosophy of the Family

We have already noted the part that Catholic family life is destined to play in the preparation of the child for death. It will be useful, therefore, to point out briefly how the Catholic philosophy of life views the family within the broader areas of society. Much of the insecurity of life results from wrong attitudes developed within the family circle during the early years of life. As the child grows normally under the protection of a properly organized home, his outlook on life becomes mature and purposeful, and the problems of advancing years find meaningful answers in the light of approaching death.

1. The Family Basic to Social Organization

The Catholic religion has always resisted efforts to undermine the structure of the family. In a society which becomes increasingly mobile and eager for new experiences, the stability of family life has been seriously affected. It is a principle of Catholic philosophy that the family is a natural society, divinely ordained as the unit of social functioning. This principle needs to be strongly reaffirmed. If children are regarded as wards of the state, the value and dignity of human life begin to suffer. Humanity is no longer something that ennobles individual men; the individual becomes expendable for the glorification of the state. Death then becomes a sacrifice to be made without any hope of personal reward. The move to terminate the lives of those who are no longer useful for society becomes stronger. Experiments on human beings for the benefit of science are made without regard for the independence of the human person. Parenthood is identified with procreation; social agencies take over responsibilities which flow naturally from the relationship between parent and child.

For the Catholic philosophy, the union of husband and wife, brought about by marriage, is meant to last until death. In the Catholic marriage ceremony the bride and groom are reminded that only death can separate them, and that the fulfillment of their marital responsibilities must take place within a permanent and stable home. Their children are not to be considered gifts to society, made through the instrumentality of the organs of reproduction. Children are God's gifts to their parents; parents share in God's power as they provide for the physical, intellectual, and spiritual growth of their children.

II. *The Source and Safeguards of Parental Responsibility*

The reality of death, though not a principal normative influence in the discharge of parental responsibility, is in the background of the efforts of Catholic parents to educate their children. To think only of life's immediate rewards and to organize family life around the enjoyment of worldly pleasure is not conducive for the strengthening of parental authority. The thought of death and of the future life will serve to remind children that their parents take the place of God within the home. The hope of achieving success in worldly careers must be brought into relation with the fear of losing the reward which a just God will bestow on those who merit it by their deeds of virtue.

This supernatural motivation, not always evident on the surface of conscious striving, is nonetheless powerful in its supporting effect on parental prestige. Few parents are free of natural defects which weaken their influence over their children. If children see their parents only for what nature has made them, they are only too likely to lose confidence in them, and to compare them unfavorably with the ideals of parenthood which their natural love of decency leads them to conceive. Every parent needs support from sources beyond his natural endowment and his own powers of activity.

As children advance in years, their parents must become increasingly aware of the need of a religious environment in the home. The Church helps to create this environment through its organized religious activity and through the encouragement and stimulation which it affords for individual devotion and prayer. The close relation between life and death, so much a part of the Catholic philosophy of life, becomes thus a hidden factor in compensating within the home for the shortcomings of parents. Parents suffer a great loss by not living up to their religious beliefs. The fear of God's punishments in the world to come adds strength and meaning to the relationship between parent and child.

III. Development of Character Within the Home

The home must provide the most effective influence for the development of moral character. The thought of death is a pivotal point around which the pattern of the Catholic personality takes specific form. It would be inaccurate and oversimplified to assert that the Catholic child is taught to live so that he may face death with equanimity and confidence. It is nonetheless true that the Catholic teaching on the meaning of death and the reality of a life after death can make the difference between a worldly life and a truly religious and spiritual life. Those for whom death is the end of personal identity or, worse still, the end of individual existence, will develop a whole attitude on life which will be different from that of those who accept as part of their faith the teaching that life on earth is a preparation for life eternal.

The personality of a naturally good man is the consequence of prolonged and coordinated effort to reach objectives that are worthwhile and substantial. To a great extent these objectives are provided by the natural resources of society. To an even greater extent, however, they must emerge from the religious teachings which have entered into the organization of family life. The Catholic character is not just something superimposed on a naturally good foundation. The influences of the Catholic religion become inseparably intertwined with the energies of nature itself in the development of the child's character.

It is a fact of life that this union of the natural with the supernatural is not always happily consummated. The Church all too often fails in its mission of making men holy. Children all too often are deprived of the advantages of a religious family life. What ought to be is not always what is. What ought to be, however, is what will be most beneficial, both for children themselves and for the society in which they are destined to make their own positive contribution of virtuous effort. If it is not accurate to say that the thought of death is what makes people truly religious, it is certainly not to be questioned that the power of the Catholic religion to build up natural character is greater because it includes the teachings of divine revelation on the rewards and punishments of the life to come.

IV. The Ongoing Influence of the Family

The child of today is the adult of tomorrow. How he reacts to death today will determine to a large extent his social attitudes in years to come and his success in meeting the reverses of life that so often precipitate emotional crises. The family, important as a formative influence during childhood and adolescence, should continue to be effective as years go on, and the relationships of its members become modified by adult maturity and old age. Children who have been taught to see death in a context of Catholic faith and hope will be likely to retain a deep sense of reverence and respect for their parents.

At the present stage of social evolution there are many obstacles to the development of natural affection between parent and child. Young people are attracted to pleasures which their parents never experienced and for which they have no present desire. The burdens of family responsibility, once borne almost entirely within the family, are now shared by a multitude of social agencies and are increasingly subject to governmental control.

We have reason to be grateful as we compare the present condition of elderly people with that which prevailed even half a century ago. As we make progress in one direction,

however, we must be careful not to go backward in another.
We must not suffer the deterioration of the love and reverence which formerly moved children to provide for their
parents in their old age. Belief in the eternal life beyond the
grave has been a powerful force in fostering respect for parents who suffer from the infirmities of old age. Aged parents
will be fortified in their preparation for death by the moral
and spiritual support of those over whom they once exercised
authority in God's Name.

C. The Catholic Teaching on Death

The Catholic philosophy of life and the Catholic philosophy
applied to the family afford a necessary background for clear
understanding of the details of the Catholic teaching on
death. Death, judgment, heaven, and hell—these are ominous
subjects of meditation when taken by themselves. As part of
a coherent interpretation of life's experiences, however, they
bring to logical completion the main directions of Catholic
philosophy which might otherwise be hard to defend against
the secularistic urge to enjoy life while we can still live it.

I. The Essential Unity of the Human Personality

That each man is a single being is a fact of human awareness that critical philosophy finds it hard to attack. The distinction in man between soul and body has sometimes been
interpreted as meaning that the soul is the human personality and the body merely a prison house in which the soul
is temporarily detained. According to such a teaching, death
would be a welcome release from an existence made completely unnatural for the soul by its union with the material
substance of the body.

This teaching has always been objected to as inconsistent
with the basic principles of divine revelation, as they touch
upon the condition of man. For the majority of Catholic
theologians the obvious unity of the human personality pre-
cludes the absolute distinction between soul and body that

would make each one a distinct being. The traditional theory that the soul is the substantial form of the body leaves much to be desired, and efforts to express it precisely give rise to much metaphysical controversy. Beyond the area of dispute, however, we are confronted with the fact of man's superiority over the rest of creation. We have noted that the spiritual soul, different from the body in its very being, affords the explanation within the individual man of his place of honor in the universe, and constitutes the foundation of human rights.

As death brings about the termination of bodily life, the teaching on the spirituality of the human soul, essentially different in its substance from the body, affords philosophical foundation for the divinely revealed truth that man will survive the fact of death and live on eternally. This doctrine must meet the objection previously noted that the whole man is made up of body and soul, and does not consist merely in the soul.

Catholic theology has always taught that in the world to come the union of body and soul, interrupted by death, will be reestablished. This means that the happiness of eternal life, the ultimate object of man's striving here below, will eventually be shared in by the body. Many secondary points connected with this teaching are dealt with extensively in Catholic theology. We note it here because it is the starting point for the presentation of what Catholics teach their children about life after death. Unless the body rises again, the happiness of man in the life to come will be objectively incomplete. Catholic theologians hold that the essential happiness of men in heaven is experienced through the higher powers of the soul. When soul and body are reunited, however, a condition of total fulfillment will be realized.

II. The Purpose of Life

It is necessary at this point only to recall and summarize certain teachings that have already been touched upon. Catholic children are taught that the activities of life are

directed objectively toward the ultimate end of possessing
God. When death occurs, a period of pilgrimage and preparation has ended. Each man has had the responsibility of
living in such a manner as to attain eternal union with God.
Divine Revelation has clarified and extended the philosophical truth that God is man's last end. To reach God is to experience the total happiness of which every pleasurable moment of this life can be only an approximation.

Catholic theology has been blamed for overinsistence
upon the relations of the future life to the present, and for
failing to deal vigorously with problems relating to individual and social justice. Whether or not this complaint is
justified, we cannot escape the fact that the individual man's
span of life extends at best over a single century, and in
most cases over a much shorter period of years. We teach
our children that the human soul will never die. Sheer
logic compels us to direct our attention to the life beyond
the grave, and to point out that we must be careful so to
pass over the present life as not to imperil our happiness for
the eternity which is to follow death.

III. *Death—the End and the Beginning*

The grief caused by death is a most natural experience.
The desire to live and to enjoy the companionship of those
we love is strong in every normal human consciousness. From
his earliest years the child of truly Catholic parents is conditioned to face the fact of death in the light of its meaning
for eternal life. One of the most consoling thoughts of the
liturgy for departed souls is that death does not take away
life but merely gives it a new direction. When the life of the
body is dissolved, an eternal dwelling place is prepared for
those who have lived consistently with their Catholic faith.
The end of all that has been valuable for temporal well-
being, death is the beginning of a new life in which the tears
of sorrow will be wiped away and the pain and misery of
bodily suffering will no longer be feared.

The Catholic religion fails in one of its essential purposes when men do not put their earthly life in its proper relation with the life to come. The Catholic religion affords deep and lasting comfort as its teachings throw light on the meaning of death, and as it causes hope to rise from the shattering experiences of sorrow which death must cause. When death is sudden, and especially when it comes after a short life, grief can be overpowering if men are left to themselves. We often note the contrast between the despondency of those who lack the support of faith, and those whose courage is supported by faith as death stalks across the pathways of life.

Perhaps we find here some confirmation of the teachings from which the Catholic attitude toward death emerges. If God is infinitely good and infinitely merciful, and if man is God's creature, the longing for a future life demands the fulfillment suggested by the teachings of divine revelation which we have set forth. Only if death is the beginning of a new life can the termination of life which death brings about lose its frustrating effect.

The Catholic child is brought up from his infancy to love God who made him and to find support in the reality of God's promises as he meets defeat and disappointment. To say that all this is pure imagination is to overlook its stabilizing influence on those who accept it and live by it. Can fantasy and mockery have such enduring and universal effects? Can the existentialist materialism which leads to despair be grounded in truth, and the Catholic idealism that builds up hope and courage be cruelly false?

IV. The Judgment

It is the teaching of the Catholic faith that, at the moment of death, God judges every man according to his works and according to his dispositions of soul. Those who have been guilty of serious violations of God's law find comfort in the hope of pardon which God holds out if they truly repent before they die. Those who live according to God's law become confirmed in the friendship with Him which will be their title to eternal happiness if they persevere in it until death.

Why God makes death the moment of judgment and decrees never to change the sentence passed at this moment on the individual soul is a question bound up intimately with the whole mystery of creation. We can never understand fully the relation between man and God. Nor can we understand, from our present point of view, the change that will come over the individual soul as it passes from the experiences of its present condition to the new understanding of its relation with God that will open up as it faces eternity.

The life that follows death will of necessity be different from that which waxes and wanes over the years of earthly existence. The possibility of repentance that continues through life will not, according to Catholic teaching, continue beyond the moment of death.

This is the basis of the doctrine of the judgment. It supposes at the moment of death a changeless fixing of the attitude toward God which has developed during life. In accordance with this attitude, God will decree for the soul an eternity of happiness or an eternity of misery; an eternal possession of God, with consequent perfect happiness that can never be lost, or an eternity of suffering which consists principally in clear understanding of the need of God and the impossibility of ever finding happiness and rest in His presence.

This is the substance of the teaching of the Catholic faith on the judgment that will follow death. The words heaven and hell, designating respectively the state of those who will be saved and those who will be lost, require much theological refinement and dissociation from imaginary elements. For the Catholic, however, heaven and hell are not products of the imagination. They correspond, on the one hand, to a condition of perfect happiness which transcends the passing joys of earthly life; and, on the other hand, to a condition of misery far more penetrating than the deepest thrusts of sorrow and pain that are felt prior to death.

The child of Catholic parents is taught to believe in the judgment that will follow death and to live in constant anticipation of it. Judgment, however, in the total structure of Catholic theology, is not a terrorizing thought, even though it is sobering and deterring. The possibility that one may reject God's friendship and thus be subject to His decree of damnation is a necessary implication of divine justice. The devout Catholic is exhorted to remember his last end, that he may never commit serious sin.

D. Death and Life in the Practice of the Catholic Religion

Catholicism, developing within the Christian tradition, has always kept the thought of death in the background of its religious activity. Christianity from a Catholic point of view has no meaning apart from its relation with the life to come. Christ did not become man to make the world a better place to live in. His mission was directed towards the happiness of heaven; He thought of the world not as an everlasting abode, but as a place of pilgrimage.

In the practice of the Catholic religion great stress is laid on the sanctification of the free activity which is concerned with man's immediate temporal needs. Much stress is laid, too, on the continuity between man's life on earth and his life for eternity. Prayers for the dead, and works of charity among the living serve likewise to direct the attention of devout Catholics to the peace that will follow suffering and strife.

It would be wrong, however, to think of Catholicism as a religion of sorrow. The road to happiness must indeed begin in self-discipline and sacrifice; there is no short cut to heaven over the easy ways of earthly comfort. The suffering of the Catholic, however, has a purifying and ennobling effect. As the child is gradually initiated into the Catholic way of life, he learns to look for the sources of true joy in the efforts he makes to be successful in the world. He is taught to project

the joys of his present experience, as he seeks them legiti-
mately, into the eternal happiness toward which his every free
act is, of its nature, directed.

I. *The Sanctification of Free Activity*

Whatever a person does freely must be directed toward
something that has value in itself. Free activity cannot be
aimless; it must have a goal. It is the function of religion to
discover those goals which are suitable for man's natural
longings and to bring the details of daily life into relation
with these goals. Seen in its relation to the ultimate goal of
life, every free action, however seemingly insignificant, has
a supernatural value that can be brought into focus by prayer
and meditation.

The child of Catholic parents is taught that religion is
not just a system of observances to be carried out at church
services and forgotten at other times. For the thoroughly indoctrinated Catholic the thought of a Sunday religion is re-
pulsive. As he assists at Mass on Sundays, and often during
the week as well, the Catholic child learns that the whole
field of his free activity must be informed by religious motivation. There can be no schizophrenic cleavage within the
Christian personality. The Catholic cannot be pious on Sundays and unscrupulous on weekdays. He cannot profess to
love God as he joins in the offering of the Mass, and be completely forgetful of the laws of God in his pursuit of worldly
gain. He cannot join with his fellow Christians at prayer,
and then break the ties which prayer has strengthened by
words and deeds directed towards evil ends.

Thousands of Catholics, following up a movement which
began a century ago, known as the Apostleship of Prayer,
begin the day by making the Morning Offering. This is a
prayerful uniting of man's will with the Will of God, made
possible through the mystery of the Incarnation of the Son
of God, born into the world of a virgin mother. As each day's
problems arise, and each day's opportunities for doing good
are made available, the Catholic seeks to direct his free activ-

ity toward the everlasting rewards of heaven. Death thus becomes the turning point at which the hope of lasting peace may be realized. The obstacles of earlier years become easier to overcome. The disillusionments which accompany waning physical strength are brightened by anticipation of God's justice and mercy in His heavenly kingdom.

II. The Relation Between the Living and the Dead

Desire to communicate with the dead has always been strong among the living. Catholic theology affords a solid foundation for the fulfillment of this desire, but the teaching authority of the Church has always discouraged efforts to enter into direct contact with departed souls. The hope of a future reward is sustained by the doctrine of the Mystical Body of Christ. As all members of the human body are united, so there is a union among all who have been baptized in Christ and never separated from Him by serious sin.

In the Constitution on the Church, promulgated by the Second Vatican Council, this truth is given authentic and vivid expression:

> Until the Lord shall come in His majesty . . . some of His disciples are still on earth; some, having died, are purified, and others are in glory; but all, in varying ways and degrees, are in communion in the same charity of God and neighbor. . . . Therefore, the union of the wayfarers with the brethren who have gone to sleep in the peace of Christ is not in the least weakened or interrupted, but on the contrary is strengthened by communication of spiritual goods. (Art. 49)

In accordance with this teaching, the faithful in the Church on earth pay honor to the saints in heaven and seek their intercession. They pray not only for one another but for the souls in Purgatory, who are being purified from the consequences of their sins and whose sufferings can be alleviated and shortened by the suffrages of the living. Those who are already in heaven likewise intercede with God for the faithful on earth and for the suffering souls in Purgatory.

This teaching of Catholic faith does much to lessen the

fear of death and to clarify the meaning of life. Veneration of the saints and prayers for the souls of the departed are so much a part of Catholic life that the child comes quickly and easily to an understanding of the truths of revelation from which they proceed. As the priest comes to administer the sacraments to the sick and the dying, children become increasingly aware of the concern of the Church for the future life. The presence of the priest at the bedside of one who is about to die, and the services held for the dead before burial and on the day of burial speak eloquently to young people about the need of preparing for eternity. As the memory of loved ones is recalled on the anniversaries of their death, sentiments of hope blend with those of sorrow.

III. Preparation for Death by Works of Mercy

One of the perennial problems of the Catholic religion is to bring the thought of death into relation with the immediate problems of daily life and to do so without creating the impression that it is wrong to experience the joys of our present existence. The Catholic religion has often been described as a good religion in which to die. Those who practice it learn that preparation for death cannot overlook the facts of life. Living usefully for others is the best way to prepare for dying. There is no contradiction between a life of active service and the desire, so plaintively expressed by St. Paul, to be dissolved and to be with Christ. (*Philippians* 1:23)

Our contemporary society sets great store by good works. This is quite consistent with the objectives of Catholic spirituality. While noting that the happiness of heaven is something essentially personal, Christian writers have always pointed out the relation between love of God and love of neighbor. The entire second chapter of the Epistle of St. James is an exhortation to works of mercy. Christ, who was no respecter of persons, loved all men, regardless of their material circumstances. The kingdom of heaven belongs to those who are rich in faith, not to those who have amassed the riches of this world.

Selfishness, often associated with good works, is less likely to predominate when those who are helped are seen as called to happiness by God. Misery, in its earthly situation, is something abominable; something to be overcome because it makes us miserable too. Poverty, whatever its cause, is a hateful condition when we think of it only as the privation of material sufficiency. To relieve the poor only that they may become rich is to meet the problem on its lowest possible level.

There must always be those who have much and those who do not have enough. Possession of wealth arouses the fear that it may be lost and the desire to compensate for future losses by every possible present gain. Giving to charity from abundance often implies the guilty desire to perpetuate the condition of need that is relieved by magnificent donations. It is hard for one who sees only this world to live in accordance with the saying that "you cannot take it with you." The concept of stewardship, which suggests that wealth is a gift of God, to be used for God's purposes, is clarified by projecting one's present generosity to others into the future life in which both giver and receiver will be happy according to merit. The thought of death moves many to share their wealth with others unselfishly and charitably.

IV. The Joy of Living

The Catholic religion must direct those who practice it toward the immediate concerns of everyday life. The thought of death, always in the background, can never be allowed to develop a habitual attitude of discouragement or of indifference toward the natural happiness which comes from honest striving for temporal rewards. There is no conflict between Christianity and humanism when humanism sets man in his proper relation with God.

Life on earth offers a great measure of happiness. The Catholic child is taught to seek this happiness in accordance with the restraints of the natural law and the ideals held out in the revelation of man's supernatural greatness. Suffering must be endured when it cannot be avoided; but it is not wrong to work mightily to remove its causes. Sacrifice must be made willingly when it is necessary for wholesome self-discipline or for the helpful service of family and friends. Sacrifice must not be thought of, however, as desirable in itself, or as the only religious approach to the happiness of heaven. The Catholic child is taught to die, but he must also be taught to live and to enjoy the comforts which social progress and charitable cooperation make possible during the years of earthly life.

Death is a stern fact of human experience. The religious life of Catholics who know the truths of their faith and live by them will not remove them from the fear of death. It will keep them, however, from being crushed by the thought of their own death and by the separation from their loved ones which breaks the peaceful course of life. Catholicism provides many comforts for those who suffer bereavement. It would be impossible to single any one such comfort, or any particular religious practice, as the avenue of approach to this most serious problem. There is no specific pattern of Catholic religious observance which concentrates on the manner in which death is to be anticipated. It is the Christian way of life, developed within the Catholic community, that teaches the child, step by step, how to adjust to the reality of death and how to overcome the natural sorrow occasioned by death.

The subject of death is by no means unmentionable among Catholics. As an aspect of the greater problem of the meaning of life, death finds an answer that is satisfying to the inquiring mind, even as it affords relief for the emotional tension which builds up in those who lose their loved ones and who must themselves come one day to the end of their span of earthly life.

Judaism, we are constantly reminded, is more than a creed; it is a way of life. Its doctrines and teachings are given practical expression in our daily actions, so that the difficult journey through life is eased and ennobled. The sages emphasize that it is the sacred duty of the Jew to conduct his life so as to make it a continuous act of service to God and to man.

The real purpose of religion is to open the heart to true joy and to strengthen the spirit in those inevitable moments of darkness and despair.

Over the centuries the rabbis have evolved a pattern of practices and rites which are concerned with every aspect of death, and these include tender regard for the dying and deep concern for the sorrowing family. The ritual of burial and the manner of mourning are prescribed to preserve, inter alia, *the qualities of taste and meaning. Moreover, the rabbis endeavored to reconcile the natural and spontaneous expression of profound grief with the reasoned and resigned self-control that the Jew is enjoined to practice. Jewish laws of mourning are many and detailed, but they always are inspired with a warm humanity; this is in pursuance of the guiding principles of the rabbis, always to adopt the "lenient view" when questions arise in connection with the laws of mourning.*

Rabbi Earl A. Grollman, D.D., has been the spiritual leader of the Beth El Temple Center in Belmont, Massachusetts, since 1951. He has served as President of the Massachusetts Board of Rabbis, the only rabbinical group in Massachusetts that serves the needs of Orthodox, Conservative, and Reform Jews.

CHAPTER IX

The Ritualistic and Theological Approach of the Jew

EARL A. GROLLMAN

FOR PEOPLE OF ALL AGES, death poses the eternal mystery at the core of our most important philosophical systems of thought. Essentially what adults transmit to the child in connection with the subject will depend largely upon their own religious resources. The wise parents will discuss the subject from the point of view of their own faith but at the child's level in an informal and casual atmosphere, while imparting love, warmth, and support as well as knowledge and belief.

Above all, the best teaching is that which elicits the creative participation of the child. The parent should strive for spiritual development rather than the positive acceptance of a theological doctrine. One should never impart a fanciful doctrine that the youngster will later need to unlearn; adults should test their own beliefs in the light of what they teach. The child, guileless as he may seem, easily senses the parents' insincerity. Adults should not indicate that they have the final answers which the offspring must accept. No one knows God fully or understands the mystery of death. The door must remain open to doubt, questioning, and differences of opinion. The youngster will better develop the capacity to understand the real implications of death when he lives in an open, loving, and truthful universe and the surviving family are open, loving, and truthful to him—when death is not associated with guilt, superstition, and unchallenging dogma.

Religion is an experience as well as belief. Children learn what they live. They live what is meaningful to them. Adults working with youngsters in relation to death are afforded the unique opportunity to offer a more meaningful religion, a more meaningful life, and to aid the children in becoming what they mean to themselves.

RITUAL

For children as well as adults, the ceremony surrounding death is of enormous significance. The Jewish faith suggests rites that play a vital role in the healing work of grief. The bereaved must realize that a loved one is gone and that the void must be filled gradually in a constructive way. He should not suppress memories or the disturbing, even guilt-producing recollections which are an inevitable part of all human relationships. Rather, shock and grief are structured by definite and solemn procedures. Joshua Liebman in *Peace of Mind* points to the wisdom of the Hebrew sages in assigning a definite period of mourning participated in by the entire family.

The wise parent should discuss the Jewish customs relating to death in a gentle and nonthreatening manner. The child should not have to wait until the death of a loved one to be hurriedly and frantically informed by a weeping mother that people are buried in special gardens or that stones or plaques are placed on each grave to indicate who is resting there. It is suggested that one explain the realities of death under more ideal circumstances, rather than with retroactive interpretation in the face of grief.

When death does occur, a child from approximately the age of seven on should be encouraged to attend the funeral. To shut a youngster out of this experience might be quite costly and damaging to his future development. He is an integral part of the family unit and should participate with them on this sad but momentous occasion. However, if the child is unwilling, he should not be forced to go or made to feel guilty because "he let the family down." If he does not attend the funeral, it may be wise to provide an opportunity at some later time to visit the cemetery and see the grave.

In Judaism, from the moment that one learns of the passing of a dear one, there are specific religious rituals to be followed which help to order one's life. The Jewish funeral is a rite of separation. The bad dream is real. The presence of the casket actualizes the experience. It transforms the process of denial to the acceptance of reality. The service itself is relatively brief and is devoted to prayers and to a description of the loved one's life and qualities that might be perpetuated by the living. By the child's attendance he, too, offers his last respects, feels enriched by being part of this person's existence, and through his presence is able to express publicly his own love and devotion. All the emotional reactions a child is likely to have to death in the family—sorrow and loneliness, anger and rejection, guilt, anxiety about the future, and the conviction that nothing is certain or stable anymore—can be considerably lessened if the child feels that he knows what is occurring and that adults are not trying to hide things from him.

Formal mourning periods of diminishing intensity follow death. After the service, the *Shivah,* first seven-day mourning period, begins. The bereaved remain at home receiving a continuous stream of condolence calls. Difficult as this may be, it helps in keeping their minds active and their attentions engaged. Also, it is important because it lends the comfort of the loving concern of family and friends. The youngster should not be arbitrarily dismissed. He should be afforded the chance to face grief and mingle with the family. Some enlightened adults have helped a child feel that he is important by allowing him to share in the family duties such as answering doorbells and telephones, helping with chores, and even in the preparation of the *Seudat Havra-ah,* the meal of consolation. He is given the opportunity to help them and be helped by them.

Following the *Shivah* comes the *Sh-loshim,* the thirty days. The mourners resume normal activity but they avoid places of entertainment, and they continue to recite certain prayers. At the end of the thirty days, ritualistic mourning is over except for immediate members of the family, when mourning continues an entire year.

The person over 13 might continue to attend the *Minyan* (daily worship) and the Sabbath services. He reads aloud the

Kaddish prayer, originally not a liturgy for the dead, but a pledge from the living to dedicate one's life to the God of Life, "Magnified and Sanctified." This is the highest approach to commemorate the memory of a loved one. Each time during the year that he recites the *Kaddish,* he reinforces both the reality of death and the affirmation of life. He openly displays his own needed concern and profound feeling of being a good son, father, brother, or husband. He participates with others who are also suffering the emotional trauma of bereavement. He belongs to the largest company in the world—the company of those who have known suffering and death. This great, universal sense of sorrow helps to unite all human hearts and dissolve all other feelings into those of common sympathy and understanding. He shares with others who give of their supporting love, affection, understanding, and compassion.

The importance of rituals to a child is dramatically portrayed in the French film, *Forbidden Games.* A girl's parents died in an air raid. She received comfort by constantly playing a game of "funeral" and providing every dead creature with an elaborate interment of flowers and ornate casket. "Playing" at burying things helped her to relive, digest, and ultimately master the shock of her parents' death. The child had succeeded in doing something for the dead and bringing relief for herself.

In the Jewish traditions of bereavement, the child could well feel that even though he should have done more for his now deceased loved one, the ritual he can at least do right. Here he can be made to understand in clear-cut, unmistakable terms what is desired of him. Perhaps by carrying out the ceremonial of daily worship, he will feel that he has regained the love he has lost, that he comes to peace with his own conscience which could personify for him the highest internal ideals. Even rituals which might seem irksome and pointless to others may be heartily welcome. They could be the sought-for punishment, the neutralizer, the deprivation that could balance off the imagined indulgence at the bottom of the guilt.

Jewish rituals are community rituals. They are performed only by those who share a religious sameness and by no one outside it. The youngster is brought into contact with those who also have a "we-feeling," a security which Freud called "the clear awareness of an inner identity, the secret of the same inner construction." The traditions create a sense of solidarity, of belongingness, the feeling that one is a member of the group with all the comfort, gratification, pride, and even pain that such a sense brings. For the ceremony is the same for all. It is definite and prescribed. If one performs it, no one can do more. In ritual, one can love his coreligionist because he does not strive against him and is not being striven against.

Judaism is strict in limiting mourning to the given periods and the customary observances. Excessive grief is taken as want of trust in God. The faith holds it as desirable that with time the havoc wrought by death should help to repair itself. Though no one is ever the same after a bereavement as he was before, he is expected, when mourning is over, to take up existence for the sake of life itself. The garment that the pious mourner rends can be sewn and worn again. The mark is there, but life resumes its course. The approach of Judaism is the climb from the valley of despair to the higher road of affirmative living. The observance of the Jewish laws and customs of mourning helps the child face reality, gives honor to the deceased, and guides the bereaved in the reaffirmation of life.

THEOLOGY

Jewish people pray to the God of Abraham, the God of Isaac, and the God of Jacob. The God of each is the same God. But each man has to find God in his own way. In a concept of death, each differs in reactions and belief. Judaism has no dogmatic creed. During the course of the centuries, many ideas have been presented.

The great scholar, George F. Moore, enumerated the many speculations of death in Jewish literature and stated: "Any attempt to systematize the Jewish notions of the here-after imposes upon them an order and consistency which does not exist in them."

In the beginning of the first Christian century, the party of the Sadducees actually rejected a belief in an afterlife; while at the same time, the Pharisees proclaimed that there was a world-to-come. The bitterest complaint against the doc-trine of the hereafter was that, by directing men's minds heavenward, it diverted them from taking action to correct social evils and encouraged a toleration of unfortunate con-temporary conditions.

Even those who believed in a life beyond considered it futile to speculate on the nature of the world-to-come. "Such knowledge," says the Psalmist, "is too wonderful for me, it is too high. I cannot attain it." The sages quoted with approval the stern caution of Ben Sirach: "Do not inquire what is beyond thine understanding and do not investigate what is hidden from thee." The Jewish philosopher, Moses Maimoni-des, asserted that when we discuss this subject we are like blind men trying to understand the nature of light. "Know that just as a blind man can form no idea of colors nor a deaf man comprehend sounds, so bodies cannot comprehend the delights of the soul. And even as fish do not know the element fire because they exist ever in its opposite, so are the delights of the world of the spirit unknown to this world of flesh."

Judaism, then, has not wholly harmonized or integrated a concept of death and the hereafter. However, in spite of the varied beliefs throughout its circuitous history, there are observed certain central and unifying patterns. These con-cepts follow.

The Inevitability of Death

"The Lord God formed man of dust from the ground, and breathed into his nostrils the breath of life, and man became a living being." (Genesis 2:7) So the Psalmist says that when God sends forth His breath, living beings, whether men or animals, are created, and when God takes His breath away, they die. (Psalms 104:29–30) When man's "breath departs, he returns to his earth." (Psalms 146:4) Ecclesiastes states with utter plainness: "The fate of the sons of men and the fate of beasts is the same; as one dies, so dies the other. They all have the same breath, and man has no advantage over the beasts . . . all go to one place; all are from the dust, and all turn to dust again." And the words of Genesis, "You are dust, and to dust you shall return."

Death is regarded by Jews as real—quite dreadfully real. It is the annihilation of life conceived in its concreteness, the rupture of the pleasures of family and friends, the destruction of the possibility of man's enjoying the praise of God. The "wise women" from Tekoa in 2 Samuel 14:14 remark, "We must all die; we are like water spilt on the ground, which cannot be gathered up again." According to Ecclesiastes 9:5, "The dead know nothing." *Sheol* is "the land of gloom and deep darkness, the land of gloom and chaos" (Job 10:21–22) and "the land of primeval ruins" (Ezekiel 26:20) ; "the land of silence." (Psalms 94:17) "In death there is no remembrance of Thee; in *Sheol* who can give Thee praise?" (Psalms 115:17) "The dead have no more for ever any share in all that is done under the sun." (Ecclesiastes 9:6) "There is no work or thought or wisdom in *Sheol,* to which you are going." (Ecclesiastes 9:10) "Are Thy wonders known in the darkness, or Thy saving help in the land of forgetfulness?" (Psalms 88:12)

Man is under "the sentence of death." (Sirach 41:3) Yet he need not fear it because "whether life is for ten or one hundred or a thousand years, there is no inquiring about it in Hades." (Sirach 41:4) And yet, perhaps we should say, therefore, "O death, how bitter is the reminder of you to one who lives at peace among his possessions, to a man without distraction, who is prosperous in everything, and who still has the vigor to enjoy his food!" (Sirach 41:1)

No form of human existence can escape the democracy of

death. It is part of the processes of birth, growth, and decay. He knows that "like the grass of the field, he is one whose place will know him no more." (Psalms 103:15) "Man that is born of woman is of few days . . . he comes forth like a flower, and withers; he flees like a shadow, and continues not . . . his days are determined, and the number of his months is with Thee, and Thou has appointed his bounds that he cannot pass." (Job 14:1–5) "Man breathes his last, and where is he? As waters fail from a lake, and a river wastes away and dries up, so man lies down and rises not again." (Job 14:10–12) He is " a wind that passes and comes not again." (Psalms 78:39)

In Judaism, death is both real and inescapable. Man knows that he must die, for death is an organic, natural, and logical part of life. For "what man can live and never see death?" (Psalms 89:48) Often in the face of death, man better understands the meaning of life.

The Affirmation of Life

Judaism is more than a creed. It is a way of life, for it is in the life of the Jew that the Jewish faith becomes real. "Better is one day of happiness and good deeds in *this* world than all the life in the *world-to-come*."

While there are beliefs in Judaism concerning death, the major emphasis is on life. Judaism stresses love of life by urging utilization of one's powers for the sanctification and ennoblement of his existence upon earth. The Jew understands that man is a mortal being, and yet at the same time man must declare: "One world at a time is enough." God's gift of life must be enjoyed to the fullest. In other words, Judaism does not ignore the mystery of death but is primarily concerned with the miracle of life. Man lives authentically by accepting not only his dying nature but his living spirit.

The priority of life is affirmed in time of death. The Hebrew Bible tells of the time when a first child was born to Bathsheba and David. The child was critically ill. David spent the whole night in supplication and refused to eat for he was prostrate with apprehension. Shortly, the infant died. The servants were afraid to tell David of the sad news. But David sensed from their behavior that the child was no longer living. As soon as his fears were confirmed, he rose from the earth, washed himself, and worshipped, then ate. His servants were puzzled over the strange contrast between his behavior before and after the child's death. David explained as follows: "While the child was yet alive, I fasted and wept; for I said, 'Who knoweth whether the Lord will not be gracious to me, that the child may live?' But now that he is dead, wherefore should I fast? Can I bring him back again?"

There is the story that when David himself died, his son Solomon posed this dilemma to the authorities: "My father is dead and lying in the sun, and my father's dogs are hungry. What shall I do?" To which, an answer was returned as follows: "Feed the dogs first, then take care of your father's body." It was not because the Jews were insensitive to the anguish of death that they established this priority but because they were keenly imbued with the affirmation of life.

Deathlessness of Man's Spirit

With the development of beliefs of other religions in retribution and resurrection, Judaism also turned its attention to what happens after death. Whatever one's belief in a world-to-come, there is the acceptance that man transcends death in naturalistic fashion. Man is immortal: *in body,* through his children; *in thought,* through the survival of his memory; *in influence,* by virtue of the continuance of his personality as a force among those who come after him; and *ideally,* through the identification with the timeless things of the spirit.

A commentator of the Bible explained this immortality of influence in a discussion of, "And Jacob lived." (Genesis 47:28) Of how few men can we repeat a phrase like, "And Jacob lived"? When many a man dies, a death notice appears in the press. In reality, it is a life-notice because, but for it, the world would never have known the man had ever been alive. Only he who has been a force for human goodness, and abides in hearts and in a world made better by his presence, can be said to have *lived*. Only such a one is heir to immortality.

In the theme of the *Midrash,* a hungry fox was eyeing some luscious fruit in a garden. To his dismay, he could find no way to enter. At last he discovered an opening through which he thought he might possibly get in, but he soon found that the hole was too small to admit his body. "Well," he thought, "if I fast three days I will be able to squeeze through." He did so, and he now feasted to his heart's delight on the grapes and all the other good things in the orchard. But lo! when he wanted to escape before the owner of the garden would find him, he discovered to his great distress that the opening was again too small for him. Poor animal! And again he had to fast three days. As he escaped, he cast a farewell glance upon the scene of his late revels saying "O garden, charming art thou, delicious are thy fruits! But what have I now for all my labor and cunning?"

So it is with man. Naked he comes into the world; naked must he leave it. After all his toil, he carries nothing away with him except the deeds he leaves behind. This is the immortality that is concerned with the effects of our lives that go on and on in this world. Whether for good or evil, this influence continues. The mother's loving caress as well as her angry slap—both continue to ruffle the surface waters and the hidden depths of life long after they occur.

Death is not the end of life—not just in terms of another possible world, but in the real and tangible sense of ongoing ideals and influence that continue shaping the affections one has held and served. Life points always to the future, when one shall become another heritage and influence, whether in ordinary personal memory, or through the thoughts and acts and decisions that give a lasting grace to ongoing human existence. The ancient Egyptians buried their dead with all the things a person needs, such as clothes, weapons, and food, and were more preoccupied with death than with life; the Hebrews, on the other hand, believed that "in the hour of a man's departure from this world, neither silver nor gold nor precious stones nor pearls accompany him, but only study and good works."

Just as man relies without fear upon the Power greater than himself during his earthly journey; just as he rests securely upon the bosom of mystery every time he falls asleep at night—so he trusts the universe beyond time also. He recognizes that it is part of wisdom not to seek to remove the veil from before birth or after death, but to live fully, richly, nobly, here and now, and make possible a society where other men can so live.

"The rabbis," wrote Louis Ginzberg, "believed in another world and often spoke of rewards awaiting the righteous after their death. Nevertheless, the development of the religious thought of the Jew showed marked tendency to fix the center of gravity of religion not in the thought of a world beyond but rather to foster and establish it in the actual life of man on earth. In this respect the scribes and the rabbis were the true successors of the prophets."

Recompense

Concerning the final outcome of man's career, many affirmed a belief that death was not nor could be the end of life. Should there not be reward for the righteous as well as punishment for the wicked? It was true that Judaism taught that men should not serve God in the spirit of "bondsmen who tend their master for the sake of wages." Still, it was held that virtue must be repaid and iniquity punished. If God is a God of Justice, and if man does not meet with perfect equity during his lifetime, then he must find it afterward. In the hereafter, the "crooked will be straight, and to each will be given according to his deserts." Thus, this world becomes an antechamber of the world-to-come where recompense and punishments are to be meted out. "Man is reminded that he must give an account to the Eternal Judge. None will escape His punishment, and no virtue will be unrewarded." (*Mish-*

na, Aboth, 4:16–17) "He who labors before the Sabbath (that is, in this world) will eat on the Sabbath (that is, in the world-to-come); but if a man does not labor before the Sabbath, how can he eat on the Sabbath day?" (*Talmud, Abodah Zarah,* 3B)

There was postulated a continued existence of the soul after death. The Hebrew expressions for soul in the Bible (*Nefesh, Neshamah,* and *Ruach*) indicated a principle of the human body which was the vehicle of all the functions of life. In the last centuries before the Christian Era, the idea developed that there was a distinction between the body and the soul. The soul was the immortal part of man that was independent of the body. "The soul," says the *Midrash,* "may be compared to a princess who is married to a commoner. The most precious gift that the husband brings to his princess fails to thrill her. Likewise, if one were to offer the soul all the pleasures of the world, it would remain indifferent to them because it belongs to a higher order of existence." The soul is the unwilling partner of the body, unwilling to be born and unwilling to die. "Man is born perforce and dies perforce."

Before the body comes into being, the soul already exists. It is pure and untainted by "original sin." Every morning the devout Jew prays, "O my God, the soul which Thou gave me is pure." The exact place of the soul cannot be determined, and this is another of the mysteries of life.

Oftentimes children, in their struggle to understand death, will ask such questions as "What happens to us after we die? Are we dead and gone forever?" Perhaps their questions can best be answered by drawing a parallel in story form: A little boy once found a bird's nest near his home which contained speckled eggs. Fascinated, he watched it for a long time until he had to take a trip to the city. Upon his return, he rushed to the nest to see the eggs. He was shocked to find that the beautiful eggs were broken. All he saw were empty shells. He wept before his father, "These beautiful eggs are spoiled and broken." "No, my son," answered his father, "they're not spoiled. All you see is the empty shell. The birds have escaped from the eggs, and soon they will be flying around in the sky. This is the way nature intended it to be. And so it is when we die. Our souls escape from our bodies . . . all that's left is the empty shell."

"But," asked the lad, "how do you know that we have a soul? You can't see it or touch it. How do you know?" The parent replied: "We don't have visible proof, but many people have faith that it is so. They believe that the soul is that part of God in us which lives on forever. And no part of God can be destroyed. They do not believe that the soul depends on the body for its existence. For example, it is amazing how many people who are totally disabled because of disease or sickness still have such wonderful minds and high spirits. There was a great man by the name of Franz Rosenzweig, whose entire body was paralyzed; he could move only one finger and nothing else. Yet, his mind was so great and his will so strong that he was able to dictate some of his greatest thoughts to his wife by the mere tapping of his finger through a code system. One cannot help but believe that there was a great spirit in him distinct from his disabled body.

"When we believe in something very much without being able to prove it, that is faith. When Columbus set out on his first voyage from the shores of Spain, he was not sure what was beyond the vision of his eye, but he had faith that the great sea had another shore. So we cannot see beyond this life, but many believe that the soul continues. You can trust in God!"

Resurrection

Still another concept of the hereafter is resurrection (*Tehiyyath Hamethem*). The earlier religion of Israel was more concerned with nationhood and conceived of retribution in national terms. Rewards and punishment were indissolubly related to the corporate people, Israel, not the single individual. It was later that resurrection was interpreted as the reunion of body and soul together standing in judgment before God. The dead will rise and then be judged as to whether they will share in the blessings of the messianic era.

Soul's Transmigration

For others, there is the belief in the transmigration of the soul *(Gilgul Hanefesh)*, where human beings after death would enter another body and thus a new life. This doctrine's acceptance was widely held by the mystical Chassidim. According to the *Kabbala,* the soul of Aaron was first reincarnated in Eli and then in Ezra.

Reform, Orthodox, Conservative

O. Lazarus in *Liberal Judaism and Its Standpoint* summarizes a Reform Jewish attitude toward death: "We cannot believe in the resurrection of the body that perishes with death. We feel, however, that there is that within us which is immortal, and is not bounded by time and space. It is this, man's soul, as it is called, which continues, so we believe, to live after the death of the body. To it, death is but an incident of life. It brings no violent change. The mere fact of death does not turn a wicked soul into a good one. When we enter the future life, our reason leads us to think that we are, at first, morally and spiritually (dare one add, even intellectually?) the same as we were before we embarked upon the 'adventure of death.' How we progress and develop towards goodness, what suffering of purification we may be called upon to endure or what rewards of pure joy we may experience, we do not know. We cannot regard death as an evil. It is universal—part and parcel, so it would appear, of God's scheme of things. It comes from Him, even as we believe life does. Both must therefore be good. Both are natural and inevitable. Why should we fear?"

The Orthodox Jew is committed to a belief in recompense, immortality, and resurrection. The scales of cosmic equity will end up in balance with the body of the dead arising from the grave to be reunited with the soul. In the presence of all the multitudes of all generations, God will pronounce judgment of bliss or damnation.

The Conservative movement has retained some of the prayers in the liturgy where belief is expressed in resurrection and immortality of the soul. For many, the concepts are not regarded literally, but figuratively and poetically. They retain the speculative rabbinic and medieval view of the soul as a distinct entity enjoying an independent existence.

Even within each of the three Jewish movements, there is the widest possible latitude for differences of opinion. There are many thoughts, yet none is declared authoritative and final. The tradition teaches but, at the same time, seems to say there is much we do not know and still more we have to learn. And even then, only God can completely discern the mysteries of life and death.

Death: A Preparation for Life

It is undeniably true that the past lives in us. It is doubly true that the future is already present and being created through man in the quality and character of the preparations he makes for death.

Life is regarded by the Hebrew Bible as coming directly from God. It was He who breathed life into the clay of the first man and who creates all living things on earth. God is the sovereign over all events of life, including death. It is the "Lord who gives and the Lord who takes." When the dark grave swallows our dearest on earth, Judaism bids us say: "It was God who gave this joy unto us; it is God who hath taken it from us to Himself. Praised be the Name of the Lord."

Man knows that he belongs to time: "The years of our life are threescore years and ten." (Psalms 90:10) He knows that "like the grass of the field he is one whose place will know him no more." (Psalms 103:15) Only God is "from everlasting to everlasting." (Psalms 90:2) The Scripture expressed the belief that life is not only holy and divine, but is granted to man as a favor from God. Long life was often considered a reward for the fulfillment of God's commandments. In the Fifth Commandment, there is a promise of longevity for those who honor their parents. The choice between good and evil is described in Deuteronomy 30:19 as the choice between life and death. In many of the passages, the wicked were punished by an untimely death.

One of the purposes of Job is to counteract the belief that goodness is equated with long life. Job sits on an ash heap in terrible pain. Satan, having received permission to deal with Job as he pleased, has caused the death of his children. Job knows he has not deserved what has been laid on him. He will not accept his friends' cruel advice that he admit doing what he did not do. He refuses his wife's suggestion that he offer God a benediction and die. He clings to God no matter what has happened or may happen. "Though He slay me, yet I will trust in Him," is one translation of his agonized faith. He realizes that an untimely death is not a punishment for evil. He must accept whatever fate God has in store for him no matter how unjust it may seem.

The end of the story appears to be a happy one. Job recovers his health and his money and has more children to love. However, the real point of the story is found in the heart of his suffering. Only when he accepts his fate, denies his guilt, and clutches at a God who had hidden His face is Job victorious. Job knows that goodness will not always lead to happiness but still always will be good. He knows that the God who hurts is still God. He knows that death is not a punishment for evil.

This does not negate the fact that suffering and death can be caused by the remissness of man. If man has the power to do right, then he must suffer when he does wrong. It is not God who causes war, but man who uses his freedom for destruction. Said Maimonides: "Man has been given free will. If he wishes to turn toward the good way and to be righteous, the power is in his own hands; if he wishes to turn toward the evil way and to be wicked, the power is likewise in his own hands." Only in this sense are life and death, good and evil, and the length of days in the province of man.

There is meaning in being reconciled to one's limitation of life. Maimonides also explained how the realization of life's brevity can at the same time invest that life with enduring significance. "People complain that life is too short, that man's life ends before he is done preparing himself for it. The truth is that while our life is short, we live as though we had eternity at our disposal; we waste too much of life. The problem is not that we are allotted a *short* life, but rather that we are *extravagant* in spending it."

One of the sages was curious about the injunction to "repent one day before thy death." Since no one can possibly know in advance the time of his death, how is it possible, he asked, to "repent one day before"? The answer: "We must therefore repent every day!" The *Talmud* relates the parable of a sailor's wife. She clothed herself in her best garments each day while her husband was at sea. When her neighbors questioned her, she replied: "My husband's plans may change or perhaps a favorable wind will bring him home earlier than he expects; I want to make sure that whenever he arrives I shall look my best." So it is with all of us. The time to prepare for death is each day of one's life. Not in the sense of being morbidly preoccupied with thoughts of death, but rather by so living that death, whenever it comes, will not be cause for incrimination of self.

The length of life has no bearing on the meaning of life. It is not the quantity of years that one accumulates which is of primary importance but the kind of life one leads—the value, the content, the idealism one bestows upon it. For an individual can reach a ripe old age without any significant meaning to his life, just as it is possible to find purpose in a relatively short span of years. The task, then, is to multiply achievements rather than years. For when man seeks only years, he is nothing more than a human adding machine. His ultimate contribution is a distinction no greater than that enjoyed by a grain of sand on a desert. If life is meaningful, then quantity is not important. The real tragedy of death occurs when men are more concerned with how long they may live rather than with how they may live. The real tragedy is not when a task is left unfinished by a worker who is called away, but when the task is never begun at all. The two least important statistics of a man's life are placed upon his tombstone—when he was born and when he died. It is not the length of one's life—rather it is the breadth of his sympathies for others; it is the depth of his understanding of life's meaning; it is the height of his aspirations that are important.

We either desecrate time or we sanctify it as we use it. The personal tragedy, the waste, lies in what we can do with time but do not—the love we do not give; the efforts we do not make; the powers we do not use; the happiness we do not earn; the kindnesses we neglect to bestow; the gratitude we have not expressed; the noble thoughts and deeds that could be ours if only we would realize why we are here. This is what we mean by the dimension of holiness in time. Is not this the meaning of the words of Ecclesiastes (4:3) which taught, "To everything there is a season, a time to every purpose under the heaven: a time to be born and a time to die; a time to weep and a time to laugh; a time to mourn and a time to dance; a time to seek and a time to lose; a time to keep and a time to cast away; a time to rend and a time to sew; a time to keep silence and a time to speak." God has made everything beautiful in its time. So we too must apportion the time of our life. Everything has a time, even for us sophisticated moderns.

Death makes life precious. It makes us want to attach our fragile and fleeting existence to that which is eternal and enduring. There is a story told about a little girl who was tacking up a new wall calendar, containing the unfamiliar figures of the new year which had just begun. "It's going to be a beautiful year," she exclaimed. Someone asked, "How do you know it is going to be a beautiful year? A year is a long time, and you never know what will happen." "Well," she answered, "a day isn't a long time. But I know it's going to be a beautiful year because I am going to take a day at a time, and make it beautiful. Years are only days put together, and I'm going to see that every day in the New Year gets something beautiful into it." "Then," the friend said, smilingly, "it *will* be a beautiful year." The child's fear will be lightened when discussion is focused not on the details of death but on the beauty of life.

In Judaism, even in the death of a loved one, one can ennoble ignoble misfortune. In many a sigh is found an insight, in sorrow a jolt out of complacency. The maxim of Jewish philosophy is, "This also for good." Every experience may be "for good" if the bereaved transforms the value potential into an instrument of spiritual stature—enlarged sympathy, courageous acceptance, and active determination. Even as the darkness eventually changes into light, so adversity may be converted ultimately into good.

The Dubner Maggid composed this parable. A king once owned a large, beautiful, pure diamond of which he was justifiably proud. It had no equal anywhere. One day, the diamond accidentally sustained a deep scratch. The king called in the most skilled diamond cutters and offered them a great reward if they could remove the imperfection from his treasured jewel. But none could repair the blemish. The king was sorely distressed. After some time, a gifted lapidary came to the king and promised to make the rare diamond even more beautiful than it had been before the mishap. The king was impressed by his confidence and entrusted his precious stone to his care. And the man kept his word. With superb artistry he engraved a lovely rosebud around the imperfection and he used the scratch to make the stem. Man can emulate that craftsman. When life bruises and wounds him, he can use even the scratches to etch a portrait of beauty, meaning, and love.

No one can determine how each individual child and his parents will react to the fact of death. The mystery still walks with our imagination and lurks in our dreams. It is good to remember that courage is not the absence of fear, but the affirmation of life despite fear. For as far as we know, only man faces life with the certain knowledge of having to die. This knowledge, this "loss of innocency," can lead him to the edge of the abyss and threaten all his actions with meaninglessness and futility. Or he can seek a bridge that will span the chasm and affirm those things which really give him life—friendship, honor, a desire for justice, love, dignity, family, friends, country, mankind. And to this end he must also help his child.

By facing the meaning of our limits as seen in death, one comes to accept the limits and possibilities of life realistically. One sees the parallel between the acceptance of one's biological death and the facing of limit and loss in everyday life. Judaism's concern is more with life in the "here" than in the "hereafter," with this world's opportunities rather than with speculation about the world-to-come.

Judaism helps its adherents of all ages to face death and to face away from it. It aids them to accept the reality of death and protects them from destructive fantasy and illusion in the unconscious denial of fact. Most important of all, the Jewish religion offers an abundance of sharing religious resources in the encounter with helplessness, guilt, loneliness, and fear. Though reason cannot answer the *why*, and comforting words cannot wipe away tears, Judaism offers consolation in death by reaffirming life.

GLOSSARY

ALAV HASHALOM — (pronounced, Ah–la–hv Ha–shaw–lome) Lit., "Peace be upon him." Phrase often used after the name of a departed male is mentioned.

ALEHAW HASHALOM — (pron., All–leh–haw Ha–shaw–lome) Lit., "Peace be upon her." Phrase used after a departed female is mentioned.

AVELIM — (pron., Ah–veh–leem) Lit., "Mourners." Laws of mourning apply in case of death of seven relatives: father, mother, husband, wife, son or daughter, brother, and sister.

BEN SIRACH, JOSHUA — (3rd pre-Christian century) Author of ancient book *The Wisdom of Jesus the Son of Sirach,* or Latin title, *Ecclesiasticus.*

CHASSIDIM — (pron., Cha–sid–eem) Pietists and mystics, followers of Rabbi Israel Baal Shem Tov (1700–1760).

CHEVRAH KADDISHA — (pron., Chev–rah Ka–dee–shaw) Lit., "Holy Brotherhood." Society whose members devote themselves to burial and rites connected with it.

DUBNER MAGGID — (1741–1804) Eminent Polish preacher and scholar, Wolf Kranz. Famous sermons interlaced with epigrams and parables.

EL MOLEH RACHAMIN — (pron., Ale–moh–lay Ra–cha–meen) Lit., "God full of Compassion." Memorial prayer recited at funerals. Dates from the 17th century. Popular Yiddish name is "Molay."

ELI — (1100, pre-Christian era) High priest at Shiloh near close of the period of the Book of Judges.

EZRA — (458, pre-Christian century) Scribe, sometimes called "Founder of Rabbinic Legalism."

GILGUL HANEFESH — (pron., Gil–gool Hah–neh–fesh) Transmigration of the soul. According to *Zohar,* "Truly, all souls must undergo transmigration." (III, 99b) Kabbalistic School of Rabbi Luria (1534–1572) believed that a soul that had sinned returned to its earthly existence in order to make amends.

GINSBERG, LOUIS — (1873–1953) Famous Talmudic and Midrashic scholar. Leading contributor to *Jewish Encyclopedia.*

HESPED — (pron., Hes–peed) Eulogy delivered by rabbi for deceased. Orations date back to Biblical times, and contain an account of life accomplishments of the departed one.

KABBALA — (pron., Kah–bah–lah) Lit., "Tradition." Applied to important complex of Jewish mystical philosophy and practice. Basic work is *Zohar* ("Splendor") which appeared at end of 13th century.

KADDISH — (pron., Kah–dish) Lit., "Holy" or "Sanctification." Aramaic prayer for the dead. Essentially a doxology, praising God, and praying for speedy establishment of God's kingdom upon earth. Recited by mourners for period of eleven months from date of burial.

KERIAH — (pron., Ka–ree–ah) Lit., "Rending." Custom of mourner tearing a section of his garment or a black ribbon as symbol of grief. Rite performed before funeral. Rent made over the left side, over the heart. To be performed standing up, for the mourner is to meet sorrow standing upright.

MAIMONIDES, MOSES — (1135–1204) Greatest Jewish philosopher and codifier of the Middle Ages.

MATZEVAH —.(pron., Mah–tzave–vah) Tombstone that is erected toward the end of the first year of interment.

MIDRASH — (pron., Mid–rahsh) Lit., "Exposition." Books devoted to Biblical interpretations. In form of homiletic expositions, legends, and folklore.

MINYAN — (pron., Mean–yahn) Lit., "Number," or "Quorum." Minimum number of ten Jewish males above the age of 13 required for public services. According to Jewish law, *Minyan* is required for community recital of the *Kaddish*.

MIRRORS — Practice of covering mirrors is not based upon explicit Jewish law. Some authorities regard practice as superstitious and discourage use. Others interpret the rite symbolically. "We ought not to gaze upon our reflection in the mirror in the house of mourning. In so doing, we appear to be reflecting upon ourselves."

MOORE, GEORGE FOOT — (1851–1931) Eminent non-Jewish Biblical scholar who wrote the monumental *Judaism in the First Centuries of the Christian Era*.

OLAM HABA—(pron., Oh–lam Ha–baw) Lit., "World to come." Maimonides explains: "The wise men call it world to come not because it is not in existence at present, but because life in that world will come to man after the life in this world is ended."

PHARISEES — Jewish religious and political party during the Second Temple period.

RABBI — Leader and teacher in the congregation. Conducts the funeral service, answers many ritual questions regarding the ceremony of death, and aids in important approach of *Menachem Avel* (pron., Mine–a–chem Ah–vel), comforting the bereaved.

SADDUCEES — Major sect among Palestinian Jews during the period of the Second Commonwealth.

SEUDAT HAVRA–AH — (pron., S–oo–dat Chah–vey–rah) Meal of consolation. Provided by friends in accordance with Talmudic injunction. "A mourner is forbidden to eat of his own food at the first meal after the burial."

SH–LOSHIM — (pron., Sh–lo–sheem) Lit., "Thirty." Mourning begins on first day of the funeral and ends on morning of the thirtieth day.

SHIVAH — (pron., Shee–vah) Lit., "Seven." Refers to the first seven days of mourning after burial.

SOUL — Biblical expressions: *Nefesh* (pron., Neh–fesh), *Neshamah* (pron., N'sha–ma), and *Ruach* (pron., Rue–ach) derive from roots meaning "breath," and "wind." Soul is the source without which there can be no life. Maimonides asserted that only that part of the soul which man develops by his intellectual efforts is immortal.

TACHRICHIM — (pron., Ta–ch–re–cheem) Lit., "Shroud." Robe in which some dead are buried. Made of white linen cloth.

TALMUD — (pron., Tahl–mude) Discussions on the text of the Mishna by the Palestinian and Babylonian scholars from the third to fifth century.

TEHIYYATH HAMATHEM — (pron., Th–chee–yaht Ha–may–teem) Resurrection of the dead. Belief that at end of time the bodies of dead will rise from grave.

UNVEILING — Tombstone consecration in which special prayers are recited, such as *El Moleh Rachamin* and the *Mourner's Kaddish*. Customary to cover the tombstone with a veil and during service for one of the mourners to unveil the stone or plaque.

YAHRZEIT — (pron., Yohr–tzite) Yiddish term for the anniversary of death. Observed by reciting the *Kaddish* in the synagogue and lighting memorial light in home.

YAHRZEIT LIGHT — Well established practice to have candle or special lamp in house of mourning for 24 hours on the anniversary of death.

YIZKOR — (pron., Yiz–kohr) Prayer, "May God remember the soul of my revered . . ." Recited on *Yom Kippur, Shemini Atzeret,* last day of *Passover,* and second day of *Shavuot.*

A child can be helped to face life in many ways. The parent starts by discovering the youngster's emotional needs. By love, the adult provides the child with a stronger, more satisfying picture of himself.

Eulalie Steinmetz Ross adds her vast knowledge of books that will contribute to the child's growth and lead to "a maturity of spirit that understands the purposes of life and accepts the mystery of death."

Formerly the Supervisor of Storytelling in the New York Public Library and the Coordinator of Work with Children in the Public Library of Cincinnati and Hamilton County, Miss Ross is Visiting Lecturer on Children's Literature and Storytelling at Simmons College. She is the compiler of three books of stories for children.

CHAPTER X

Children's Books Relating to Death: A Discussion

EULALIE STEINMETZ ROSS

INTRODUCTION

FROM EVERY EXPERIENCE that a child has he takes what he needs at the moment for mental, emotional, or spiritual growth, for grow he must: it is his nature to do so. The experience of reading a book can contribute to the child's growth, and the better the book, the more vigorous the growth. The best of children's books can help the child come ultimately to a complete realization of himself in relation to himself and the complex world around him. Books can give him the wisdom and strength to "rivet and publish himself of his own personality" as Walt Whitman says, and from that striving come to a maturity of spirit that understands the purpose of life and accepts the mystery of death.

Children's books then as an enhancement of life and death will be considered here. Those books written expressly for the child on the subject of death are best recommended to him by the priest, or rabbi, or minister of his faith. Such books will speak to the child against the background of his religious teachings and in terms he understands, for they are mostly publications of denominational presses.

The books in this survey are from the mainstream of children's literature. Death occurs in them as an integral part of the story and the presentation is honest, not morbid or sentimental. The teach-a-lesson story has never been accepted by children. Even in the stark days of Puritan theology when books abounded devoted to the holy lives and joyous deaths of children, the boys and girls found their own antidote for such grim fare in the chapbooks with their folk tales of sturdier characters and livelier action.

There is no need to belabor the point. The books mentioned here have food for the child's growth in them. Trust the child to find it. They are books written from an author's heart and speak directly to the spirit of the child. There is education here in the truest sense of the word. Elizabeth Gray Vining, that remarkable Quaker who was tutor to the Japanese Crown Prince and herself the author of distinguished children's books, says that the reading of a good children's book leaves a little residue behind in the heart of the child: a freshly realized concept, an awakened awareness to the glory of God's world, a glimpse of the mystery that comes at life's end. It is these accumulated residues that help the child grow in grace and in the understanding of God and man.

PICTURE BOOKS FOR THE YOUNGER CHILD

In the picture books for the smallest child there are no intimations of immortality. The child is so recently of the quick that there is little need in his spring-green world for an understanding of the dead. Rather, there are books for him that reflect in word and picture the love and security of his family circle, his first advances out of that circle toward friendship, his exciting discovery of abstract ideas, his growing awareness of God, and his delight in the small wonders of nature. The warmth and beauty and tenderness of such picture books help crystallize the child's sense of security in his real world. When older he is sustained in emotional crises by this sense of security; it enables him to endure whatever may befall him with greater stability.

Family Relationships

Of all the family members the mother, is by the very nature of her role, the first person on whom the small child depends for his well-being. This dependence and happy relationship is demonstrated in a number of lively picture books. Robert McCloskey's *Blueberries for Sal* tells in words, and pictures the color of ripe blueberries, how one small girl and one bear cub get their mothers mixed up on Blueberry Hill.

Naturally it is the mothers who are upset when they discover their mix-matched state, not the children. In *One Step, Two* . . . Charlotte Zolotow's small heroine walks with her mother down to the corner. "See!" says the child. "See!" And any two-year-old understands the urgency of that small finger pointing at a crocus, a bluebird, the milkman, clothes prancing on a line, the school bus. The gay pictures in springlike colors are by Roger Duvoisin. Helena's mother gives her frequently "the little loving, and the little hugging" that all small children need; but when Genevieve in her French–English asks her mother for the same dosage a toy cooking stove is offered instead—"a little 'ovin.' " This gentle story of children and mothers is told in words and pictures by Eleanor Estes and has for its title—of course—*A Little Oven*.

In Margaret Wise Brown's *The Runaway Bunny* a small rabbit and his mother play a beguiling pretend game of hide-and-seek with the mother finding her son wherever he hides, whatever he becomes. The pictures by Clement Hurd invite the reader to hunt for the bunny, too. Perhaps this would be a good place to make the point that small children identify themselves completely with the leading character in their picture books whether he be a human being, a bunny as is the case here, a steam shovel, a dog, or whatever. Another rabbit that is in essence all of childhood is Peter Rabbit as created by Beatrix Potter in *The Tale of Peter Rabbit*. Peter is one of a family unit, he misbehaves as all children do, he suffers as a consequence, but in the end he is safely home with mother—even though his dietary indiscretions in Mr. McGregor's garden give him camomile tea instead of milk and blackberries for supper. Gene Zion's *Harry the Dirty Dog* has somewhat the same theme as *The Tale of Peter Rabbit:* the misbehaving child. But when Harry returns to all his dear families from a day on the town he isn't recognized and he has to discover for himself how he can be converted from a dirty black dog with white spots to a clean white dog with black spots. Ping leaves home, too—Ping is a Chinese duck—but he is glad enough at the end of an almost

fatal day to return to the wise-eyed boat on the Yangtze
River where he settles down with "his mother and his father
and two sisters and three brothers and eleven aunts and seven
uncles and forty-two cousins." The unusually literate text
of *The Story of Ping* is by Marjorie Flack. Kurt Wiese made
the pictures.

Little Toot is a tugboat in New York harbor, but essentially he is the dawdling, playing child who cares not about
doing the few things he should. Even Grandfather Toot is
out of patience with his frivolous grandson, but when Little
Toot redeems himself it is Grandfather who blasts the news
of his heroic deed all over the harbor. Hardie Gramatky is the
creator of *Little Toot* in pictures and story. Children find the
cheeky little tug very much like themselves and, naturally
then, very likable. There is a grandfather in another book
that is a favorite with the small children even though it is
intended as a reader. This is *Little Bear's Visit* by Else Holmelund Minarik. Little Bear first appeared in a book that bore
his name as its title and was devoted to his pleasant adventures with his mother and his animal friends. *Father Bear
Comes Home* brings the male parent into the series—Father
Bear is a fisherman, what else?—and *Little Bear's Friend* introduces the first human to the bear establishment. There is
much understanding of the young child in all these engaging
stories but it is most evident in the first book mentioned, *Little Bear's Visit,* which is based on that unique relationship
that exists between grandparent and grandchild. As has been
said these books are intended to be used as readers, but they
read aloud well to children as small as Little Bear, and the
old-fashioned pictures by Maurice Sendak are delightful.
Helen E. Buckley writes of the grandfather-grandchild relationship in her picture book, *Grandfather and I.* In all the
hurrying world, only a grandfather and his grandson have
the time to walk leisurely, stop, look, and then just "walk
along, and walk along." Paul Galdone did the pictures for
this book and there is a nice contrast between the strolling

pair and the other rushing members of the family. Again, the building of a sense of security.

Sisters are a part of the family, and in Charlotte Zolotow's *Do You Know What I'll Do?* an older sister tells her younger brother all the loving and imaginary things she will do for him: bring him a shell, blow on his nightmare, tell him her dreams, and—last of all—when she is grown up and married "bring you my baby to hug. Like this." The demonstrated hug is charming as pictured by Garth Williams, who illustrated the book.

In Thomas Handforth's *Mei Li* it is a brother who makes it possible for his small Chinese sister to experience a day at the city Fair. Exciting as the day is, Mei Li is wearily happy to return home where she is proclaimed "the princess who rules our hearts." Mr. Handforth's spacious illustrations for his story are beautiful and Mei Li, with her candle-top pigtail, is an appealing heroine.

And so to the last picture book to be discussed here that reflects the child in his relations with the various members of his family. This one reflects also the first breaking of the mother-child-father bond, the first independent step in the world alone. Momo is a Japanese–American child who receives on her third birthday red rubber boots and a blue umbrella. So proud is Momo of her gifts that the first day she uses them she walks to nursery school "straight, like a grown-up lady." And the first day she uses them is also the first day she walks alone without holding her mother's or her father's hand. Taro Yashima wrote and illustrated *Umbrella* from an incident in the life of his own daughter. Perhaps that is why small children respond to the book so completely.

Friendship

As Momo leaves the protective and loving hands of her parents for a measure of independence so do all children venture forth in their own good time to find new experiences outside the shelter of home and family. Reading of such experiences in picture books encourages the timorous child to take the first fearful step by showing him the added delights that friendship can bring into his life. There is another picture book about Momo that does just this. Momo is a big girl now and the story concerns the friendship she is finally able to establish between herself and the shy little boy next door. Taro Yashima did this picture book from life also and it is called *Youngest One*. Louis Slobodkin's *One Is Good but Two Are Better* pictures for the child all the good and gay things he can do with a playmate. It is a grandfather writing and illustrating this book: he knows the ways of small children. In *Play with Me*, by Marie Hall Ets, a yellow-haired little girl learns how to make friends with the small creatures of the meadow: by sitting still and letting them come to her on their own terms. Her growing delight in their friendly advances is shown in the picture only by the movements of her eyes and an ever-widening grin of pure bliss.

There is no more friendly creature in the realm of children's literature than Johnny Crow who did dig and sow till he made a little garden and then invited the whole animal world to share it with himself. There are three books about this cheerful crow all written and illustrated by Leslie Brooke: *Johnny Crow's Garden, Johnny Crow's Party,* and *Johnny Crow's New Garden*.

Abstract Ideas

The books surveyed so far reflect in concrete stories the love a child knows in his family circle and the friendships he enjoys when he goes forth into the world. Joan Walsh Anglund has most successfully put these two abstract ideas into miniature books for children. Perhaps the books speak so directly and understandably to the young child because Miss Anglund wrote and illustrated them for her own small children. *Love Is a Special Way of Feeling* begins with mother love and ends with "Love is a happy feeling that stays inside your heart for the rest of your life." *A Friend Is Someone*

Who Likes You lists animal friends as well as human, cautions against rushing and hurrying so fast lest friends be passed by, and advises wisely that "Sometimes you have to find your friend." The backs of two little girls, arms entwined and heads together, is the charming illustration with which the book ends.

God

To the love of family and friends the small child soon adds the love of God. A picture book that helps him understand what God is like is Florence Mary Fitch's *A Book about God*. Miss Fitch's quietly reverent text is perfectly illustrated by Leonard Weisgard with water colors that are in part gentle, in part majestic—always beautiful. The last page of text reads: "All things beautiful are like God. God is like all these and more . . . No one can count the stars in the sky. No one can count the ways God shows His love." The illustration for this evokes the Twenty-third Psalm. This is a book for children of all faiths. Another picture book that speaks serenely in word and picture of God's love is *A Child's Good Night Book* by Margaret Wise Brown. The text describes the animals and children that are asleep and, at the end, two guardian angels offer a prayer for their safekeeping through the night. The moving quality of the book comes from the illustrations of Jean Charlot, whose strong line manages to convey strength encompassing tenderness. Françoise's *The Thank-You Book* also extends a child's horizon to include God's love. A little girl thanks all the things that have contributed to her happiness: the hen that lays her egg for breakfast; the cat who keeps her company when she is sick; the house that shelters her; and, finally, "Thank-you to God who gives us everything."

God's World

The young child's eyes are soon wide at the wonders of the world around him. He sees with a clear vision, a fresh spirit, and an eager heart. If he can sustain through the years this sensitivity to nature's beauty he will have within him a fountainhead of comfort when sorrow comes. There are many picture books of nature for the small child, to reflect and reinforce the facts of his first observations, but only a few manage to include his wonder.

White Snow, Bright Snow does this as it describes the first snow of winter with a simple text by Alvin Tresselt and striking illustrations by Roger Duvoisin. Janice May Udry in *A Tree Is Nice* sees all the wonderful things a tree can mean to a child: it can fill up the sky, a swing can hang from it, it is a good place to lean your hoe when you rest, you can pick apples from it. Marc Simont's pictures, alternately in color and black-and-white, make trees look as green and strong as they are. The seashore is treasure trove to the young child: the tidal pools that are just his size, the shells of mysterious shapes and jingling sounds, the sand to puddle and play in. *On My Beach There Are Many Pebbles,* by Leo Lionni, pictures in soft gray colors the odd stones that young beach-combers delight in gathering. Mr. Lionni puts the stones to-gether in queer combinations and produces fishpebbles and goosepebbles and even peoplepebbles. There is much of tex-ture and shape in this fascinating book. Alice Goudy helps the youngest child in his shell collecting in her *Houses from the Sea.* Her words and Adrienne Adams's soft watercolors tell the child just as much as he cares to know about the common shells he can pick up on almost any beach in this country.

Finally, there is Robert McCloskey's *Time of Wonder* that manages to include every phase of this discussion: the security of the family circle, friendships outside of the home, an awareness of God's presence, and the wonders of His world. *Time of Wonder* comes from Mr. McCloskey's island home in Maine and describes in rhythmic words and beauti-ful watercolors one summer spent on the island in the com-pany of his two young daughters. There are ferns unrolling their fiddleheads, gaggling sea gulls, friends to belly-whopper and dog-paddle with, a hurricane that shrieks in with the tide, and arms to hold you fast against the wind's fearful roar. There is overall a sense of God's presence, a sense of peace that comes from this book, and the child feels it when the story is read to him and he looks at the accompanying pictures.

These then are picture books, written with grace and distinctively illustrated, that reinforce and enhance the world of love and beauty that should be the inheritance of every child. Such a world gives him emotional security in his childhood and emotional stability in his adult years. It is this stability that will sustain him when he makes acquaintance with death and must cope with its finality.

BOOKS FOR THE OLDER CHILD

After the child has mastered the mechanics of reading he turns to the body of children's literature for sustenance of mind and spirit. Here, with life, will he find death, for the best of children's books represent life as a whole, encompassing death. He will meet death in folk and fairy tales, in fantasies, in myths, in hero tales from epics and sagas, in historical novels, in family stories, in animal adventures, in contemporary biography, and in the singing lines of poetry. In reading these representations of death he will unconsciously acquire some tolerance for the enigma, and the ability to contend with it when it moves within his periphery.

Folk and Fairy Tales

Death in folk tales is the customary end for the various creatures of evil: witches, dragons, giants, stepsisters, and stepmothers. It is not allotted as a punishment to be suffered, but comes as a decisive end that is anticipated and justified. Death is quick, extremely tidy, and, once accomplished, forgotten about. There is no need here to go into detail concerning such folk tales for there are hundreds of them and they come readily to the mind of any adult: "Rapunzel," "Hansel and Gretel," "Snow White," "The Tinder Box," "Rumpel-

stiltskin," "The Robber Bridegroom"—to name but a few.
For those who may have need of it there is at the end of this
section, just before the general bibliography, a selective list
of folk tales from various countries and in good editions.
These stories are read with pleasure by the children, they
read aloud even better, and they are at their best when they
are told, as folk tales are supposed to be.

Hans Christian Andersen wrote his own versions of many
of the folk tales of the north. He also wrote creative fairy
tales, and in these his acceptance of life and death as one
entity are most evident. He assumed that children could accept this and he must have been right in his assumption for
those stories that include death are the most beloved by
children today. The little mermaid dies herself rather than
sacrifice the life of the prince she loves to regain her fish
tail. Karen's "soul flew on the sunshine up to God, and there
there was no one who questioned her about her red shoes."
The Tin Soldier and the little dancer come to an end together in the flames of the nursery fire with only a tin heart
and a blackened spangle left of their love. The little match
girl went away "in splendor and joy, high, high up towards
heaven." The fir tree is burnt up after its hour of shining
beauty. Two editions of Andersen that are well-translated
and illustrated are: *Forty-Two Stories,* translated by M. R.
James and illustrated by Robin Jacques, and *Hans Andersen's Fairy Tales,* translated by L. W. Kingsland and illustrated by Ernest H. Shepard. Marcia Brown has made a
lovely picture book for the younger children of "The Steadfast Tin Soldier."

Oscar Wilde wrote several fairy tales that deal with death.
The least sentimental of them all is "The Selfish Giant." The
symbolism in the story is understood best by the Christian
child, for the small boy in the giant's garden is Christ, but
the ending in its honesty is for all children. The giant is
dead. Adults, insecure because of their own muddled ideas
about death, often say the giant is "sleeping" when telling
this story or reading it aloud. They say, uneasily, that they

are protecting the children. This is nonsense, and robs the story of its strength. The giant is dead. A good collection of Oscar Wilde's stories is *The Happy Prince,* illustrated by Philippe Jullian.

There is a Japanese legend of the Buddha's death that has somewhat the same ending as "The Selfish Giant." It is about a cat who longed to have a cat in the painting her master was making of the Buddha's farewell to the animals as he prepared to die. This could not be because the cat had refused homage to the great teacher. In the end a miracle is accomplished, the cat *is* in the picture, curved under the compassionate hand of Buddha himself. When the cat sees the painting she dies of joy. Elizabeth Coatsworth tells this story for American children in *The Cat Who Went to Heaven* and Lynd Ward has illustrated it with portraits of the animals as they come to say goodbye to Buddha. This is a serene book that speaks to the spirit.

(A factual book that gives the child some sense of Oriental religious beliefs, including those that have to do with death, is *Their Search for God* by Florence Mary Fitch.)

Fantasy

From folk and fairy tales it is but a glass-slippered step to the literature of fantasy. Much of this literature for children is in the form of the allegory where truths are half-seen and shadowy, and where each child is free to make his own interpretation depending on the experiences he brings to the reading. Such a book is George Macdonald's *At the Back of the North Wind,* which ends in the death of its small hero, the boy Diamond. There is a mystical, haunting quality to Diamond's adventures with the swirling north wind, and because in time these adventures become more real to Diamond than life itself it seems right that he should die and go to the back of the north wind forever.

Antoine de Saint-Exupéry's *The Little Prince* is another allegory, full of mystical symbolism, and almost defying analysis, for it means different things to different people, and the meanings change with every reading. Like poetry *The Little Prince* has to be read again and again, for with each reading comes new understanding, fresh comprehension. The story concerns a slight princeling who comes upon the author as he works on his disabled plane in the Sahara Desert. There follows a series of conversations of life on the planet from which the little prince came, of a flower and baobab trees that grow there, of life and death, of the mystery of the desert, of foxes and snakes. In the end the little prince dies from a snake bite, expected and awaited. He tells the author: ". . . You will suffer. I shall look as if I were dead, and that will not be true . . . You understand . . . It is too far. I cannot carry this body with me. It is too heavy. But it will be like an old abandoned shell. There is nothing sad about old shells . . ." Perhaps the kernel of truth at the heart of this fantasy is in this statement by the fox: "It is only with the heart that one can see rightly; what is essential is invisible to the eye." The author's delicate watercolors perfectly complement the gossamer and illusive quality of this tale.

There is a touch of mysticism to Carolyn Sherwin Bailey's otherwise sturdy story of a doll whose body is an apple twig and head is a hickory nut. Miss Hickory is her name and also the name of Miss Bailey's book. Miss Hickory is hardheaded and she keeps her sap flowing even when she is forgotten by her small mistress and must spend the New Hampshire winter in an abandoned robin's nest. In the spring Miss Hickory loses her head to a hungry squirrel, but this isn't the end of Miss Hickory; ah no, instead it brings her a new kind of life, a life that covers her first with apple-blossoms and then with apples, round and red. It can happen if you keep your sap flowing, and there is a small miracle to help. Ruth Gannett's lithographs illustrate every dramatic incident in the book, including Miss Hickory's flowering after losing her head.

C. S. Lewis in his books about the mythical kingdom of Narnia writes of the eternal struggle of good versus evil, life versus death. The lion Aslan represents the forces of good and is the creator of Narnia, which he sang into existence. The White Witch is the leader of the evil forces. Into this land come four children through an attic wardrobe, and thereafter their fates and the fate of Narnia are inexorably joined together. The first book about Narnia is *The Lion, the Witch and the Wardrobe,* and usually after children have had a taste of this they gallop through the other six titles.

In her science-fiction fantasy, *A Wrinkle in Time,* Madeleine L'Engle writes also of the struggle of good versus evil, life versus death. In her book three children tesseract—take a tuck in time—to another planet where the father of two of them is being held prisoner by IT, a shapeless, howling, evil mind. IT gets possession of one of the children too and almost causes the death of his soul. A chant of love defeats IT, for love is the one force that is incompatible with evil. The children respond to the contemporary setting of *A Wrinkle in Time* and absorb while reading it a philosophy as old as time itself.

Myths

Let us tesseract a bit ourselves and go back in time to a brief consideration of the myth in this survey of children's literature that has to do with death. In mythology there are gods of death as well as life and the geography of their dwellings is equally well defined. Edith Hamilton's *Mythology,* because of its modern look, is perhaps the most inviting book in this field for today's child. It offers him a good background discussion of mythology before presenting the myths themselves. The emphasis is on the myths of Greece and Rome and the hero stories connected with the Trojan war. A brief final chapter treats of Norse mythology. A supplementary book of Greek myths is illustrated by Helen Sewell in a classical-modern style that is most effective. The selections are from Bulfinch's *Age of Fable* and the book is called simply *A Book of Myths.* A more inclusive telling of the Norse myths is to be found in Dorothy Hosford's *Thunder of the Gods.* Included here is the story of the death of Balder the Beautiful, the beloved of the gods, slain by a blind man who did not know that the weapon the evil Loki thrust in his hands was the fatal Mistletoe wand. All grieved for Balder, all save one, and because she would not weep Balder remained with Hela in the great hall of the dead "and the earth was never again as fair to gods or men." A story to stretch the spirit and nourish the heart.

Hero Tales and Legends

Miss Hosford has made an equally simple yet moving retelling of the Beowulf story for children, *By His Own Might*. The epics and sagas present to the child great heroes who have no fear of death, who strive mightily, letting death come when it will. Beowulf faces death three times: with the monster Grendel, with Grendel's fierce mother beneath the sea, and with the dragon of the treasure hoard. Beowulf never falters in his tasks; even when the dragon has given him the fatal wound he rallies to slay the beast.

The stories of King Arthur lift the spirit of the child for here too are men who live with death, but will not admit to the fear of death and so weaken and cripple their heroic hearts. Howard Pyle's *The Story of King Arthur and His Knights* sustains, in words and pictures, the noble spirit of the Arthurian stories. It is interesting to note that in the death of Arthur a phenomenon occurs that is in many hero tales: the dying hero is mysteriously spirited away to return when his people have need of him.

Ireland has two legendary heroes who moved over the green isle when the high kings sat at Tara: Cuchulain, the Red Hound of Ulster, and Finn McCool, who led the Fellowship of the Fianna in bright adventure. These men are cut from the same heroic cloth as Beowulf and Arthur, but a few strands have been woven into the material that are pure Irish: grandiloquence, mysticism, faëry lore, and lusty humor. Rosemary Sutcliff in *The Hound of Ulster* retells the Cuchulain story, and Ella Young in *The Tangle-Coated Horse* relates episodes from the Fionn Saga. Finn McCool, like Arthur, is not supposed to be dead but asleep to rise again when Ireland has need of him. "Some day his battle-shout will make a gladness in the hills and in the hearts of men."

Historical Novels

Two historical novels for children are based on legends and both have youths for heroes who sacrifice themselves for their countries. There is no fear of death here but an exaltation of the human spirit that is communicated to the child reader. Harry W. French's *The Lance of Kanana* is the story of an Arabian boy who saved his country from a Roman invasion in the fourth century. He does so by drawing upon inward spiritual resources, by using his wits, and by hurling one spear—the only spear he ever lifted for Allah and Arabia. That spear saves his country, frees his father from imprisonment, and brings about his own noble death. *The Trumpeter of Krakow,* by Eric P. Kelly, tells of a Polish boy of the thirteenth century who, in the face of a marauding Tartar horde, sounded the Heynal—the hymn to Mary— triumphantly from a church tower in Krakow. A Tartar arrow ended the hymn on a broken note and on that broken note the Heynal ends today in memory of a brave youth who died for Poland, a symbol of heroism. Once, in another century, the hymn was finished and from that circumstance comes a story rich in the imagery, the superstitions, and the customs of the Middle Ages.

Rosemary Sutcliff writes distinguished historical novels for the older child. One such, *Knight's Fee,* has to do with a dog-boy who rises from the lowest position on a feudal estate to become the knight of the castle, the lord of the manor. There is a moving chapter when the boy, sorrowful and reluctant, receives his heritage from the hands of his dying Norman lord.

In *The Bronze Bow* by Elizabeth George Speare death is represented as a corroding, motivating force in the heart of a young Jewish boy whose parents were crucified by the Romans. Daniel's song of revenge is David's "He trains my

hands for war, so that my arms can bend a bow of bronze . . ."
until Jesus makes him understand that only love can bend a
bow of bronze, only love can conquer the Romans.

Harry Behn evokes with extraordinary clarity and understanding the peoples of prehistoric times in *The Faraway
Lurs*. Lurs are the bronze trumpets blown by the priests of
the Sun People when speaking with the sun. The struggle
in the story is between the Sun People and the Forest People,
and it culminates in the human sacrifice of a maiden of the
Forest People. As far removed as we are from the understanding of such a sacrifice, we are convinced it is right and
even beautiful, so mystically has Mr. Behn handled the incident. "In a moment her fear was gone, swept away by the
sunny stillness of the forest, the timeless voice of peace. She
opened her eyes and smiled as she thought of Wolf Stone
waiting for her in the glade only a little distance away. She
drank deeply [of the poison]."

Family Stories

Death occurs in many family stories that are written for
the child, even as it comes to many families in real life. The
most sorrowful of all is perhaps the death of Beth in Louisa
Alcott's *Little Women*. It is a tender farewell Beth takes of
life surrounded by the loving family that constituted her
world. In *Little Men* Miss Alcott writes of another death,
that of Meg's husband, kindly John Brooke. There is much
here that is good of the funeral service, and a glimpse for
the child reader of a love that can be a benediction to a
grieving wife.

Lucinda Wyman has experiences with death in the two
stories written about her by Ruth Sawyer: *Roller Skates* and
The Year of Jubilo. In *Roller Skates* it is the death of fragile
little Trinket whom Lucinda "borrowed" from time to time,
a borrowing that was as good for Trinket as it was for Lucinda for it helped gentle her stormy spirit. After Trinket's
death Lucinda writes in her diary: "What is hard to understand is how death divides you in two. Something goes and

something stays." Even to understand that much was wisdom for a ten-year-old. *The Year of Jubilo* brings death closer to the Wymans for it is the father himself who dies, forcing the family into a different way of life. In the adjustment, Lucinda, now fourteen, grows up. Lucinda Wyman is a sturdy, vigorous heroine who can shake up the more docile souls who may read of her escapades even as she shook up her more ladylike cousins, the four Gazelles.

In *Meet the Austins,* by Madeleine L'Engle, a child, orphaned when her father's jet explodes, comes to live with the Austin family. The child's reaction to the shock of her father's death is to parade her grief, demand sympathy, and behave generally in an insolent, sullen way totally unfamiliar to the Austins. In time, the security that emanates from their loving family circle contains the orphan and she becomes an Austin too.

An outsider brings discord to another home, albeit the outsider is a doll and the home a dolls' house. Rumer Godden writes so convincingly of dolls and makes such real characters of them that one forgets almost that they are made of plush, and wood, and celluloid, and china. It is Birdie, the celluloid doll in *The Dolls' House,* who is the heroine of the story in spite of her empty little head where words and ideas knock about like pebbles. When Marchpane, the intruder, lures the baby too close to a burning candle it is Birdie who thrusts him away from the flame—and burns up herself. "There was a flash, a bright light, a white flame, and where Birdie had been there was no more Birdie." Only a doll perhaps, yet such is the genius of Miss Godden's pen that Birdie's "death" is a moving experience for the child reader.

In three stories for children death comes with shocking suddenness. How the characters react to death provides motivation for the stories. In Ester Weir's *The Loner* the only person who had ever been kind to a homeless, nameless boy is killed before his eyes, caught by her yellow hair in a potato digging machine. The boy takes to the road in wild grief and desperate loneliness, not knowing he is moving to a happier

destiny that will give him a family, a name—David, and a
flock of sheep to tend. The flooding Ohio River claims the
lives of the mother and father in Florence Musgrave's *Marged,*
leaving only the grandmother, the small son, and the embit-
tered daughter as the family unit. Marged is bitter because
it was in a sense the grandmother's fault that the parents died:
she refused to leave the home in time for higher and safe
ground. Only when Marged realizes how terrible a burden
this knowledge is to the grandmother, and that death took
from her an only son, do the two women come to terms and
peace. It is surging water that takes the lives of Jiya's parents
too, but this water comes from the sea in a great tidal wave.
Pearl Buck tells the story of Jiya's tragedy in *The Big Wave.*
She tells too how his foster-father with wisdom and gentle-
ness helps Jiya recover from his shock, accept death, and live
again with a heart free of bitterness. This is a stark, short
story and Miss Buck has put in it much of the Japanese philosophy of death: "To live in the presence of death makes us
brave and strong . . . To die a little later or a little sooner
does not matter. But to live bravely, to love life, to see how
beautiful the trees are and the mountains, yes, and even the
sea . . . in these things we Japanese are a fortunate people.
We love life because we live in danger. We do not fear death
because we understand that life and death are necessary to
each other."

Animal Tales

Death occurs in many animal stories written for children. In Rudyard Kipling's Jungle Books death is the penalty when the Laws of the Jungle are broken. There is no
redress. There is a kind of Victorian moral rectitude to the
jungle of Mowgli, the Man-Cub, which enables him to live
as a brother with wolf, bear, python, and panther. In Zachary Ball's *Bristle Face* and Marjorie Kinnan Rawlings' *The
Yearling* animal pets must be killed. In *Bristle Face* it is a
mercy killing, lest the blinded hound dog kill himself at the
next hunt. In *The Yearling* the killing is a matter of survival,

lest the fawn eat the food that sustains the Baxter family in their Florida backwoods home. The deaths of dog and fawn deeply affect the boys who own them; the terrible grief of Jody Baxter washes away his youth and leaves a man in its place.

The death of a spider has moved many children as E. B. White describes it in his fantasy of the barnyard, *Charlotte's Web*. Charlotte dies as spiders must after they have laid their eggs. Unfortunately this happens at the Fair Grounds, but with the help of Templeton the rat and the pig Wilbur the eggs are brought safely back to the barn. They hatch in good time and through her children Charlotte achieves immortality.

Heroes of Today

The courageous heart speaks to the teen-age reader from the accounts of those who have met death but recently and in their early years. *The Diary of a Young Girl* by Anne Frank is at once an autobiography of life and death, demonstrating how magnificently the human spirit of a blithe young girl can ignore the shadow of death and an almost impossible way of life to emerge in triumphant normalcy. As Anne Frank writes from her attic prison of doing this and that "later on" it is the reader who realizes a sharp distress, for there was no "later on" for this Jewish victim of Hitlerism.

John Gunther's son Johnny died of a brain tumor at the age of seventeen after hosting the disease for fifteen months. Mr. Gunther writes of that struggle in *Death Be Not Proud* "so that they [children] and their parents may derive some modicum of succor from the unflinching fortitude and detachment with which he rode through the ordeal to the end." It is not only succor that Mr. Gunther's book gives to a young person but a glimpse of the courageous heart, his as well as Johnny's.

Cancer killed Tom Dooley too in the brightness of his manhood. He was thirty-four years old when he died. He, like Johnny Gunther, held fast to life so long as he was able. "The jagged, ugly cancer scar went no deeper than my flesh. There was no cancer in my spirit." "I must, into the burnt soil of my personal mountain of sadness plant the new seedlings of my life. I must continue to live." Both of these quotations are from Doctor Dooley's *The Night They Burned the Mountain.* This book, *Deliver Us from Evil,* and *The Edge of Tomorrow* have been abridged and made into one book for young people, *Doctor Tom Dooley, My Story.* This is a good thing, for Doctor Dooley's story is best told in his own words.

Lewis Mumford's son, Geddes Mumford, was killed in World War II when he was nineteen. In *Green Memories* Mr. Mumford writes of his son so selflessly that the reader is reconciled to the tragedy of a young man of great promise dying before his time. This moving book is not written particularly for young people, but it will do them no harm to read it. It is not a tragic book in any sense of the word but a curiously sunny one. The reading of it may help the young person to understand similar tragic deaths when they occur in his own circle, and it will give him some insight into the heart of a loving parent.

Poetry and Other Literary Forms

Singing lines of poetry often hold for the reader the essence of his own experience in life. So can it be for his experiences with death. The lines can be found in any poem and they are quickly recognized. They leap out at us and we say, "This is the way it is! This is the way it will be!" Such singing lines help cast out the fear of death by clarifying its mystery and they bring solace to the grieving heart when death comes. They do all this with words of soaring beauty that in themselves are a benison to the spirit.

A child finds in poetry these same singing lines to hold in his mind until his heart has need of them: lines that will help him understand death some day and accept it. It would be impossible to discuss here all the volumes of poetry wherein a child might find his own peculiar treasure; suffice to name those poets who write directly to the child heart, and those collections of poems, selected from the whole realm of poetry, that have been made with the child in mind.

In *Windy Morning* Harry Behn, a contemporary poet, writes of the wonders and experiences that have brought delight to his own young children. Another contemporary poet, David McCord, sings of the things children know from seeing and feeling and touching in *Take Sky.* Mr. McCord's touch is light and his deft use of words gives them fresh meaning. Robert Louis Stevenson writes of the child in relation to the world around him, and the child within himself, in his loved collection *A Child's Garden of Verses.*

The great English poet, Walter de la Mare, gave of his genius to the children and published a number of poetry collections for them. His *Rhymes and Verses* comprises his own selection from these various collections. In the introduction to one of these collections, *Bells and Grass,* is Mr. de la Mare's oft-quoted statement: "I know well that only the rarest kind of best in anything can be good enough for the young." This applies aptly to the verses he wrote for children. It also applies to the poetry of his fellow countrywoman, Eleanor Farjeon. Miss Farjeon's poems sing and dance and prance straight into the heart of the child. *Eleanor Farjeon's Poems for Children* is the most inclusive collection of her children's poems.

Selections from two of America's great poets have been made with the young reader in mind: *You Come Too,* by Robert Frost, and *Early Moon,* by Carl Sandburg.

Walter de la Mare has chosen poems that have delighted him for two anthologies: *Come Hither* is for the "young of all ages," *Tom Tiddler's Ground* is for the younger reader. Both contain expressions of Mr. de la Mare's thoughts on poetry in general and, more specifically, on the individual poems included in the anthologies. There is no particular arrangement to *Tom Tiddler's Ground,* but the child reading it will have the delightful sense of rambling leisurely through the whole world of poetry with a kindly companion, stopping to sniff a poem here, sample another there.

This Way, Delight really is a delight not only because of its discriminating selection of poems by Herbert Read, but also because of its most attractive format. Each page has its own poem with generous margins to set off its beauty, like the work of art it is. This is not the rule in anthologies. The airy illustrations of Juliet Kepes add another note of grace and beauty to the anthology.

Poetry has always been a source of deep delight to Annis Duff, and this is apparent in the anthology of poetry she compiled with Gladys Adshead, *Inheritance of Poetry*.

In Geoffrey Grigson's anthology, *The Cherry Tree*, there are two sections on death: "O Mortal Man" and "Life and Death." Mr. Grigson is of the contemporary English world of letters, and his anthology of some 500 poems is directed to "all those of whatever age, who are young." This is a book for the browsing young person.

A Book of Comfort has for its compiler Elizabeth Goudge, whose sensitivity as a writer and a person can be depended upon to give her selection taste and imagination. It is unfortunate that the title of this anthology may keep the young person from discovering the poems gathered together under: The Glory and Wisdom of Creation, Delighting in Each Other, Faith, Tribulation (a section here is devoted to poems relating to death), and Living in the World of the Imagination. Each of these parts begins with "The comfort of . . ." too, more's the pity.

In John Mason Brown's book of essays, *Morning Faces*, there is one essay, "The Long Shadow," which discusses the effect death has had on Mr. Brown's own children and their young friends. This is not written especially for young people, but its wisdom and common sense should appeal to them. Although most of the essays in *Morning Faces* are light and gay this one is quietly serious.

For the child the most frightening manifestation of death perhaps is the coffin with the dead body straight and stiff within it. The child who reads "Blue Silver" from Carl Sandburg's *Rootabaga Stories* may have this fear alleviated, for the American poet writes here with delicacy and beauty of a child's funeral. "So they made a long silver box, just long enough to reach from her head to her feet. And they put on her a blue silver dress and a blue silver band around her forehead and blue silver shoes on her feet. There were soft blue silk and silver sleeves to cover her left arm and her right arm—the two arms crossed on her breast like the letter X." And the king of the country decreed: "We shall put the crossed arms in the alphabet; we shall have a new letter called X, so everybody will understand a funeral is beautiful if there are young singing playmates."

Writers with Carl Sandburg's breadth of vision and depth of compassion write of death for children, write of it creatively and as a natural part of the experience we call living. In such writings death is not a negative force but a positive one shaping the life currents that flow from it; it may be a physical tragedy, but from the tragedy comes spiritual triumph; it is not an end, but the beginning of a new influence, a new motivation, a new understanding. In such writings the death of the body and the withdrawal of a human spirit from association with the living is presented for the child to absorb and ponder over, strengthening as he does so the inner resources that will help him cope with death when it moves within his confines. As a child learns of life from the books he reads, so may he learn of death which is a part of life. The books discussed in this short essay may help him in his pursuit of grace and understanding.

NOTES, REFERENCES, BIBLIOGRAPHIES

PROLOGUE

Alpert, Augusta. "A Brief Communication on Children's Reactions to the Assassination of the President," in *The Psychoanalytic Study of the Child,* XIX. New York: International Universities Press, Inc., 1964.

Anthony, Sylvia. *The Child's Discovery of Death.* London: Kegan Paul, Trench, Traubner & Co., Ltd., 1946.

Arnstein, Helene S. *What to Tell Your Child About Birth, Illness, Death, Divorce, and Other Family Crises.* Indianapolis: The Bobbs-Merrill Company, Inc., 1960.

Barnes, Marion J. "Reactions to the Death of a Mother," in *The Psychoanalytic Study of the Child,* XIX. New York: International Universities Press, Inc., 1964.

Bro, Marguerite H. *When Children Ask.* New York: Harper and Brothers, 1956.

Brown, F. J. *The Sociology of Childhood.* New York: Prentice-Hall, Inc., 1939.

Chaloner, L. "How to Answer the Questions Children Ask About Death." *Parents' Magazine,* 37, November 1962.

English, O. Spurgeon, and Pearson, Gerald H. *Emotional Patterns of Living.* New York: W. W. Norton & Company, Inc., 1963.

Feifel, Herman. "Death—Relevant Variable in Psychology," in Rollo May, ed., *Existential Psychology.* New York: Random House, Inc., 1961.

———. *Meaning of Death.* New York: McGraw-Hill, Inc., 1959.

Fulton, Robert (ed.). *Death and Identity.* New York: John Wiley & Sons, Inc., 1965.

Furman, Erna. "Treatment of Under-Fives by Way of Their Parents," in *The Psychoanalytic Study of the Child,* XII. New York: International Universities Press, Inc., 1957.

Furman, Robert A. "Death of a Six-Year-Old's Mother During His Analysis," in *The Psychoanalytic Study of the Child,* XIX. New York: International Universities Press, Inc., 1964.

———. "Death and the Young Child," in *The Psychoanalytic Study of the Child,* XIX. New York: International Universities Press, Inc., 1964.

273

Gibney, Harriet H. "What Death Means to Children." *Parents' Magazine,* March 1965.

Gittelsohn, Roland B. *Man's Best Hope.* New York: Random House, Inc., 1961.

God in Our Widening World. Manual for Teachers of the Primary Course. Grades 1, 2, 3. Greenwich, Connecticut: Seabury Press.

Goddard, Carolyn E. *Primary Manual.* Boston: United Church Press, 1963.

Goodman, David. "When a Loved One Dies." *The Boston Traveler,* Tuesday, March 9, 1965, p. 35.

Gorer, Geoffrey. *Death, Grief, and Mourning.* Garden City, New York: Doubleday & Company, Inc., 1965.

Gruenberg, S. M. *The Encyclopedia of Child Care and Guidance.* Garden City, New York: Doubleday & Company, Inc., 1954.

Hunter, Edith F. *The Questioning Child and Religion.* Boston: Beacon Press, 1956.

Hurlock, Elizabeth B. *Adolescent Development.* New York: McGraw-Hill Book Company, Inc., 1955.

Jackson, Edgar N. *For the Living.* New York: Channel Press, 1965.

――――. *Telling A Child About Death.* New York: Channel Press, 1965.

――――. *Understanding Grief.* New York: Abingdon Press, 1957.

Kliman, Gilbert. *Prevention and Minimization of Childhood Pathogenic Experiences.* Unpublished paper. 1966.

Lambert, Clara. *Play: A Child's Way of Growing Up.* New York: Play Schools Association, 1947.

Langdon, Grace, and Stout, Irving W. *Bringing Up Children.* New York: The John Day Company, Inc., 1960.

Lee, R. S. *Your Growing Child and Religion.* New York: The Macmillan Company, 1963.

Levin, Phyllis Lee. "Breaking the News of Death." *The New York Times Magazine,* February 21, 1965.

Lichtenwalner, Muriel E. "Children Ask About Death." *International Journal of Religious Education,* June 1964.

Lindemann, Erich. "Symtomatology and Management of Acute Grief," *American Journal of Psychiatry,* 101, 1944, 141–148.

McDonald, Marjorie, M.D. "A Study of the Reactions of Nursery

School Children to the Death of a Child's Mother," in *The Psychoanalytic Study of the Child*, XIX. New York: International Universities Press, Inc., 1964.

Mohr, G. J. *When Children Face Crises*. Chicago: Spencer Press, Inc., 1952.

Nagy, Maria. "The Child's Theories Concerning Death." *Journal of Genetics and Psychology*, 73, 1948, 3–27.

Osborne, E. *When You Lose a Loved One*. New York: Public Affairs Committee, 1958.

Parkhurst, Helen. *Exploring the Child's World*. New York: Appleton-Century-Crofts, 1951.

Polner, Murray, and Barron, Arthur. *The Questions Children Ask*. New York: The Macmillan Company, 1964.

Sherrill, Helen H., and Sherrill, Lewis J. *Interpreting Death to Children*. National Council of the Churches of Christ, 475 Riverside Drive, New York, 1956.

Wolf, A. M. W. *Helping Your Child to Understand Death*. Child Study Pamphlet, 1958.

CHAPTER I

1. Paradoxically, however, death, according to this same theology, was fundamentally alien to man; it was not originally a condition of his existence. Rather, it was a divine penalty levied on man for his original sin — a transgression, however, which was expiable. Christianity teaches that although we may experience a temporal death, by atonement it is possible to be returned to God in heaven; failure to atone for original sin condemns man to hell. In either case, there is implicit the idea that man will ultimately cheat his temporal death; whether redeemed or damned it is believed that a personal identity follows each man into eternity. Thus traditional Western theological thought has explicitly and implicitly demonstrated what Freud and others have since observed — namely, man's inability to envision the irrevocable death of his "self."

2. The story of Frankenstein is the story of a prideful man who arrogantly seeks to emulate God by creating life. He succeeds but his success is short-lived. His creation not only runs amok, threatening the world with destruction, but eventually turns on its creator. In the story of Dracula, it is not a matter of striving to challenge God but rather it is a matter of inadvertently coming

upon or accidentally conjuring up His great adversary — the Devil. Man in this morality play is caught between transcendental forces beyond his knowledge or control. Good struggles with evil for his soul. Only his belief in God and the efficacy of the cross before the power of evil permit man to ward off this new onslaught against himself. The death of Dracula, however, provides only a respite from such attacks because evil itself remains.

3. This convergence was seen particularly in modern television with such programs as "The Munsters," "The Adams Family," "I Married an Angel," "My Favorite Martian," etc. In these popular situation comedies, evil was normal and temporal while manifestations of good were witty, bright, naughtily irreverent people who displayed their "special" powers to solve domestic problems or repair electrical appliances. The traditional role of the "mysterious stranger" who rights wrongs and protects the innocent from evildoers is now in the hands of the masters of parody. The leap from the heroics of the Lone Ranger to the antics of Batman is only the distance between two generations, but in another sense it is the culmination of forces which have been emerging in America for many decades. Batman is in the long tradition of the "mysterious stranger" but has no longer an ideology that will sustain him. Like Frankenstein's monster who now, it will be observed, is a docile and comical "Munster" (and an embalmer to boot), Batman has become an object of ridicule and humor in the mass media.

4. The kidney machine is an "artificial kidney" to which a person suffering from end-stage kidney disease (uremic poisoning and congestive heart failure) may be attached. Each patient using the machine has a U-shaped tube imbedded in his forearm. At specified intervals (usually twice a week for several hours) this tube is hooked up to the artificial kidney and through the chemical process of dialysis the blood of the patient is cleansed of harmful wastes. (For a more detailed explanation of the workings of the machine, see Shana Alexander, "They Decide Who Lives, Who Dies." *Life,* Vol. 53, No. 19 (November 9, 1962), pp. 102–125.)

5. A few of the factors used in making the selection of patients who may use the machine are: 1) age and sex of the patient (no one over the age of 45 is eligible); 2) marital status (the married are given prior consideration); 3) number of children

(the larger the family of young children, the greater the chance of being chosen) ; 4) type of occupation and educational background (those with a record of past performance and a high future potential in an occupation which will somehow "contribute" to society are given the most serious consideration) ; 5) emotional stability, with particular regard to the patient's ability to accept the treatment and its restrictions. (See Shana Alexander, *op. cit.*) . The trend to equate "worth" with "achievement" has been noted and decried by John W. Gardner, President, Carnegie Foundation for the Advancement of Teaching. In a short editorial statement he says, "human dignity and worth should be assessed only in terms of those qualities of mind and spirit that are within the reach of every human being. This is not to say that we should not value achievement. We should value it exceedingly. It is simply to say that achievement should not be confused with human worth. The more we allow the impression to get abroad that only the college man or woman is worthy of respect in our society, the more we contribute to a fatal confusion, which works to the injury of all concerned." (Reprinted in *The Minneapolis Morning Tribune,* February 23, 1967, editorial page.)

6. At this juncture, one cannot help drawing parallels between developments of this kind in America and the events that occurred in Germany during the early 1930's. The beginnings of the Nazi crimes were small. At first, there was only the subtle shift in the perspective of physicians that there was such a thing as a life not worthy of living or that one person had a greater claim to life than another. In 1931 Bavarian psychiatrists were publicly discussing sterilization and the euthanasia of persons with chronic mental illness. In 1936 Hitler ordered euthanasia for these persons. All state hospitals were to report on those persons who had been ill for five years or more and who were unable to work. Reports were made to boards of leading psychiatrists who passed judgment. A "Charitable Transport Company for the Sick" carried patients to "Charitable Foundations for Institutional Care" where they were put to death. The victims were all those unable to work and considered nonrehabilitable. Within a few years, about 275,000 Germans were put to death. From that established base it was merely a matter of "logic" to include the Gypsy, the Jew, and all other "enemies" of the state. (See Leo L.

Alexander, "Medical Science Under Dictatorship," *New England Journal of Medicine,* Vol. 241, No. 2 [1949], pp. 39–47.)

7. For an extended discussion of the cryonic movement, see Robert C. W. Ettinger, *Prospect of Immortality,* Garden City, New York: Doubleday & Company, Inc., 1964.

8. Robert Fulton, *The Sacred and the Secular: Attitudes of the American Public Toward Death,* Milwaukee: Bulfin, 1963.

9. Herman Feifel, "Older Persons Look at Death," *Geriatrics,* 11, 1956, pp. 127–130.

10. Robert Fulton, *op. cit., passim.*

11. In 1961, 60.9% of all deaths occurred in a hospital or institution — 48.3% occurred in a short-stay hospital and 12.6% occurred in resident institutions. (United States Department of Health, Education, and Welfare, *Hospitalization in the Last Year of Life: United States, 1961,* Washington, D.C.: Public Health Service Publication No. 1000, series 22, no. 1, 1965, table 2, p 15.) For discussions of death in a hospital setting, see Avery D. Weisman and Thomas P. Hackett, "Predilection to Death," in Robert Fulton (ed.) , *Death and Identity,* New York: John Wiley & Sons, Inc., 1965, pp. 293–329; David Sudnow, *Passing On,* New York: Prentice-Hall, Inc., 1966; and Barney G. Glaser and Anselm L. Strauss, *Awareness of Dying,* Chicago: Aldine Publishing Company, 1965.

12. United States Department of Health, Education, and Welfare, *The Facts of Life and Death,* Washington, D.C.: Public Health Service Publication, No. 600, revised edition, 1965, table 4, p. 4.

13. The Bureau of the Census has estimated that in 1975 there will be more than 21 million persons over the age of 65 and in 1980 there will be approximately 23 million in this age group. (United States Department of Commerce, *Current Population Reports, Population Estimates Projection of the Population of the United States by Age and Sex, 1964–1985,* Washington, D.C.: United States Department of Commerce, 1964, table E, p. 5.

14. Franz Borkenau, "The Concept of Death," in Robert Fulton (ed.), *Death and Identity, op. cit.,* pp. 42–56.

15. That is, given the number of deaths per year at approximately 1,800,000 and an average household size of 5 (only 11.1% of United States households in 1960 consisted of more than 5 people) the statistical probability of a death occurring within a

household is 1 in 20 per year. Obviously, the smaller the household size the lower the probability of a death occurring within it each year. (United States Bureau of the Census, 1960 Mortality Statistics and United States Bureau of the Census, *Current Population Reports,* Series P-20, no. 106 (January 9, 1961), table 3, p. 13.)

16. Different authors have noted the tendency for the threat of mass death to undermine the meaning systems of modern society. See, for example, Robert J. Lifton, "On Death and Death Symbolism: The Hiroshima Disaster," *Psychiatry,* 27, 1964, pp. 191–210; Geoffrey Gorer, "The Pornography of Death," in *Death, Grief, and Mourning,* Garden City, New York: Doubleday & Company, Inc., 1965, pp. 192–199; and Frederick J. Hoffman, *The Mortal No: Death and the Modern Imagination,* Princeton, New Jersey: Princeton University Press, 1964.

17. See, for instance, Martha Wolfenstein and Gilbert Kliman (eds.), *Children and the Death of a President,* Garden City, New York: Doubleday & Company, Inc., 1965; Bradley S. Greenberg and Edwin B. Parker (eds.), *The Kennedy Assassination and the American Public: Social Communication in Crisis,* Stanford, California: Stanford University Press, 1965; and Bureau of Social Science Research, *Studies of Kennedy's Assassination,* Washington, D.C.: Bureau of Social Science Research, 1966.

18. Paul B. Sheatsley and Jacob J. Feldman, "The Assassination of President Kennedy: A Preliminary Report on Public Reactions and Behavior," *Public Opinion Quarterly,* 28, 1964, pp. 189–215.

19. Erich Lindemann, "Symptomatology and Management of Acute Grief," *American Journal of Psychiatry,* 108, 1944, pp. 141–148.

20. Karl Stern, Gwendolyn M. Williams, and Miguel Prados, "Grief Reactions in Later Life," *American Journal of Psychiatry,* 108, 1951, pp. 289–294.

21. Herbert J. Barry, Jr., "Significance of Maternal Bereavement Before the Age Eight in Psychiatric Patients," *Archives of Neurological Psychiatry,* 62, 1949, pp. 630–637.

22. Mervyn Shoor and Mary H. Speed, "Delinquency as a Manifestation of the Mourning Process," *Psychiatric Quarterly,* 37, 1963, pp. 540–558.

23. Geoffrey Gorer, *Death, Grief, and Mourning, op. cit., passim.*

24. United States Department of Health, Education, and Welfare, *The Facts of Life and Death, op. cit.,* table 13, p. 11.

25. Edmund H. Volkart and Stanley T. Michael, "Bereavement and Mental Health," in Robert Fulton (ed.), *Death and Identity, op. cit.,* pp. 272–293.

26. 1,813,549 Americans died in 1963. Of this total, 60.5% were deaths of persons age 65 or older. Deaths of male adults age 65 or older accounted for 56.0% of all male deaths; and deaths of women in this same age category accounted for 66.3% of all female deaths. Deaths of children under the age of 15 accounted for 7.5% of the total deaths that year. (United States Department of Health, Education, and Welfare, *The Facts of Life and Death, op. cit.,* table 13, p. 11.) For an extensive account of the relationship between death and demography as well as the social and cultural consequences of this relationship, see Robert Blauner's insightful essay, "Death and Social Structure," *Psychiatry,* vol. 29, no. 4 (1966), pp. 378–394.

27. In addition to the research previously referred to, a study of deaths in military action in World War II showed that the bereaved had great difficulty believing in and accepting the reality of the death of their kin because they had no opportunity to see the body or witness its disposal. See Thomas D. Eliot, "Of the Shadow of Death," *Annals of the American Academy of Political and Social Science,* 229, 1943, pp. 87–99.

28. Charles W. Wahl, "The Fear of Death," in Robert Fulton (ed.), *Death and Identity, op. cit.,* pp. 56–66.

29. In the face of the arguments that young people typically are indifferent to or unaffected by death is the finding of Roberta Sigel that the young people of the country, according to their own reports, were at least as emotionally involved in the events surrounding President Kennedy's death and burial as were their parents. She concluded that among children, teen-agers, college students, and adults response similarities to the assassination were more marked than were the discrepancies. (The N. O. R. C. report which in certain respects contradicts the findings of this study was based upon the opinions of parents regarding their children's reactions.) Roberta S. Sigel, "Television and the Re-

actions of School Children to the Assassination" in Bradley S. Greenberg and Edwin B. Parker, *op. cit.*, pp. 199–219.

CHAPTER II

1. Sylvia Anthony, *The Child's Discovery of Death: A Study of Child Psychology,* London: Kegan Paul, 1940, New York: Harcourt, Brace & World, Inc., 1940.

2. James George Frazer, *The Golden Bough: A Study in Magic and Religion,* New York: The Macmillan Company, 1947, p. 11.

3. Sigmund Freud, "Creative Writers and Day Dreaming," in *The Complete Psychological Works of Sigmund Freud,* standard edition, London: Hogarth Press, 1959, vol. IX, p. 145.

4. Sigmund Freud, "Negations," in *The Complete Psychological Works of Sigmund Freud,* standard edition, London: Hogarth Press, 1961, vol. XIX, p. 236.

5. Sigmund Freud, "On Narcissism," in *The Complete Psychological Works of Sigmund Freud,* standard edition, London: Hogarth Press, 1957, vol. XIV, pp. 82–102.

6. *Ibid.*

7. Sigmund Freud, "On Narcissism: An Introduction," in *Collected Papers,* London: Hogarth Press, 1948, vol. IV, pp. 32–39.

8. Sigmund Freud, "The Psychopathology of Everyday Life," in *The Complete Psychological Works of Sigmund Freud,* standard edition, London: Hogarth Press, 1960, vol. VI.

9. Maria Nagy, "The Child's Theories Concerning Death," *Journal of Genetics and Psychology,* 73, 1948, 3, 4, 26, 27.

10. Gregory Rochlin, "The Loss Complex: A Contribution to the Etiology of Depression," *Journal of the American Psychoanalytical Association,* 7, 1959, 299–316.

11. Gregory Rochlin, "The Dread of Abandonment: A Contribution to the Etiology of the Loss Complex and to Depression," in *The Psychoanalytic Study of the Child,* New York: International Universities Press, Inc., 1961, vol. XVI, pp. 451–470.

12. Paul Schilder and David Wechsler, "The Attitude of Children Towards Death," *Journal of Genetics and Psychology,* 45, 1935, 406.

13. The supposition of a death instinct, to which Freud (see

his "The Ego and the Id" in *The Complete Psychological Works of Sigmund Freud,* standard edition, London: Hogarth Press, 1961, vol. XIX, pp. 3–66) gave credence, although stating categorically that it was not a psychological phenomenon, led him into fruitless speculation and drew others into endless controversy for decades. The continuing speculation no longer interests most psychoanalysts but it seems to retain polemical viability in some academic circles. (See N. Brown's *Life Against Death,* New York: Random House, 1959, pp. 87–134.) Confusing speculation with clinical findings leads to overlooking that the notions about a death instinct are being associated with self-destructive acts and behavior arising as specific conflicts connected with unbearable destructive wishes toward a valued object which are instead directed toward oneself. Others since Freud are responsible for the continued confusion by failing to note his comment that if such instincts are present they are "mute."

14. Reference here is to secondary narcissism. Primary narcissism forms one of the hypotheses of the libido theory. It is deduced rather than observed and is perhaps best indicated by the autoerotic and the instinctual processes, in contrast to secondary narcissism, which develops as a part of the ego.

CHAPTER III

1. I. Alexander and A. M. Adlerstein, "Affective Responses to the Concept of Death in a Population of Children and Early Adolescents," *Journal of Genetics and Psychology,* 93, 1959, 167–177.

2. Silvia Anthony, *The Child's Discovery of Death,* New York: Harcourt, Brace & World, Inc., 1940.

3. Jacques Choron, *Death and Western Thought,* New York: The Crowell-Collier Publishing Company, 1963.

4. Jacques Choron, *Modern Man and Mortality,* New York: The Macmillan Company, 1963.

5. Herman Feifel (ed.), *The Meaning of Death,* New York: McGraw-Hill, Inc., 1959.

6. Robert Fulton (ed.), *Death and Identity,* New York: John Wiley & Sons, Inc., 1965.

7. Arnold Gesell and Frances L. Ilg, *The Child from Five to Ten,* New York: Harper and Brothers, 1946.

8. Barney Glaser and A. L. Strauss, *Awareness of Dying,* Chicago: Aldine Publishing Company, 1965.

Notes. References, Bibliographies 283

9. Earl Grollman, unpublished manuscript.

10. I. Huang and H. W. Lee, "Experimental Analysis of Child Animism," *Journal of Genetics and Psychology,* 66, 1945, 69–74.

11. Robert Kastenbaum, "Engrossment and Perspective in Later Life: A Developmental-field Approach," in Robert Kastenbaum (ed.), *Contributions to the Psychobiology of Aging,* New York: Springer, 1965, pp. 1–18.

12. Robert Kastenbaum, "Time and Death in Adolescence," in Herman Feifel (ed.), *The Meaning of Death,* New York: McGraw-Hill, Inc., 1959, pp. 99–113.

13. Robert Kastenbaum and R. B. Aisenberg, *The Psychology of Death,* New York: Springer, in press.

14. G. Klingberg, "The Distinction Between Living and Not Living Among 7–10-year-old Children with Some Remarks Concerning the So-called Animism Controversy," *Journal of Genetics and Psychology,* 105, 1957, 227–238.

15. Adah Maurer, "Adolescent Attitudes Toward Death," *Journal of Genetics and Psychology,* 105, 1964, 75–90.

16. Adah Maurer, "Maturation of Concepts of Death," *British Journal of Medicine and Psychology,* 39, 1966, 35–41.

17. Jessica Mitford, *The American Way of Death,* New York: Simon and Schuster, Inc., 1962.

18. N. McLaughlin and Robert Kastenbaum, "Engrossment in Personal Past, Future and Death," paper presented at annual meetings of the American Psychological Association, September 2, 1966.

19. Maria H. Nagy, "The Child's View of Death," *Journal of Genetics and Psychology,* 73, 1948, 3–27 (reprinted in Feifel, above).

20. Jean Piaget, *The Child's Conception of Physical Causality,* (translated by M. W. Gabian), New York: Harcourt, Brace & World, Inc., 1930.

21. Jean Piaget, *The Construction of Reality in the Child,* (translated by M. Cook), New York: Basic Books, Inc., 1954.

22. R. W. Russell, "Studies in Animism: II. The Development of Animism," *Journal of Genetics and Psychology,* 56, 1940, 353–366.

23. Paul Schilder and David Wechsler, "The Attitude of Children Towards Death," *Journal of Genetics and Psychology,* 45, 1934, 406–451.

24. Colin Scott, "Old Age and Death," *American Journal of Psychology,* 1896, 67–122.

25. Millicent Shinn, *Biography of a Baby,* Boston: Houghton Mifflin Company, 1900.

26. Albert J. Solnit and Morris Green, *Modern Perspectives in Child Development,* New York: International Universities Press, Inc., 1963, pp. 217–228.

27. A. L. Strauss, "The Animism Controversy: Re-examination of Huang-Lee Data," *Journal of Genetics and Psychology,* 78, 1951, 105–113.

28. Adriaan Verwoerdt, *Communication with the Fatally Ill,* Springfield, Illinois: Charles C. Thomas, Publisher, 1966.

CHAPTER IV

1. R. E. Bradbury (ed.), *New and Accurate Description of the Coast of Guinea,* New York: Barnes & Noble, Inc., 1966.

2. E. E. Evans-Pritchard, "Witchcraft Explains Unfortunate Events," in William A. Lessa and Evon Z. Vogt (eds.), *Reader in Comparative Religion,* New York: Harper and Brothers, 2nd ed., 1965, pp. 277–282.

3. D. Forde, "Death and Succession: An Analysis of Yako Mortuary Ritual," in Max Gluckman (ed.), *Essays on the Ritual of Social Relations,* Manchester: Manchester University Press, 1962, pp. 89–123.

4. John Greenway and Melville Jacobs (eds. and compilers), *The Anthropologist Looks at Myth,* Austin and London: University of Texas Press, 1966.

5. Michael J. Harner, "Jivaro Souls," *American Anthropology,* 64, 1962, 258–272.

6. Edward Norbeck, *Religion in Primitive Society,* New York and Evanston: Harper & Row, Publishers, 1961, pp. 159–164.

7. Julian Steward (ed.), *Handbook of South American Indians,* vol. 3, Bureau of American Ethnology, bulletin no. 143, 1948, p. 88.

CHAPTER VI

1. Margaret Schoneberger Mahler, "On Sadness and Grief in Infancy and Childhood: Loss and Restoration of the Symbiotic Love Object," in the *Psychoanalytic Study of the Child,* New York: International Universities Press, Inc., 1961, vol. XVI, pp. 332–351.

2. Gregory Rochlin, "The Dread of Abandonment: A Contribution to the Etiology of the Loss Complex and Depression," *Psychoanalytic Study of the Child,* XVI, 1961, 451–470.

3. Lauretta Bender, *Aggression, Hostility, and Anxiety in Children,* Springfield, Illinois: Charles C. Thomas, Publishers, 1953, p. 63.

4. Anna Freud, *Normality and Pathology in Childhood,* New York: International Universities Press, Inc., 1965, p. 58.

5. Norman Paul, "The Mourning Experience in Family Therapy," unpublished paper presented to the Psychological Counseling Department, Arlington Public Schools, Massachusetts, March 1966.

6. A. C. Cain and J. Fast, "Children's Disturbed Reactions to Parent Suicide," *American Journal of Orthopsychiatry,* 36, October 1966, 873–880.

7. R. Behrens, M. Kraushaar, C. Rohrbough, and E. Rosenberg, *A Descriptive Study of Elementary School Children Who Have Sustained a Major Loss,* unpublished master's thesis, Simmons College School of Social Work, June 1964.

8. John Bowlby, "Childhood Mourning and Its Implications for Psychiatry," *American Journal of Psychiatry,* 118, December 1961a, 481–498.

CHAPTER VII

1. Geoffrey Gorer, *Death, Grief, and Mourning,* Garden City, New York: Doubleday & Company, Inc., 1965.

2. Robert Fulton (ed.). *Death and Identity,* New York: John Wiley & Sons, Inc., 1965.

3. Erich Lindemann, "Symptomatology and Management of Acute Grief," *American Journal of Psychiatry,* CI, 1944.

4. James A. Knight, introduction to *For the Living,* New York: Channel Press, 1963.

5. Sigmund Freud, *Collected Papers,* London: Hogarth Press, 1950.

6. Otto Rank, *Psychology and the Soul,* Philadelphia: University of Pennsylvania Press, 1950.

7. Nandor Fodor, *The Search for the Beloved* and *The New Interpretation of Dreams,* New York: Hermitage Press, 1949.

8. Jean Piaget, *The Language and Thought of the Child,* New York, Meridian Press, 1955; *Judgment and Reasoning in the*

Child, New York: Humanities Press, 1947; *The Child's Conception of the World,* Totowa, New Jersey: Littlefield, Adams, & Company, 1960; *The Child's Conception of Physical Causality,* Totowa, New Jersey: Littlefield, Adams, & Company, 1960; *The Moral Judgment of the Child,* New York: Free Press, n.d.; *The Psychology of Intelligence,* Totowa, New Jersey: Littlefield, Adams, & Company, 1960; *Play, Dreams and Imitation in Childhood,* New York: W. W. Norton & Company, Inc., 1962; *The Child's Conception of Number,* New York: Humanities Press, n.d.; *The Origin of Intelligence in Children,* New York: W. W. Norton & Company, Inc., 1963; *The Construction of Reality in the Child,* New York: Basic Books, 1954.

9. Carl Rogers, *On Becoming a Person,* Boston: Houghton Mifflin Company, 1961.

10. Abraham Maslow, *Toward a Psychology of Being,* Princeton: D. Van Nostrand Company, Inc., 1962.

11. Viktor Frankl, *The Doctor and the Soul,* New York: Alfred A. Knopf, Inc., 1955; *From Death-Camp to Existentialism,* Boston: Beacon Press, 1955.

CHAPTER VIII

Becque, Maurice, C.SS.R., and Becque, Louis, C.SS.R. *Life After Death.* New York: Hawthorn Books, Inc., 1960.

Didier, Jean-Charles. *Death and the Christian.* New York: Hawthorn Books, Inc., 1961.

Eminyan, Maurice, S.J. *The Theology of Salvation.* Boston: Daughters of St. Paul, 1960.

Garrigou-Lagrange, R., O.P. *Life Everlasting.* St. Louis: B. Herder Book Company, 1952.

Mersch, Emile, S.J. *Morality and the Mystical Body.* New York: P. J. Kenedy & Sons, 1939.

Philipon, M. M., O.P. *The Sacraments in the Christian Life.* Westminster, Maryland: Newman Press, 1953.

Vaughan, John S. *Life After Death.* New York: Benzinger Brothers, Inc., 1902.

CHAPTER IX

Anthony, Sylvia. *The Child's Discovery of Death.* London: Kegan Paul, Trench, Trubner & Co., Ltd., 1946.

Arnstein, Helene S. *What to Tell Your Child About Birth, Illness, Death, Divorce, and Other Family Crises.* Indianapolis: The Bobbs-Merrill Company, Inc., 1960.

Barnes, Marion J. "Reactions to the Death of a Mother." *The Psychoanalytic Study of the Child,* XIX, New York: International Universities Press, Inc., 1964, pp. 334–357.

Barish, Louis and Rebecca. *Basic Jewish Beliefs.* New York: Jonathan David, Publishers, Inc., 1961.

Bookstaber, David. *The Idea of the Development of the Soul in Medieval Jewish Philosophy.* Philadelphia: Maurice Jacobs, Inc., 1950.

Clark, Walter. *The Psychology of Religion.* New York: The Macmillan Company, 1958.

Cohon, Samuel S. *Judaism, A Way of Life.* Cincinnati: Union of American Hebrew Congregations, 1948.

Feifel, Herman. *The Meaning of Death.* New York: McGraw-Hill, Inc., 1959.

Feldman, Abraham J. *The Concept of Immortality in Judaism — Historically Considered.* Titner Memorial Lecture.

Gittelsohn, Roland B. *Man's Best Hope.* New York: Random House, Inc., 1961.

Gordon, Albert I. *In Times of Sorrow.* New York: United Synagogues of America, 1949.

Greenberg, Sidney. *A Modern Treasury of Jewish Thoughts.* New York: Thomas Yoseloff, 1960.

Gruenberg, S. M. *The Encyclopedia of Child Care and Guidance.* Garden City: Doubleday & Company, Inc., 1954.

Hertzberg, Arthur. *Judaism.* New York: Washington Square Press, Inc., 1963.

The Holy Scriptures. Philadelphia: The Jewish Publication Society of America, 1917.

Jacobson, David S. *Death.* Universal Jewish Encyclopedia 3. New York: Universal Jewish Encyclopedia Company, 1943.

Jackson, Edgar N. *Telling a Child About Death.* New York: Channel Press, 1965.

Katz, Robert L. "Counseling the Bereaved." *Central Conference of American Rabbis Yearbook,* 1953, LXIII, 465–469.

Lasker, Arnold A. "When Children Face Bereavement." *Conservative Judaism,* 1964, XVIII, 53–58.

Lazarus, O. *Liberal Judaism and Its Standpoint*. London: The Macmillan Company, 1937.

Liebman, Joshua L. *Peace of Mind*. New York: Simon and Schuster, Inc., 1946.

Linn, Louis, and Schwarz, Leo. *Psychiatry and Religious Experience*. New York: Random House, Inc., 1958.

Montefiore, C. G., and Lowe, H. A. *Rabbinic Anthology*. London: The Macmillan Company, 1938.

Moore, George Foote. *Judaism*. Cambridge: Harvard University Press, 1946.

Noveck, Simon. *Judaism and Psychiatry*. New York: United Synagogues of America, 1956.

Ostow, Mortimer, and Scharfstein, Ben-Ami. *The Need to Believe*. New York: International Universities Press, Inc., 1954.

Parkhurst, Helen. *Exploring The Child's World*. New York: Appleton-Century-Crofts, Inc., 1951.

Pool, David de Sola. *Why I Am a Jew*. New York: Bloch Publishing Company, 1951.

Rabinowicz, H. *A Guide to Life, Jewish Laws and Customs of Mourning*. London: Jewish Chronicle Publications, 1964.

Schwartzman, Sylvan D. *Orientation to God, Prayer, and Ethics*. Teacher's Manual. Experimental Edition, Hebrew Union College, Jewish Institute of Religion, 1961.

Steinberg, Milton. *Basic Judaism*. New York: Harcourt, Brace, and Company, 1947.

When You Lose a Loved One. Public Affairs Pamphlet, 22 East 38th St., New York, 1958.

Wolf, Arnold J. *Challenge to Confirmands*. New York: Scribe Publications, Inc., 1963.

CHAPTER X

ASSOCIATIVE READING

Duff, Annis. *Bequest of Wings*. New York: The Viking Press, Inc., 1944.

———. *Longer Flight*. New York: The Viking Press, Inc., 1955.

Eaton, Anne Thaxter. *Reading with Children*. New York: The Viking Press, Inc., 1940.

———. *Treasure for the Taking*. Revised edition. New York: The Viking Press, Inc., 1957.

Hazard, Paul. *Books, Children and Men.* Translated by Marguerite Mitchell. Boston: The Horn Book, Inc., 1947.

Meigs, Cornelia, and others. *A Critical History of Children's Literature.* New York: The Macmillan Company, 1953.

Moore, Anne Carroll. *My Roads to Childhood.* Boston: The Horn Book, Inc., 1961.

Sayers, Frances Clarke. *Summoned by Books.* New York: The Viking Press, Inc., 1965.

Smith, Lillian H. *The Unreluctant Years.* Chicago: American Library Association, 1953.

Viguers, Ruth Hill (ed.). *The Horn Book Magazine.* Boston: The Horn Book, Inc., 1942 to date.

Viguers, Ruth Hill. *Margin for Surprise.* Boston: Little, Brown and Company, 1964.

PICTURE BOOKS DISCUSSED FOR THE YOUNGER CHILD

Anglund, Joan Walsh. *Love Is a Special Way of Feeling.* New York: Harcourt, Brace & World, Inc., 1960.

———. *A Friend Is Someone Who Likes You.* New York: Harcourt, Brace & World, Inc., 1958.

Brooke, L. Leslie. *Johnny Crow's Garden.* New York: Frederick Warne & Co., Ltd., 1904.

———. *Johnny Crow's New Garden.* New York: Frederick Warne & Co., Ltd., 1935.

———. *Johnny Crow's Party.* New York: Frederick Warne & Co., Ltd., 1907.

Brown, Margaret Wise. *A Child's Good Night Book.* Illustrated by Jean Charlot. New York: William R. Scott, Inc., 1943.

———. *The Runaway Bunny.* Pictures by Clement Hurd. New York: Harper and Brothers, 1942.

Buckley, Helen E. *Grandfather and I.* Pictures by Paul Galdone. New York: Lothrop, Lee & Shepard Company, Inc., 1959.

Estes, Eleanor. *A Little Oven.* New York: Harcourt, Brace & World, Inc., 1955.

Ets, Marie Hall. *Play With Me.* New York: The Viking Press, Inc., 1955.

Fitch, Florence Mary. *A Book About God.* Illustrated by Leonard Weisgard. New York: Lothrop, Lee & Shepard Company, Inc., 1953.

Flack, Marjorie, and Wiese, Kurt. *The Story of Ping*. New York: The Viking Press, Inc., 1933.

Françoise. *The Thank-You Book*. New York: Charles Scribner's Sons, 1947.

Goudey, Alice E. *Houses from the Sea*. Illustrated by Adrienne Adams. New York: Charles Scribner's Sons, 1959.

Gramatky, Hardie. *Little Toot*. New York: G. P. Putnam's Sons, 1939.

Handforth, Thomas. *Mei Li*. New York: Doubleday & Company, Inc., 1938.

Lionni, Leo. *On My Beach There Are Many Pebbles*. New York: Ivan Obolensky, Inc. (An Astor Book), 1961.

McCloskey, Robert. *Blueberries for Sal*. New York: The Viking Press, Inc., 1948.

———. *Time of Wonder*. New York: The Viking Press, Inc., 1957.

Minarik, Else Holmelund. *Father Bear Comes Home*. Pictures by Maurice Sendak. New York: Harper & Row, Publishers (An I Can Read Book), 1959.

———. *Little Bear*. Pictures by Maurice Sendak. New York: Harper & Row, Publishers (An I Can Read Book), 1959.

———. *Little Bear's Friend*. Pictures by Maurice Sendak. New York: Harper & Row, Publishers (An I Can Read Book), 1960.

———. *Little Bear's Visit*. Pictures by Maurice Sendak. New York: Harper & Row, Publishers (An I Can Read Book), 1961.

Potter, Beatrix. *The Tale of Peter Rabbit*. New York: Frederick Warne & Co., Ltd., 1903.

Slobodkin, Louis. *One Is Good But Two Are Better*. New York: The Vanguard Press, Inc., 1956.

Tresselt, Alvin. *White Snow, Bright Snow*. Illustrated by Roger Duvoisin. New York: Lothrop, Lee & Shepard Company, Inc., 1947.

Udry, Janice May. *A Tree Is Nice*. Pictures by Marc Simont. New York: Harper & Row, Publishers, 1956.

Yashima, Taro. *Umbrella*. New York: The Viking Press, Inc., 1958.

———. *Youngest One*. New York: The Viking Press, Inc., 1962.

Zion, Gene. *Harry the Dirty Dog*. Pictures by Margaret Bloy Graham. New York: Harper & Row, Publishers, 1956.

Zolotow, Charlotte. *Do You Know What I'll Do?* Pictures by Garth Williams. New York: Harper & Row, Publishers, 1958.

———. *One Step, Two* . . . Illustrated by Roger Duvoisin. New York: Lothrop, Lee & Shepard Company, Inc., 1955.

FOLK TALES

Folk tales are usually read by children when they are in the fourth and fifth grades.

Boggs, Ralph Steele, and Davis, Mary Gould. *Thre Golden Oranges*. Pictures by Emma Brock. Spanish. New York: Longmans, 1936.

Chase, Richard (ed.). *Grandfather Tales*. Illustrated by Berkeley Williams, Jr. American-English folk tales. Boston: Houghton Mifflin Company, 1948.

———. *Jack Tales*. With an appendix compiled by Herbert Halpert. Illustrated by Berkeley Williams, Jr. Boston: Houghton Mifflin Company, 1943.

Fillmore, Parker. *The Shepherd's Nosegay*. Edited by Katherine Love. Illustrated by Enrice Arno. Stories from Finland and Czechoslovakia. New York: Harcourt, Brace & World, Inc., 1958.

Finger, Charles. *Tales from Silver Lands*. Woodcuts by Paul Honoré. South American. New York: Doubleday & Company, Inc., 1924.

Grimm, Jacob and Wilhelm. *Household Stories*. Translated by Lucy Crane. Illustrated by Walter Crane. Ann Arbor, Michigan: University Microfilms, Inc., 1966.

———. *Tales from Grimm*. Freely translated and illustrated by Wanda Gág. New York: Coward-McCann, Inc., 1936.

———. *More Tales from Grimm*. Freely translated and illustrated by Wanda Gág. New York: Coward-McCann, Inc., 1947.

Haviland, Virginia. *Favorite Fairy Tales Told in France*. Illustrated by Roger Duvoisin. Retold from Charles Perrault and other French storytellers. Boston: Little, Brown and Company, 1959.

Jacobs, Joseph. *English Fairy Tales*. Illustrated by John D. Batten. Third edition, revised. New York: G. P. Putnam's Sons, 1892.

———. *More English Fairy Tales*. Illustrated by John D. Batten. New York: G. P. Putnam's Sons, n.d.

MacManus, Seumas. *Hibernian Nights*. Introduced by Padraic Colum. Illustrated by Paul Kennedy. Irish. New York: The Macmillan Company, 1963.

Nic Leodhas, Sorche. *Heather and Broom*. Illustrated by Consuelo Joerns. Tales of the Scottish Highlands. New York: Holt, Rinehart and Winston, Inc., 1960.

Ransome, Arthur. *Old Peter's Russian Tales*. Illustrated by Dmitri Mitrokhin. New York: Thomas Nelson & Sons, 1917.

Thorne-Thomsen, Gudrun (ed.). *East o' the Sun and West o' the Moon*. With other Norwegian folk tales. Revised edition. Evanston, Illinois: Row, 1946.

Uchida, Yoshiko. *The Dancing Kettle and Other Japanese Folk Tales*. Illustrated by Richard C. Jones. New York: Harcourt, Brace & World, Inc., 1949.

Wheeler, Post. *Russian Wonder Tales*. Containing twelve of the famous Bilibin illustrations in color. Revised edition. New York: Beechhurst, 1946.

BOOKS DISCUSSED FOR THE OLDER CHILD

The figures in parenthess at the end of each title entry refer to the age when children read the book. These are approximations only, for children read as individuals, each according to his ability and his interests of the moment.

Adshead, Gladys L., and Annis, Duff (compilers). *Inheritance of Poetry*. Decorations by Nora S. Unwin. Boston: Houghton Mifflin Company, 1948. (All ages)

Alcott, Louisa M. *Little Men*. Illustrated by Hilda van Stockum. Cleveland: The World Publishing Company (Rainbow Classics), 1950. (10–13)

———. *Little Women: or, Meg, Jo, Beth, and Amy*. Illustrated by Barbara Cooney. New York: The Crowell-Collier Publishing Company, 1955. (10–13)

Andersen, Hans Christian. *Forty-Two Stories*. Translated from the Danish by M. R. James. Illustrated by Robin Jacques. New York: Barnes & Noble, Inc., 1959. (9–10)

————. *Hans Andersen's Fairy Tales.* Translated by L. W. Kingsland. Illustrated by Ernst H. Shepard. New York: Henry Z. Walck, Inc., 1962. (9–10)

————. *The Steadfast Tin Soldier.* Translated by M. R. James. Illustrated by Marcia Brown. New York: Charles Scribner's Sons, 1953. (8–9)

Bailey, Carolyn Sherwin. *Miss Hickory.* With lithographs by Ruth Gannett. New York: The Viking Press, Inc., 1946. (9–10)

Ball, Zachary. *Bristle Face.* New York: Holiday House, 1962. (10–12)

Behn, Harry. *The Faraway Lurs.* Cleveland: The World Publishing Company, 1963. (10–14)

————. *Windy Morning.* New York: Harcourt, Brace & World, Inc., 1953. (7–9)

Brown, John Mason. *Morning Faces.* A book of children and parents. Illustrations by Susanne Suba. New York: McGraw-Hill, Inc. (Whittlsey House), 1949. (14 to all ages)

Buck, Pearl S. *The Big Wave.* Illustrated with prints by Hiroshige and Hokusai. New York: The John Day Company, Inc., 1947. (10–14)

Bulfinch, Thomas. *A Book of Myths.* Selections from Bulfinch's *Age of Fable.* With illustrations by Helen Sewell. New York: The Macmillan Company, 1942. (10–14)

Coatsworth, Elizabeth. *The Cat Who Went to Heaven.* Illustrated by Lynd Ward. New York: The Macmillan Company, 1958. (10–12)

De la Mare, Walter. *Bells and Grass.* Illustrated by Dorothy P. Lathrop. New York: The Viking Press, Inc., 1942. (9–12)

————. *Come Hither.* A collection of rhymes and poems for the young of all ages. Illustrated by Warren Chappell. New edition. New York: Alfred A. Knopf, Inc., 1958. (11 to all ages)

————. *Rhymes and Verses.* Collected poems for children. Illustrated by Elinore Blaisdell. New York: Holt, Rinehart and Winston, Inc., 1947. (9–12)

————. *Tom Tiddler's Ground.* New York: Alfred A. Knopf, Inc., 1962. (10–14)

Dooley, Thomas Anthony. *Doctor Tom Dooley, My Story.* New York: Farrar, Straus & Company (Ariel Books), 1960. (16 to any age)

Farjeon, Eleanor. *Eleanor Farjeon's Poems for Children*. Philadelphia: J. B. Lippincott Company, 1951. (9–12)

Fitch, Florence Mary. *Their Search for God*. Ways of worship in the Orient. New York: Lothrop, Lee & Shepard Company, Inc., 1947. (10–14)

Frank, Anne. *The Diary of a Young Girl*. Translated from the Dutch by B. M. Mooyaart-Doubleday. New York: Doubleday & Company, Inc., 1952. (13 to any age)

French, Harry W. *The Lance of Kanana*. A story of Arabia. New York: Lothrop, Lee & Shepard Company, Inc., 1940. (10–14)

Frost, Robert. *You Come Too*. Favorite poems for young readers. With wood engravings by Thomas W. Nason. New York: Holt, Rinehart and Winston, Inc., 1959. (11–16)

Godden, Rumer. *The Dolls' House*. With pictures by Dana Saintsbury. New York: The Viking Press, Inc., 1948. (9–10)

Goudge, Elizabeth (compiler). *A Book of Comfort*. Illustrations by Gloria Kamen. New York: Coward-McCann, Inc., 1964. (All ages)

Grigson, Geoffrey (compiler). *The Cherry Tree*. New York: The Vanguard Press, Inc. 1962. (All ages)

Gunther, John. *Death Be Not Proud*. A memoir. New York: Harper and Brothers, 1949. (14 to any age)

Hamilton, Edith. *Mythology*. Illustrated by Steele Savage. Boston: Little, Brown and Company, 1940. (11–16)

Hosford, Dorothy. *By His Own Might*. The battles of Beowulf. Drawings by Laszlo Matulay. New York: Holt, Rinehart and Winston, Inc., 1947. (10–14)

———. *Thunder of the Gods*. Illustrated by Claire and George Louden. New York: Holt, Rinehart and Winston, Inc., 1952. (10–14)

Kelly, Eric P. *The Trumpeter of Krakow*. Decorations by Janina Domanska. New edition. New York: The Macmillan Company, 1966. (11–14)

Kipling, Rudyard. *The Jungle Book*. Black and white illustrations throughout by J. Lockwood Kipling, W. H. Drake, and P. Frenzeny. New York: Doubleday & Company, Inc., 1894. (9–11)

———. *The Second Jungle Book*. With illustrations by J. Lockwood Kipling. New York: Doubleday & Company, Inc., 1895. (9–11)

L'Engle, Madeleine. *Meet the Austins.* New York: The Vanguard Press, Inc., 1960. (10–12)

———. *A Wrinkle in Time.* New York: Farrar, Straus & Company (Ariel Books), 1962. (10–14)

Lewis, C. S. *The Lion, the Witch and the Wardrobe.* A story for children. Illustrated by Paul Baynes. New York: The Macmillan Company, 1960. (9–12)

MacDonald, George. *At the Back of the North Wind.* Illustrated by Harvery Dinnerstein. New York: The Macmillan Company (A Macmillan Classic), 1964. (9–10)

Mumford, Lewis. *Green Memories.* The story of Geddes Mumford. New York: Harcourt, Brace & World, Inc., 1947. (16 to any age)

Musgrave, Florence. *Marged.* The story of a Welsh girl in America. New York: Farrar, Straus & Company (Ariel Books), 1956. (10–13)

Pyle, Howard. *The Story of King Arthur and His Knights.* New York: Charles Scribner's Sons, 1903. (10–14)

Rawlings, Marjorie Kinnan. *The Yearling.* With pictures by N. C. Wyeth. New York: Charles Scribner's Sons, 1939. (11 to any age)

Read, Herbert (compiler). *This Way, Delight.* Illustrated by Juliet Kepes. A book of poetry for the young. New York: Pantheon Books, Inc., 1956. (10–14)

Saint-Exupéry, Antoine de. *The Little Prince.* Translated from the French by Katherine Woods. New York: Reynal and Company, Inc., 1943. (9 to any age)

Sandburg, Carl. *Early Moon.* Illustrated by James Daugherty. New York: Harcourt, Brace & World, Inc., 1930. (11–14)

———. *Rootabaga Stories.* Illustrations and decorations by Maud and Miska Petersham. New York: Harcourt, Brace & World, Inc., 1922. (10–12)

Sawyer, Ruth. *Roller Skates.* Illustrated by Valenti Angelo. New York: The Viking Press, Inc., 1936. (10–12)

———. *The Year of Jubilo.* Drawings by Edward Shenton. New York: The Viking Press, Inc., 1940 (10–14)

Speare, Elizabeth George. *The Bronze Bow.* Boston: Houghton Mifflin Company, 1961. (11–14)

Stevenson, Robert Louis, *A Child's Garden of Verses.* Illustrated by Jessie Willcox Smith. New edition. New York: Charles Scribner's Sons (Scribner Illustrated Classics) , 1955. (4–9)

Sutcliff, Rosemary. *The Hound of Ulster*. With drawings by Victor Ambrus. New York: E. P. Dutton & Co., Inc., 1963. (11–14)

————. *Knight's Fee*. Illustrated by Charles Keeping. New York: Henry Z. Walck, Inc., 1960. (11–14)

Weir, Ester. *The Loner*. New York: David McKay Co., Inc., 1963. (11–16)

White, E. B. *Charlotte's Web*. Pictures by Garth Williams. New York: Harper & Row, Publishers, 1952. (8–10)

Wilde, Oscar. *The Happy Prince*. The complete fairy stories of Oscar Wilde. Illustrated by Philippe Jullian. London: Gerald Duckworth & Co., Ltd. (distributed in the United States by The Macmillan Company) , 1952. (9–10)

PT 76 901

PT 76 301